Survival Kit for New Secondary Teachers:

Empowering Educators
for Classroom Success

Emma S. McDonald, M.Ed.
Educator

Dyan M. Hershman
Educator

Inspiring Teachers Publishing, Inc. / Garland, Texas

All Art Work reprinted by permission under license or otherwise.

Art Work: 6th grade students at Spring Valley Elementary in Richardson, Texas (1997)
Michael Morgan
Little Wing's Clipart Collection
Texas Agricultural Extension Service
Florida First/Second Wave IFAS/ TAEX Clipart Collection
ClickArt
Microsoft Publisher
ClipArt.com

DEDICATION

This book is dedicated to our loving husbands, Sean and Matt, and our children, Joshua, James, Mason, and Kylie. Without their unfailing support and help this book would not have been possible!

In addition, we'd like to dedicate this book to our parents, Captain and Mrs. Charles O. Barker and Lt. Colonel and Mrs. Michael J. Ferguson. They have given us the drive and discipline to tackle any task with enthusiasm and determination. Without their love and support we would not be the teachers we are today!

We'd also like to dedicate this book to our beloved students who we have taught. It is from them we have learned so much about the art of teaching and learning.

Lastly, we'd like to dedicate this book to our great friend and constant supporter, Reta Bukin. Although she is no longer with us, her constant sense of purpose and boundless energy continues to inspire and sustain us in our quest to help new teachers.

Acknowledgements

Thank you to the 1997-98 6th grade students at Spring Valley Elementary School in Richardson, TX for providing much of the art work found in this book!

We would like to acknowledge several schools, professors, and teachers for their hard work and dedication to the teaching profession.

Spring Woods Middle School, Houston, Texas
Handley Middle School, Fort Worth, Texas
Spring Valley Elementary, Richardson, Texas
Borman Elementary, Denton, Texas
Maurine Graves, teacher, Spring Branch ISD
Alice Ann McDuffy, teacher, RISD
Missy Norrell, teacher, Ft. Worth ISD
Emory University Education Department
University of North Texas Education Department
University of Houston Education Department
All of our education professors
All the excellent teachers we have worked with in our years of teaching
Our TPC Interns

We would also like to especially thank the following people:

Vaughn Gross for her support and help with the production of earlier versions of this book

Sandy Nobles and the Master Teachers in RISD for reading over our book and providing insightful comments

Reta Bukin for being our constant cheerleader, support, editor, and friend

Table of Contents

Detailed Table of Contents

FOREWORD

Dear New Teacher:

We wrote this book to openly share experiences and strategies to help you become a well-prepared teacher. Some of them we developed on our own. Others are ideas that were shared with us by other teachers, some we know were told to us, and others we simply have no clue where they came from. Regardless, successful teachers have a funny way of taking information they see, read, or hear and adapt it to their own classroom. While an original idea may have come from a college text-book, professional book, professor, or colleague, teachers shape these teaching tools to fit their own classroom needs. This is called "professional sharing", and is done by educators everywhere. We encourage you to take the ideas from this book and modify them as you see fit so that they will work for you.

We believe we have covered most of the questions and problems you will encounter as you prepare for and enter the teaching profession. Please realize, however, that it is impossible to cover EVERY question or problem as each school and each classroom is unique.

Remember, the more effort you put into these strategies and ideas, in fact, the more effort you put into teaching itself, the more effective you will be in the classroom. When our students have an effective teacher from the very first day, they are more successful learners. We sincerely hope that you use the ideas found within this book to help smooth your first several years in the classroom. However, remember that this book is meant as a starting point, not a program. Successful teachers are constantly striving to improve as they gain experience.

Below are some of the reasons why we wrote this book. Since some probably sound familiar to you, and all are addressed in the pages to follow, we believe that Survival Kit for New Teachers will continue to be of great value to you for several years to come.

"How do I talk to parents or hold a conference?"

"Where do I start when looking for a teaching job?"

"How do I report and handle student misbehavior?"

"What am I supposed to do on the first day of school?"

"What am I supposed to teach each day?"

"Who do I go to when I have questions?"

"I'm so frazzled! Somebody help me, PLEASE!"

The life of a new teacher is full of unfamiliar experiences and questions. Let's face it, who has time to stop and ask?

The ideas and strategies within this book offer a road map to navigating the world of teaching.

Being a Professional

Entering the teaching profession is a noble act. By being a teacher you can have a profound impact on our society as a whole. In shaping young minds, we influence many lives and guide the learning of our future leaders. This being said, it is important for teachers to be positive role models in schools and in the community. The way we are perceived by those around us influence whether we are considered part of a profession or just glorified babysitters.

As Vivian Troen and Katherine Boles so eloquently state in their book, who's teaching your children?

> "...teaching is a complex skill that requires specialized training. Once we understand that teaching is much more than simply conveying information from one person to another, certain truths begin to emerge, and persistent myths disappear." (p. 148)

Teachers can have an impact on how we are percieved by society if we all make a concerted effort to demonstrate our professionalism.

Being a professional teacher requires:

- Training beyond initial course work
- Dedication through extra effort and time
- Professional appearance and demeanor
- Positive interpersonal skills
- Working collaboratively with other educators
- Continuing professional education throughout career
- Resourcefulness and flexibility

Within this chapter you will find many tips and strategies for working as a professional with your students, parents, colleagues, and the community as a whole.

I know that the field of teaching is considered a profession.

What does that mean?

Field Training

All educators are required to do some sort of field work before attaining their teaching certificate. This includes both university trained and alternatively certified teachers. When working in a field situation, many interns find themselves working closely with a veteran teacher within the school. Here are some strategies to make this a positive learning experience for you.

Learn all you can from your experiences whether positive or negative.

Perhaps your cooperating teacher has a personality and teaching style that is very dissimilar to your own. From these experiences, jot down ideas of what you will and will not do in your classroom.

Observe other teachers

- Gather new ideas
- Observe a variety of teaching styles
- Observe different classroom management techniques
- Observe different teacher/student interactions

Become involved in the school

- Volunteer for committees and other school projects
- Attend staff development and faculty meetings
- Sit in on parent meetings to observe positive interactions
- Attend school events such as open house, grade level meetings, parent nights, etc.
- Be an active participant whenever you can

Plan and Team Teach with Veteran Teachers

Planning lessons and team teaching with a veteran teacher provides first hand experience in good lesson design and presentation. When preparing to student teach, talk with your cooperating teacher about using the following format to help you ease into full classroom duties.

1) Classroom observations - several days
2) Team planning of lessons to be presented by veteran teacher while you observe
3) Team teaching of lessons planned together
4) Independent delivery of lessons planned together
5) Independent planning and delivery with veteran observation

Hint:

The more involved you become within the school, the more likely you will be to garner positive recommendations from other teachers and perhaps even one or more of the administrators.

Set aside time to debrief

It is important to take time and debrief throughout your field work experience. This gives both you and the veteran teacher a chance to engage in discourse about observations of each other.

• **Feedback shared by veteran to help you improve**
You need to know both the positive aspects of your lesson as well as ways to be more effective. Without this type of constructive feedback, you have fewer chances to grow as a professional.

• **Reflect on teaching practices you observed**
Talk with the veteran teacher to determine his/her reasoning behind different teaching strategies and lesson presentation styles. Reflect in a journal or through discussion ways that you will or will not incorporate what you've seen in your own classroom. Specifically, you might ask for copies of lessons, handouts, and other procedures you felt were very effective.

 **Collect Ideas and Materials**

• Use a 3-ring binder with tabbed sections to organize
• Sections might include: Classroom Management, Special Education, ESL, Different subject areas, Assessment, Parent Communication, Technology ideas, etc.
• Gather materials from teachers during observations
• Also store student samples and copies of your own lessons to use later when creating a professional portfolio

 Working in Difficult Situations

There may be times where you are faced with a difficult situation while working with your supervising teacher. Whether it is a personality conflict or differing attitudes about teaching practices, it is in your best interest to maintain a professional demeanor.

• Be diplomatic *"You can catch more flies with honey than vinegar."*
• Work to solve problems through mediation and compromise
• Remember, you are a guest in their classroom
• Respect the experience and knowledge of veteran teachers even if you don't agree with their strategies
• Be humble
• Keep open communication with your professor to keep him/her informed of the situation
• Try to work with a variety of teachers within the school building to gain different perspectives and ideas

"Always act in a professional manner no matter what."

 Hint:

Be professional:

Show up on time.
Dress appropriately.
Maintain consistent attendance.
Refrain from gossip.
Be diplomatic.
Maintain a positive attitude.

Dedication

Teaching Is Not An 8 to 3 Job

Although students get out at 2:30 or 3:00, teachers do not. It takes time outside of school hours to organize and manage your classroom, plan lessons, develop positive relationships with parents, work collaboratively with school staff, and attend professional development sessions to enhance your teaching strategies. Teachers have a heavy load. After all, our mission is educating our future leaders. Be prepared to work anywhere from 8 to 12 hours (or more) just like other professionals in the business world.

Maintaining a Professional Appearance and Demeanor

Being a professional includes maintaining a certain type of appearance and demeanor. Think about other professionals in the world. Generally they are sharply dressed and use appropriate language for their field. When seeing a doctor or lawyer, you expect a certain level of speech and attire. When that does not occur, do you still feel confident in that person's abilities? Now apply that to how others in the community view you as a professional educator.

Dress Professionally

We understand the need for special areas teachers, such as Art, Vocational, and P.E. teachers, to wear practical clothes, not a 3-piece business suit. But please, no baggy t-shirts and stretch pants! What kind of image does this present to students, parents, and other members of the local community?

Appropriate Attire

Although there are many cute styles of clothing available, not all are appropriate to wear when working in a professional environment teaching adolescents. Remember that you will be kneeling, bending, and often leaning over to help students. Check your outfit before you leave home to be sure that it remains appropriate.

- Nice slacks/pants
- Blouses or collared shirt
- Skirts of a reasonable length (no mini's)
- Teacher vests and ties

Dedication Means:

- Participating in meetings
- Tutoring after school
- Joining committees
- Calling parents
- Attending school events
- Staying after school to plan
- And more!

Hint:

If you are doing a hands-on project with students, such as making adobe bricks with mud and straw, you'll need to wear practical clothes. Blue jeans are fine for this occasion, but not ones with paint stains and holes in the knees.

 **Appropriate Demeanor**

The language we use with students, parents, and other educators helps to define us as professionals. Use care when talking. Be aware that others are responding to your level of dialogue. Before you get ready to say something, think through what you plan to say before you say it. This will help keep you from making serious communication mistakes.

Demeanor also is the way in which you carry yourself. Good posture (ie - standing up straight, personal grooming, etc.), all play a part in whether or not you appear professional. Below are some tips for maintaining a professional demeanor.

- Refrain from using slang
- Be aware of your body language and facial expressions
- Be diplomatic in your relations with other colleagues, students, and parents

Interpersonal Skills

Our interactions with others can be either positive or negative depending on our interpersonal skills. Look at the tips below to help you have positive relationships with your colleagues.

√ Be respectful to all school staff including office staff, maintenance staff, paraprofessionals, and others.

√ Acknowledge the experience of veteran teachers even if you don't agree with them.

√ When implementing innovative strategies, be prepared to support your ideas with appropriate background reading and research.

√ Be considerate of others.
- Inform other school staff when utilizing school resources, going on field trips, holding an assembly.
- Always ask before taking supplies or using resources.
- Don't make assumptions.

√ When working with others, be diplomatic in making suggestions or sharing ideas.
For example, If another teacher leads the planning of a lesson and you want to input your ideas, you could say, "What do you think about (insert idea)?"

Approaching a situation with a humble and agreeable tone is more effective than being confrontational.

"Remember, everything you say and do reflects upon your professionalism."

Teacher Testimony
"I remember once when I was a new teacher, I decided to send an unruly student out of the class. Since we could not use the hallway as "time-out," I decided to send him to another teacher's room. Later she approached me quite upset because I had caught her off guard with this action. When the student unexpectedly arrived, she was not prepared to deal with him.

I learned how important it is to check with other teachers before making this kind of a decision. Had she and I talked about this type of situation earlier and worked out the details, she would have been prepared."

Collaboration with Others

As soon as you enter the school, you are part of a community and will be working with other professionals. Collaboration is not only important because it makes your job easier, but it also benefits the students. You know the saying, "Two minds are better than one." Whether you are working with a mentor, special area instructor, or the office staff, it is beneficial for all to engage in a sharing of ideas and resources.

Become a part of the School Culture and Community

√ Work closely with Mentor

The mentor is your guide to the school culture. This person can offer advice in a variety of situations. Your mentor helps you gain access to established networks within the school. They can also be an advocate and speak up for you in important situations. Lastly, your mentor can help you stay true to your goals by holding you accountable. They can check and evaluate your work, giving you feedback on your progress.

√ Team teach with Mentor or other veteran teachers

Once again, we feel that Vivian Troen and Katherine Boles have accurately described the importance of team teaching in the school. Here is what they have to say:

"Numerous studies conducted both in the United States and in other countries, notably China and Japan, have shown that teachers become more proficient by continually working on curriculum, demonstration lessons, and assessments together. Research shows that not only does working in teams improve the practice of teaching; it also eliminates the isolation inherent in most teachers' work lives." (p. 150)

> *"Collaboration with other teachers increases your abilities and benefits your students."*

Teacher Testimony
"Team teaching can be extremely helpful as long as both teachers take an equal part in the planning and lesson delivery. During my first year of teaching, I team-taught with a veteran teacher and it was a very positive experience. We were each in charge of outlining lessons and activities for different weeks. Once a week we met after school and together used the outlines to write full-scale lesson plans. During our team-teaching, we each presented the lesson during one class period. First my mentor would teach the lesson to both of our classes while I monitored/ helped students and observed her teaching techniques. Later in the day, when we had English I classes again, I taught the lesson while she observed and offered help to the students. As we became more comfortable with each other, we would often interject timely comments to further the discussion/lesson. In this way, we were both teaching and students were getting the benefit of two different perspectives. At the end of the year I felt that I had learned a lot from my mentor."

√ Participate in vertical planning teams

Due to the isolation often experienced by teachers, student learning can become disjointed between grade levels. Therefore, many schools have implemented Vertical Planning Teams to build consistency from one year to the next.

Example: Seventh grade teachers and eighth grade teachers meet together to determine benchmarks (where students need to be at the end of the year/ skills learned) for student progress.

Additionally, it is helpful for students when teachers agree on certain terminology to use in different subject areas.

Example: Students are exposed to the term "pre-writing" early on as a means for brainstorming and gathering ideas. This same term is used throughout their schooling and across subject areas.

√ Participate in other school committees

Working with others as a team in a committee situation helps us network with other teachers in the school and build a camaraderie. There are times when we may feel that being a part of a committee is just another item added to our already large workload. Think of this as a type of "break" from the usual routine of redirecting behavior. All day you are surrounded by adolescents. When do you have time to be part of an adult group?

√ Attend school events to show support

Become a part of the school community by being visible at school events. Students and parents want to see you actively involved. They are invested in their neighborhood school and want to know that you are part of the community. Additionally, students love it when you show up for their art shows, science fairs, sports events, carnivals, etc..

√ Working with other Special Areas teachers and para-professionals

When planning lessons, be sure to include your special area teachers such as Art, Music, PE, Special Education, and ESL. Why? Their input can be valuable for student learning as well as to make connections for students between subject areas. Additionally, these teachers are fantastic sources of expertise in their field and can provide you with ideas, support, and resources.

For example, when studying the continent of Africa, you might approach the Art teacher to do a unit on African masks. Also, the music teacher could provide different types of music from that culture.

Parent Testimony

"As the parent of a non-sighted child, I have seen the value of teachers working together for the benefit of my son. The classroom teacher plans lessons with the speech teacher and the VI (Visually Impaired) teacher to make sure that my son can take part in the fun and exciting lessons going on in the classroom.

Although the regular teacher is wonderful, the special area teachers can offer specific ideas to make the lessons more meaningful for my son.

As a parent, this type of collaborative effort really impresses me!

Professional Development

It is important for teachers to continually increase their knowledge about effective teaching practices to implement in the classroom. This new knowledge is often gained through staff development either within the school or from outside sources. For those of us who have been in the profession for a while, we come to think of staff development as torture equal to any medieval stretching machine. However, staff development should be a time of professional growth and continuing education. Here are some things you can do to turn a potential waste of time into a valuable learning experience.

Take the Learning into Your Own Hands

Remember that YOU are the one who needs to benefit from this information. Come to the session with an open mind and a willingness to learn. Just as our students need to be open to what we teach them, so should we be open to what others have to teach us. You never know what jewel of an idea or strategy that you may discover. Remember that this is life-long learning.

Do Not Bring Anything Else to Do

Although you run the risk of being bored, take a chance and be proactive in your learning. If you don't bring any other tasks with you to the workshop, you won't be tempted to start working on them when the presenter is speaking. It is difficult to listen and learn when your mind is focused on other tasks. While others may be grading papers, looking over lesson plans, or some other task, ask yourself, *"Are they missing out on potential ideas for their classroom?"*

Request Meaningful Activities and Information

Before the workshop begins, speak with the presenter and request that they give practical ways to apply and implement the information throughout their presentation rather than all at the end or only in a handout. If you let the person in charge know what you are looking for ahead of time, he/she may be able to adapt the presentation to meet your requests.

Don't Be Afraid to Ask Questions

Go ahead and speak up. If something is confusing to you, raise your hand and ask for clarification. The workshop will not do you any good if you sit through half of it confused. Most likely if you are confused, several others are too. Also, ask for examples of how strategies presented would work in the classroom. Don't wait until the end to ask your questions, but instead ask when the question is pertinent.

Hint:

If you have questions during a presentation, but don't feel it is appropriate to interrupt the speaker, write them down on an index card. Then, when the time is right, you will have not forgotten what you were planning to ask.

This strategy can also be used with comments or ideas of your own that you wish to share with others around you. Write them down, and then at a break in the presentation, feel free to share.

Go With a Positive Attitude

We are always saying this to our students and it applies to us as well. If you walk into a staff development with a poor attitude and no intention of learning anything, then you will have a wasted day. If, however, you walk in with an open mind and positive attitude, you just may get several great ideas to use during the school year. I find that sometimes I get ideas, not only from the workshop itself, but also from casual conversations or side conversations happening during the workshop.

Encourage Others Around You to Maintain a Positive Outlook

We all know teachers who prefer to sit in the back and complain about the workshop before it even begins. This negative attitude can infect everyone around that person which causes a chain reaction through the room. Instead of responding to a negative comment with a negative comment of your own, try to infect that person with your positive attitude. You might try pointing out something positive for each negative comment that is said. If all else fails, move to another seat so that you are not distracted.

Provide Specific Constructive Feedback to Presenters

If the workshop still ends up making it on your "worst" list, let those in charge know why it was a complete bust. Don't forget to start out with one or two positive comments first. Be sure to offer a couple of suggestions for correcting the problems. Sometimes those who are presenting staff development forget how to be good teachers. Your comments may help someone else have a great staff development in the future. Who knows, perhaps one day you'll find yourself presenting to a group of teachers and will appreciate helpful feedback from them.

> *"An effective teacher seeks ideas from a variety of sources and presentations to use in the classroom."*

> *"Attitude can be infectious, whether positive or negative. How do you want to influence others?"*

Resourcefulness and Flexibility

Teaching is a profession of constant change and movement. At a moment's notice a school-wide assembly may be called, interrupting an important lesson. Additionally, students are often unpredictable in their thoughts and actions which means that you need to be prepared to handle a myriad of situations. Being flexible also means being able to utilize resources on hand and go-with-the flow when necessary.

> *For example*: If a Pep-Rally or other type of assembly is called at the last minute, how will that affect your lesson plans? What will you require of your students to make up for this loss? Will you rearrange your plans to compensate? How will this affect your testing schedule? Also, how does this affect your planning period and the tasks you have set for yourself to accomplish?

These are just some of the things you need to be prepared to handle.

Situations like the one above (and others) can cause serious frustration and stress. A teacher's professional life is full of stressful events. In talking about stress, we recently attended a professional workshop where the presenter stated, "Stress makes you stupid." What he meant was that when you are working in stress mode, you are not performing at your optimum level.

As a new teacher you will experience even more stress in trying to assimilate and apply everything you've learned into becoming an effective teacher. It takes time to get your own routine and procedures perfected, which will help relieve much of your stress. Until then, what can you do to take some time out for yourself? Below are some "Stress Busters" to help you along.

Take Time Outs

We give our students time outs when they need a break to cool off and get back on task. Why not give yourself one every now and then? When you are feeling a little hot under the collar and are ready to strangle somebody for something...anything... that's the moment you need to take a time out.

Turn away from the situation, go out into the hallway, and collect yourself. You'll find that even with a small amount of distance your blood pressure will lower, and you will have a fresh look at the situation.

"Don't feel that you are alone. Everyone feels stressed out and frustrated their first year in the classroom. This is common and it will pass!"

"Even veteran teachers have their moments of stress, though it may look like they have it all together."

"Like a tree, bend with the wind. Try not to snap."

Take Time for You

Our life is not meant to be spent inside grading papers all the time! You need to take some time for yourself. Leave those papers at school at least one night a week and treat yourself to something fun. Go see a movie, attend a happy hour, cruise the mall, or get to the gym. There is more to life than teaching and, let me tell you, there will always be more papers to grade.

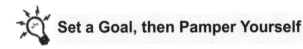

Set a Goal, then Pamper Yourself

Set a goal for yourself such as, "I'll plan lessons for next week." Then, when you've reached your goal, pamper yourself! Treat yourself to a relaxing bath, a nice dinner out, or a great dessert. Although these are things you should be doing for yourself every now and again anyway, you might feel better about doing them if you know you've accomplished at least one goal.

5 Minute Exercises

If you are feeling exceptionally stressed, try some of these 5 minutes exercises:

- Count slowly to ten. Breathe deeply in on the odd numbers, and breathe out on the even numbers.

- Tighten your body from head to toe. Then, slowly relax the muscles in your body starting with the toes and working your way up the neck and shoulder muscles.

- Do a few small circular muscle stretches with your wrists, ankles, and neck.

- Close your eyes and imagine a place where you feel happy and relaxed. Keep that image in your mind when you are stressed.

- A moment of meditation goes a long way towards serenity.

Teacher Testimony
"My first year of teaching I made it a priority to take one day off a week from my usual after-school, into the night, working-like-a-dog, routine. Every Wednesday I went to the local movie theater and watched a $2.50 movie. As a movie buff, this was a real treat for me and helped me remember that there IS life in the world outside of school."

CONCLUSION

Upon reading this chapter we can conclude that teaching is a stressful, intense, unpredictable and difficult job. Teaching carries a heavy burden. However, with the right attitude, level of dedication and coping strategies at your fingertips, teaching is also the most rewarding career in the world! For the same reasons that make it hard, it is also exciting, challenging, and fun! Teaching is never dull. It is a wonderful career choice made all the better with a positive attitude.

Additionally, when we act as education professionals, we change the public's view of teaching. Since the early 1900's teachers have often been viewed as nothing more than "glorified babysitters." It is time to change this perception and as the future generation of teachers, it is up to us to change it! Remember, the more we dress and act like professionals, the more we will be treated as such.

Additional Resources

Who's Teaching Your Children?
by Vivian Troen and Katherine C. Boles

Making Teaching a True Profession
by J. D. Saphier

Teaching as the Learning Profession: Handbook of Policy and Practice
by Linda Darling-Hammond (Editor) and Gary Sykes (Editor)

Questions for Reflection

1) In what ways can you become involved in the school as a student teacher or intern?

2) Do you feel you come across as a professional to others? Why or why not? What are some ways you could help others see you as a professional?

3) Think about the way you relate to others. What are some positive and negative reactions you've experienced when working with other people? What kinds of changes might you make to your interpersonal skills to receive more positive reactions than negative?

4) Why is collaboration among teachers so important? Support your reasons.

5) What is your attitude towards professional development workshops? How does this attitude affect your ability to learn and apply new information? What are some ways you can be sure to get the most out of a professional development workshop?

Suggested Activites

1) Create a 3-ring binder with the following tabbed sections (as applicable to you):

- Classroom Management
- Reading
- Math
- P.E.
- General Teaching Strategies
- Special Education
- Writing
- Art
- Assessment
- Parent Communication
- ESL
- Science
- Music
- Technology

Begin gathering materials to place within this binder for future reference. OR, organize materials you've already gathered into this binder for easy reference.

2) Approach your Cooperating Teacher, Mentor Teacher, or a veteran teacher on your grade level with the idea of team teaching a few lessons. Keep a journal reflecting on the process, ways that you benefited, and ideas to improve future team teaching efforts.

3) Plan a strategy for taking time for yourself. What is something you can do away from school one day a week? What might you do during the day to help relieve stress? Type up your plan and post it on your refrigerator, computer screen, desk, bathroom mirror, and any other place where you will be reminded to take time for yourself.

Notes/ Reflection on Chapter

Before School Starts

I just got hired and school starts in a couple of weeks.

Where do I begin?

While you may feel overwhelmed with a new job and all that it entails, there are a few important things to do before school starts that will help you later on. As a well-prepared teacher, one of the most important things that you can do for yourself and for your students is getting organized before the first bell rings on the first day. This will make your life so much easier and will provide a smooth beginning for everyone.

You can't know everything by osmosis.

There are so many small details in the day to day operation of a school that you need to be aware of. The veteran teachers in your school already know where to find necessary materials and supplies, and on top of that, know what materials and supplies they need!

Who do I ask?

If your school provides a Mentor Teacher, this person would be an excellent resource. Also, the school secretary and librarian are both a treasure trove of knowledge. Some questions you may want to ask are:

Where do I find:

- School/ Class Schedule?
- Class lists with addresses and phone numbers?
- Hall/ Office passes?
- Detention forms?
- Paper for the copier?
- Substitute information?
- Resource materials for the classroom?
- Classroom supplies?
- Discipline/ office referrals?
- Insurance information?
- School rules/ code of conduct?
- Computers & computer programs available?
- Maintenance request forms?
- Any other important papers you might need (ask the secretary)?

More Questions to Ask...

√   **Do I need a special Lesson Plan book/ Grade Book and where can I get one?**

√   **How are supplies handled in this school? Do we buy our own or does the school provide them?**

√   **How are curriculum materials, field trips and other necessary items funded?**

Quick Tips

"A well-prepared teacher asks questions and seeks out answers."

💡 Check out the school library or teacher workroom.

- Most schools keep their supplies either in the library or in a teacher workroom. This can also include the overhead projector and overhead carts.

- Take some time to look through the cabinets, drawers and bookshelves for resources you could use during the year.

- Explore every nook and cranny and you may find treasures galore!

Hint: **Take some time to talk to the librarian. This person is often the keeper of supplies and resources and may be able to show you what the school has to offer in the way of materials.**

💡 Sign up for the TV/VCR in advance.

- Most teachers want to reserve the TV/ VCR for specific days, such as the day before a holiday, the last day of school, etc. If you wait too long to sign up, you may find that there are none left.

- Do you know where to sign up for a TV/VCR? Usually the Librarian handles these transactions.

- These days many teachers have presentation stations which may include a TV/VCR combination. If you have one of these in your classroom, you will not need to worry about this issue.

"The librarian is often the keeper of supplies and resources."

Join School Organizations

Most schools require 100% participation in the school PTA. After all, the T stands for Teacher. Another organization you may be asked to join is the Social/ Morale club. If you do not join before school starts, you may be so overwhelmed that you will forget.

Keep a ream of paper stashed in your room for emergencies.

You never know when the copier will run out of white paper, or when you will need white paper for projects. Therefore, it is important to always have some in your room.

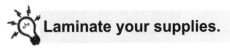

Laminate your supplies.

Don't hang anything on your walls without laminating them first. Teacher stores charge for lamination and they can be expensive. However, almost every school has a laminator that you can use for free.

WARNING: Check to see whether *YOU* can use the laminator. Some schools only allow *ONE PERSON* to run the laminating machine.

Also, many school districts have a Media Center where teachers can laminate for free or at a reduced cost. Retail copy and print shops can do these same services, but the fee is often quite costly.

Some things you many want to laminate:

√ Posters

√ Student work from previous experience

√ Strips of colored construction paper for later use to make die cut letters, etc.

√ Clip art for bulletin boards

√ Manila folders that you may want to use all year

√ Pages from illustrated calendars to use as journal starters or for classroom decoration

"Your district Media Center may be able to laminate your classroom posters to save you time and money."

Gather Supplies

You will need all of these items before school begins to help you get organized and ready for the new year. Check to see if your school/district gives you these supplies before you spend your own money. Also, check to see how generous your school is with supplies.

You may end up having to buy supplies at a later date, but these items are well worth spending the money if you have to.

- Tubs or crates

- Letter trays

- Desktop filing

- Drawer organizers

- Overhead pens

- Transparency film

- Electric pencil sharpener

- Three hole punch

- Manila folders

- Boarder for bulletin board

- Plastic shoe boxes with lids

- Office supplies including scissors,tape, stapler, staples, paperclips,pencils, pens, rubber bands, etc.

"How generous will your school be with supplies?"

"A well-prepared teacher brainstorms a list of supplies needed for the classroom."

Hint: You do not have to do everything yourself. Do not be afraid to ask questions. Most of the seasoned teachers in the school are more than willing to help you out, but they do not want to make YOU feel uncomfortable by offering advice. No one will think you are stupid for asking questions.

Write or Call Students Before School Starts

The year gets off to a positive start when you welcome the students through a postcard, letter, or phone call.

Your welcome message should include:

- An introduction of who you are
- The name of your class and your room number
- A statement expressing your excitement to meet that student
- A statement about the upcoming year

Example:

August 9, 20__

Welcome to the new school year. My name is Mrs. Jackson, and I will be your English 101 instructor. I look forward to meeting you in room 302 on Monday, August 14. Please come to class prepared with a spiral notebook, a three ring binder, and one novel you read this summer. Also, please don't forget to bring your imagination and your brain!

Sincerely,
Mrs. Jackson

Other Tips for Communicating with Students and Parents

- Don't forget to translate this letter into another language when appropriate.

- Create a web site complete with a picture of you that explains more about who you are, your educational training background, and any previous teaching experience (student teaching).

- Put your web site address on your postcard/ welcome letter so that students and parents with computers can get to know you better!

"A well-prepared teacher makes students feel welcome even before school starts"

Hint:

Keep in mind that student schedules are often not finalized until a day or two before school starts. This can make it very difficult and even impossible to send a note or letter home to every students before school starts.

If you have a general letter typed out and copied, request a set of labels from the attendance officer for the students on your roster. This will help speed along the process.

Other Options

Instead of sending home a postcard, other ways of welcoming students before school starts include:

- Fold-over note cards
- Colored paper
- Designer stationery
- Phone call
- Home visits

Type up a letter, save it, and print it out on colorful paper rather than handwriting each student a letter.

This is helpful for teachers who have several classes of students!

Welcome Letter Example

August 9, 20___

Dear Parents and Students,

Welcome! My name is Paul Richards and I am pleased to have you in my class this year. This is my first year with Spring High School. I moved to this area from Atlanta, Georgia recently with my wife. I graduated from the University of Georgia with a BS in Biology and have experience with sophomores and juniors. I am looking forward to seeing you in Biology II this semester.

All students need to come to class prepared with the following:

Three-ring binder	college ruled paper	graph paper
Onion skin paper	pens/pencils	spiral notebook

I have also attached our syllabus for this semester as well as my classroom procedures for your information. Please keep this copy somewhere visible so that you can reference it easily.

Communication is very important to me. I want you as students and parents to feel comfortable asking questions and sharing concerns. If you would like to contact me before school starts with any specific needs, I will be available during the day at the school number 555-789-4355 after August 12th. School starts August 17th and I look forward to meeting you in room 312.

Mr. Richards   *www.richards.aol.com*

 Hint: If you do not know your curriculum for the year, check your State Standards or Essential Elements for the grade/subject you'll be teaching. This will help you begin the planning process.

Every State Department of Education has a website. You can get a listing from the US Department of Education at www.ed.gov/

Home Visits

Some principals require their teachers to
conduct home visits before school begins.
When visiting a student's home, the teacher
can gain a better understanding of the
financial and time resources available to
the family. This is also a good time to meet

additional family members, and observe parent-child interactions
within a comfortable setting for the family. A home visit will also
help the teacher gain a more realistic picture of the student and
his or her home life.

Why?

- Home is often more of a relaxed and non-threatening
  environment than school.

- Students often come to class with much more enthusiasm
  than when the teacher is a complete stranger.

- Parents are more comfortable with the teacher in charge
  of their child.

Tips

- Don't forget about safety issues. Be sure that at least one
  other person knows where you are. If you have a mobile
  phone or pager, keep it with you at all times. Use common
  sense at all times.

- Not all families will want to invite you into their home. Offer to
  meet at a local restaurant or park near the school for your
  intial visit.

- When meeting students and their family for the first time,
  keep the conversation light. Know ahead what you will and
  won't tell them so that you won't be caught off guard by
  questions.

- Do not direct the entire conversation. Allow the student and
  parent opportunities to ask questions and lead the
  discussion.

- Be aware of your comments. Every comment and action has
  a consequence. That consequence can be either positive or
  negative. Be very careful in what you say and do.

"Be professional and appropriate at all times when meeting with students and parents."

"A well-prepared teacher is aware of cultural differences when meeting with families."

"Pull out your resources, or search the internet on different cultures to prepare for meeting families.

Remember, a wrong comment or action could jeopardize a positive relationship."

Read the Cumulative folder for each student

This may sound time consuming, but it really only takes five to ten minutes for each student.

Information included in the cumulative folder:

"Cumulative folders supply important information about students!"

- Health records

- Previous report cards

- Special Education information

- ESL information

- Information on family situations

- Comments from previous teachers

- Test resuts

- Helps teacher not make assumptions in regards to the student

---

Teacher Testimony

My first year of teaching I did not read the cumulative folders for my students because I did not want to pre-judge them. I felt it important to make my own assessment of each student instead. One day while reprimanding a student I made the comment, "If your behavior does not improve, I will have to call your mother." As it turns out, the student's mother had died the year before. By not reading the Cumulative folder I made a serious mistake which jeopardized my relationship with that student for the rest of the year.

Hint:

Take it ten folders at a time. Do not feel pressured to read 150 folders all at once. Set aside some time each day to read through a few folders. Before you know it, you'll be done!

Make notes for yourself in your own student folders or on index cards.

Remember, this is not for judgement purposes. If you want to wait until you've had a chance to meet the students before reading the folders, that is fine. Just remember that this information will help you in understanding why the student may be behaving a certain way. You may also learn some important ways to interact with each student for positive results.

Getting Organized

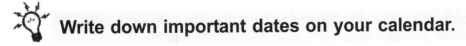

Write down important dates on your calendar.

Every school has a SCHOOL CALENDAR.

This calendar marks important school holidays, functions, meetings, etc. Any time you or your grade level has an important event, you need to make sure you put this on the big calendar so everyone else knows what is going on.

- Before school starts you need to write down dates that are already on the school calendar into your own personal/ desk calendar. This way you will not be caught off guard or schedule conflicting meetings or conferences.

- Be sure to immediately mark down dates given to you through school memos. Then throw them away or file them in a binder chronologically. This type of paperwork can drown you the first six weeks of school and can get easily lost.

- Make sure you write down any staff development meetings that are required by your school or district as well as school holidays.

Organize your filing cabinet.

It is important that you decide how to organize your filing cabinet before school starts because you won't have a chance later on. There are several ways to do this.

- **By drawer**
  Each drawer has a different purpose.
  - student folders
  - lesson/ thematic folders
  - administrative information (certification, staff development, insurance, committees, clubs, etc.)
  - extra materials

- **Alphabetically**

"Record important school events and meetings on your own calendar to help you with scheduling and with planning lessons."

"A well-prepared teacher is organized."

> *"Organization is the key to a successful year"*

Set up a manila folder for each student.

Create your own file on each student with a manila folder. These folders are excellent for keeping documentation on:

- student behavior
- parent communication
- student information records
- special classes information
- absent/ tardy notes
- anything else that pertains to that student
- office referrals

This will be your saving grace if you or the school needs to go to court for anything dealing with the student.

DO NOT EVER THROW THESE RECORDS AWAY

It is vital to document all forms of parent communication (phone calls/ letters/ conferences)!

Teacher Testimony

My first year of teaching I had a very difficult student who was constantly in trouble. After a few months I had a pretty large file of all his transgressions. Right around Thanksgiving this student brought a gun to school and was expelled. His parents then withdrew him from the school on the pretext that they were moving. Unknowing of the consequences, I threw away his student record thinking that he was no longer our problem. A few months later he returned, and the school prepared to testify against him in court proceedings. I was asked to submit my files on this student. Unfortunately all of the documentation I had gathered was long gone. The school was still able to expel the student, but only because other teachers had kept their records.

Create Student Mailboxes

Each student should have a place to call their own in the classroom to keep folders, novels, papers, and personal supplies organized. An inexpensive way to create mailboxes is to get plastic crates and hanging file folders with tabs. You can also set aside a filing cabinet with one drawer per class period. Just be sure students can access their mailbox!

√ Mailboxes are handy for storing school supplies on the first day of school before students begin using them.

√ They work very nicely for handing out graded papers without taking up class time to do so.

√ When students are working on research or group projects, mailboxes are a good place to keep class work so that it won't get lost.

Hint:

It would be helpful to staple a **PARENT PHONE RECORD** form on the inside left of this folder for record keeping purposes. A sample phone record can be found in the back of the Parent Communication Chapter.

"Do not throw away your student files, even if the student withdraws from your school."

Teacher Testimony

For the longest time my classroom was in a constant state of chaos with papers and supplies floating around everywhere. I finally decided to get organized and set up mailboxes. I used hanging file folders and dedicated one for each student in my class. Students keep their journals, books, and unfinished folders in their mailbox. I also keep a folder labeled "graded work" in each. Once a day either I or my teacher helpers file graded student work into these folders. The students can then pull the work out of that folder and put it in their binder to take home. It has really kept the classroom less messy and I don't feel like I'm wasting class time every day to pass back student work!

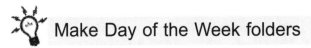 Make Day of the Week folders

Day of the week folders are an invaluable tool for classroom organization. As teachers, we are faced with the challenge of staying organized on a day-to-day basis. Day of the week folders help us manage paperwork and materials in two main ways:

1. A place to hold materials

- During the week, as you plan for lessons later that week or the following week, you will begin to gather materials such as copies of handouts, etc.

   Example: Tuesday during your planning period you research information, gather materials, and make copies for Thursday's lesson. Immediately you place these materials in the Thursday folder so that they are ready to be used. Otherwise, they end up in piles on your desk, cause clutter, and often are lost when you need them!

- If you have a special test or form for students to complete on Friday, stick these in your Friday folder for that class.

- If you have a field trip on Wednesday, then put all of the necessary information, forms, entrance tickets, etc., into the Wednesday folder for that class.

2. Relieves Stress and Promotes Professional Appearance

Situation: You have a flat tire on the way to work Tuesday morning, and your principal must tend your class for an hour or so until you arrive, which would she appreciate more?

   a)   A mass of papers piled on the desk with your lesson plans somewhere in your room, but she doesn't know where they are.

   b)   A Tuesday folder placed neatly on your desk with lesson plans, warm-up activities, materials, copies, and a substitute folder inside, all ready to go.

Hint:

Use plastic shoe boxes with lids to store supplies such as scissors, crayons, tape, etc..

These also make great storage places for supplies used by student groups. Label each box with the table number or name so that students can easily locate the supply box for their group.

"A well-prepared teacher has lessons and materials ready ahead of time and organized in one location."

"Before you leave each day, place the sub folder inside your Day of the Week folder just in case you need to be absent the following day."

Using Day of the Week folders not only give you a more professional appearance, but you will actually feel more calm and prepared every morning when you follow these Day of the Week folder guidelines. It truly makes for a smooth start to every day.

 Hint:

Get everything ready for the next day BEFORE you leave the classroom. Set up your chalkboard with the date, agenda, objectives, and warm-up activity.

Prepare your Day of the Week folders to be used the following day. Be sure your lesson plans and materials for the day are inside.

Lay them flat on your desk so that it is the first thing you or anyone else sees when approaching your desk. Put the sub folder inside the first period folder, just in case.

Setting up the Day of the Week folders

Use manila folders and label each one with the day of the week (ie - Monday, Tuesday, etc.). Use different colored folders to color code each day of the week. **This is an excellent organizational tool!**

You need to:

- Create a different folder for each class you teach. For example, a teacher who has two sessions of English 101 and three sessions of American Lit will have two of each daily folder.

- Be sure you label each folder with the title of the class for easy reference.

- Folders not in use should stay in the filing cabinet in a hanging folder for each day. If you use hanging files with a gusset (a bottom), you'll be able to make copies of handouts ahead of time and store them in the appropriate place.

Hint:

1) Laminate the folder so they will last.

2) Put a stand-up file holder on your desk to hold the folders in an easily accessible place.

3) Put all materials for each day's lesson in the folder. (ie - copies, lesson plans, newsletter, activites, etc.) Be sure to put enough copies for each class period per subject taught.

Teacher Testimony

One day I remember in particular where I was very late for school. My son was sick and I had to wait for my mother to come over and watch him. By the time I arrived to my classroom, school had been in session for over an hour. I was frantic! I walked inside to find the principal standing there working with my kids (panic attack). As he left, he smiled and said, "Thanks for having everything ready to go today. Keep up the good work." I am so glad that I had my board set up the afternoon before and my lesson plans in the day's folder right on my desk!

 Make a Substitute Folder

Taking the time to put together a folder for substitutes is an excellent way to stay organized when you are absent from school. As a teacher you are judged on how well your classroom runs even when you are not there. You are expected to make things easier for a substitute who is a guest teacher in your school.

Across the nation there has been a huge shortage of substitute teachers available. The biggest reason for this deficit of "guest teachers" is the lack of respect and support from school staff and faculty. This includes a lack of prior preparation, communication, and acknowledgment.

One way you can ensure that substitutes will want to come to your classroom is to provide them with detailed plans, instructions, and classroom policies/procedures. If these necessary tools are readily accessible, the substitute teacher will be more comfortable and confident about leading your class through the day. This will more than likely result in a problem free day for both the sub and the students!

When leaving instructions for "guest teachers," be sure to offer detailed explanations of how your classroom management system works. When you determine your classroom procedures and motivational techniques, be sure to type them up and place them, not only in your teacher binder, but also in the sub folder.

You also want to have alternative plans that can be used at any time during the year. Oftentimes grade levels, departments, or teams plan for special units or lessons that require everyone to have full participation. If you are absent, your team may decide to do different lessons on that day.

Also, the school may call for an assembly or other type of event may occur that will disrupt your scheduled plans. If you have alternate plans which are easy to implement and follow, your substitute will have a much easier time of adapting to an unexpected situation.

Additionally, your substitute may not understand your plans and may not feel qualified to implement lessons or activities. Having alternate plans with hand-outs ready alleviates this potential frustration for the sub and students.

"A well-prepared teacher has a substitute folder with important information, alternate lessons and activities ready to be used."

Checklist for Substitute Folder

You may be able to get a Sub folder from a teacher store or your school secretary. However, if you cannot find a pre-made folder, it is very easy to make your own out of a manila or pocket folder. The following items should be included:

_____ **Seating chart**

_____ **Class schedule**

_____ **Easy stable lesson plans**
   -substitutes tend to work best with paper/pencil activities that can be easily monitored and explained.

_____ **Daily instructions**
   -classroom procedures explained in detail, lunch schedule for teacher and students, and students who are pulled out for special classes.

_____ **Class roll**

_____ **Sponge activities/ creative writing ideas**
   -just in case they finish lesson early

_____ **A form for them to report back to you**

_____ **Helpful students**

_____ **Names and room numbers of grade level/ team members**

"Returning to the classroom after an absence can be either a pleasure or a pain depending on how prepared You were for having a substitute teacher in your class."

Hint:

Type out your classroom procedures and other information that will not change too much over time. Save this file for future reference. Next year you can open the file, make the necessary changes, print it out, and you are ready to place the new information into your substitute folder.

Use a generic response form using Bloom's Taxonomy that can be used for any type of reading, both fiction and non-fiction. See the form in the back of the Reading/Writing chapter for reference (p. 216-217). Have a class set of this form in your substitute folder ready for use. Be sure to replenish your supply when you return to school. See page 234-235 for a description of Bloom's Taxonomy.

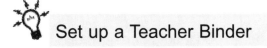 **Set up a Teacher Binder**

An excellent way to organize yourself and your units is to create a binder for yourself. Within this binder you can keep your classroom information, lesson plans and handouts organized for each six weeks period. The binder should be organized with tab dividers and contain the following sections:

1. Student information section:

   - Student list (you'll get this a few days before school starts)
   - Seating chart
   - Textbook records
   - ESL and Special Ed lists and schedules
   - Student locker and class job information

2. Calendars/ Schedules section:

   - Library
   - Counseling
   - Computer lab
   - Elective/ special areas
   - Lunch schedules
   - Daily classroom schedule
   - A calendar with important district, school, grade level, and personal dates marked.
   - Classroom management procedures

3. TEAM Planning section:

   - Middle school teachers may want to keep an extra section for notes taken during team planning.

   - The more records you keep, the more you are safeguarded against problems in the future.

4. Extra Forms section:

   - Hardcopies of forms such as parent communication, bonus points, certificates, free homework coupons, etc.

> *"A well-prepared teacher has class information organized in an easily accessible location"*

> *"Keep yourself organized with a three-ring binder."*

Course Binders

- Keep one binder for each course you'll be planning (each prep)

- In the front of each should be a planning calendar that shows an overview of the entire grading period

- Grading period lesson plans and daily handouts are kept in this binder.

- Keep everything in chronological order to make planning easier the following year. You might use tabs for organization.

- Transparencies can be attached through hole-punched clear plastic covers – look for these in office supply stores.

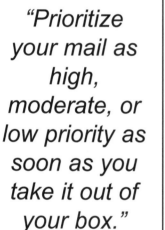

At the end of each grading period, you could transport this section into another three ring binder and clearly label it for future reference with the name of the unit.

Many teachers like to plan at home rather than in the classroom. If you have a binder, this will cut down on the number of manila files you will have to take back and forth between school and home. It will also simplify your preparation for the next year.

Note of Warning:

- The more records you keep, the more you are safeguarded against problems in the future.

- Your school may give you a binder that holds the teacher manual and other information for the school and district. **READ IT CAREFULLY!**

- If you ask your principal or another veteran teacher a question which is already answered in the Teacher Manual, they will be very irritated!

- The school's teacher manual is another great place to store memos, newsletters, or other paperwork you receive from the school. Create an additional tabbed section in the notebook if necessary.

"Don't let paperwork pile up on you!"

"Prioritize your mail as high, moderate, or low priority as soon as you take it out of your box."

"File memos and other papers as soon as you read them."

Set up your Classroom

Your room should reflect you and your teaching style. It should be completely set up before the first student arrives. A first impression is everything for students and parents.

- Make a sketch of your ideal classroom.

- Look to see how you can meet that image. What do you need? What do you already have?

- Make necessary changes to your sketch.

- Try it out and see how it works. It may take you several tries until you are completely satisfied.

- Think about the flow of your room. Where do you want your students looking? Where is your overhead screen, presentation station, chalkboard, and bulletin board?

Ask yourself:

- Should I use rows or groups of desks?
- Should I use tables?
- How easily will I be able to move between students?
- Can we all get out of the classroom quickly in an emergency?

- Do I want a writing center?
- Do I want a reading corner?
- Do I want learning centers?
- Do I want a conference area?
- Do I want an arts area?

- Do I want a Brain Challenge area with enrichment activities for further study?

- Should I have a computer station?

- How will the teacher area look?
    - where will you put your desk? filing cabinets? shelves?
    - think about easy access to curriculum materials
    - think about visual monitoring of students
    - will you be sitting behind your desk frequently or not?
    - do you need your own personal space?

"Your room will reflect your personality and teaching style. What does your room say about you as a teacher?"

Create a Learner Centered Environment

The environment we create for our students is equally as important as the content we teach and the learning strategies we use. This applies to all teachers of all age groups from pre-school to graduate school. The environment includes the atmosphere, the traditions we set, the furniture arrangement, the centers or special areas within the room, and the decorations. All of these things add up to create either a positive or negative environment for students.

On the previous page we discussed classroom layout, furniture, and setting aside special areas for student use. Here we will discuss classroom traditions, attitudes, and decorations to help create a positive learner-centered environment.

1) **Students should feel welcomed and inspired to learn from the moment they walk through your door.**

- Decorate Your door with a theme or slogan. Some examples include:

-Blasting off to Learning
-Come Explore Learning in Room 32   -Soar the Heights
-A class slogan such as:
"Learning is Victory!" or "Learning=Success!" or "Using Our Minds to Conquer the World!"

- Greet students with a smile.

2) **Create traditions within your classroom.** These are fun actions or events that students look forward to experiencing each day or week.

- Every Friday we read from our Acts of Kindness box.
- Whenever we read a story, one student gets to introduce the reader.

3) **Classroom walls and bulletin boards are covered with thought provoking and stimulating material.**

- Motivational posters
- Language rich
- Humorous posters
- Manners and Character Building posters

Remember: Students will be more motivated to learn in an environment that is stimulating. Blank walls = Blank Minds

"What kind of traditions could you create in your classroom?"

 **Bulletin Board Ideas**

Some bulletin boards you'll want to create on your own, especially at the beginning of the year. However, think about different ways you can take the ideas below and get your students involved in locating information and creating their own bulletin boards. This encourages higher level thinking and creativity.

- Quotable Quotes

- What's New - to post classroom, school, community, and world events

- Centers - Use a board to post brain challenges or learning center activities for students to complete

- Miss Manners - posting manners posters or tips of etiquette

- Famous Authors - teacher can post information or have students research 1 author and post their findings on the board.

- Famous Mathematicians, Scientists, Artists, Musicians, Sports figures, People in History (same as above)

- Careers

- Highlight a concept being taught

- See What We're Doing - post student work

- Who's Who in Room____ (spotlight students & their work)

- Who Am I? - show a baby picture and offer clues. Students guess who that person is

- Classroom Expectations

- Class Slogan

- Theme - changes with each unit

"A well-prepared teacher utilizes bulletin board space to enhance student learning."

Create a class/ daily schedule

When making a schedule, try to think in terms of time rather than subject periods.

Middle school teachers have only 45 or 50 minutes to schedule per subject/ class period taught

Example: English - 50 minutes - 9:00 AM to 9:50 AM

9:00-9:05 - Daily Oral Language (call roll, etc.)

9:05-9:10 - Go over DOL - (grammar lesson)

9:10-9:25 - Mini-lesson -(writing skill)

9:25-9:45 - Writing time -(students work on individual writing pieces)

9:45-9:50 - Clean up/ Closure

Some schools have block scheduling which generally lasts 1 and 1/2 hours

Example: Social Studies - 90 minutes - 9:00 AM to 10:30 AM

9:00-9:15 - Daily Geography (call roll, etc.)

9:15-9:25 - Discuss answers to Daily Geography

9:25-9:55 - Lesson

9:55-10:20 - Activity to enhance lesson (group work, etc.)

10:20-10:30 - Closure/ Clean up

Before School Checklist

_____ Laminate supplies

_____ Set up room
        _____ arrange desks/tables
        _____ set up reading corner
        _____ set up other special areas (writing center, learning centers, etc.)
        _____ post classroom expectations and consequences posters
        _____ organize filing cabinets

_____ Set up student mailboxes/ cubbies

_____ Create Day of the Week folders

_____ Create individual student folders

_____ Set up gradebook

_____ Write welcome postcards to students
        _____ mail postcards/letter

_____ Create a class schedule

_____ Create a substitute folder

_____ Organize a Teacher Binder

_____ Write out lesson plans for first day
        _____ second day?
        _____ third day?

Hint:

Be aware that many districts require you to start work at least four days before the kids start. **THIS WILL NOT BE ENOUGH TIME TO PREPARE.**

Several of those days will be spent in staff development, new teacher training, and school meetings. You will probably be given one day or 1/2 day to work alone in your classroom. It is wise to get your classroom keys the day you are hired or as soon as possible thereafter.

Substitute Report Form

DATE: _____

TODAY WE...

Use this space to report what was actually done during class. What activities did you do, how much of the lesson plans did you cover, what else did you do that was not on the original lesson plan, etc..

The following problems occurred:

Use this space to describe any serious behavior or other type problems. Be specific and report the facts without emotion. Use the back of this page if necessary.

Problem: Action Taken:

Problem: Action Taken:

Problem: Action Taken:

Problem: Action Taken:

The following students were exceptionally good and/or helpful:

CONCLUSION

There are so many different tasks that must be done before school starts, it can be overwhelming. However, they are necessary to ensure that you start the year well-prepared. Veteran teachers know that the more prepared we are at the beginning of school, the more effective we are throughout the year. It is important to keep in mind that the more time you spend in your classroom before school starts, the more you will get done and the better prepared you will be.

Additional Resources

So Much Stuff, So Little Space: Creating and Managing the Learner Centered Classroom by Susan Nations, Suzi Boyett, Steven Dragon

Begin With the Brain: Orchestrating the Learner-Centered Classroom by Martha Kaufeldt

Questions for Reflection

1) What do you plan to put in your substitute folder? Why do you feel these elements are necessary?

2) Why do you feel it is or is not important to have a mailbox available for each student in your classroom? How would you implement this idea in your classroom?

3) Do you think it is important to create a positive learner centered environment in the classroom? Why or Why Not?

4) What do you feel is top priority to be done before school starts to be well-prepared? Explain why you feel these activities are vital for a successful start to the school year.

Suggested Activites

1) Create your own Day of the Week folders to be used in your classroom.

2) Design the ideal classroom set-up for yourself using a computer draw program or "good old-fashion" construction paper. Include the following items, and more of your own:
   - Desk arrangements
   - Teacher work station
   - Computer stations
   - Learning Centers
   - Some type of "Book Nook"

Don't forget the details of how you plan to make this a warm and welcoming learning environment for students.

          © 2003 Survival Kit for New Secondary Teachers

Notes/ Reflection on Chapter

Classroom Management

Good management is vital to a successful classroom. The best time to think about how our classroom will work is before school starts. In this chapter you will find various ways to have a smooth classroom through proactive management and discipline strategies.

As teachers we need to strive for positive relationships with our students - one that has clear expectations, but is based on mutual respect, communication and kindness. Just because we are in control and expect appropriate behavior does not mean that we need to be cold or distant.

Teachers can help to create a positive and motivating classroom environment by:

√ Being friendly
√ Having a sense of humor
√ Having a good rapport with students
√ Effectively communicating our desires and expectations
√ Understanding that students cannot read our minds
√ Being organized
√ Being well-prepared

Teachers are much more than just babysitters, managers, and timekeepers, they are also leaders. This role has much more importance than one realizes on the overall classroom climate. A leader guides, shapes, teaches, motivates, corrects, directs, and encourages his/her "platoon." In a teacher's case, the proper leadership style is crucial so that chaos doesn't rule!

My room is all set up and ready to go, but I'm not sure how to make everything flow smoothly.

Where do I begin?

"Leading your platoon takes effort, communication, dedication and respect!"

Classroom Leadership Styles

The three main leadership styles teachers use in the classroom are:

Teacher as Dictator
Teacher as Free-Spirit
Teachers as Balanced Leader

Teacher as Dictator

The teacher who acts as a dictator is often afraid of losing control, so he/she resorts to maintaining a very distant and stringent relationship with students. This often results in a relationship that is businesslike, firm, and authoritarian.

Characteristics of a Dictator Leadership Style:

- No room for group discussions or banter of any sort

- Routines are strictly adhered to

- Flexibility is not commonplace

- Tasks are performed in a quiet and efficient manner

- Students are not encouraged to be individuals and active participants in the lesson

- Students are required to conform to the teacher's way of learning

- Creative thinking is not encouraged

- Memorization and "skill and drill" are the main learning styles of this classroom

Although predictability and routine can be a positive classroom feature, this type of leadership is often boring and squelches creativity. It promotes a dull and resentful environment instead of one filled with active learning and excitement.

Rarely does a teacher accomplish a smooth running classroom by resorting to dictatorship. Students are more likely to rebel, complain, and misbehave because they are not intrinsically motivated.

"The Dictator Leadership style does not promote a positive classroom climate."

Teacher as Free Spirit

An ingredient in the free-spirit recipe is a teacher who is more than likely unorganized and unprepared which results in a choppy and incomplete presentation. Students are kept waiting while the teacher mentally decides what to do next and looks for materials. Students get confused and distracted easily which results in disruption after disruption. This in turn results in more "breaks" as the teacher must stop to deal with unruly behavior.

Characteristics of a Free Spirit Leadership Style:

- Teacher wants to be a "buddy" with the students rather than an authority figure.

- Students end up making most classroom decisions without guidance.

- Lesson plans are loosely sketched and student digressions dictate the course of the lesson rather than the teaching objective.

- Students are given maximum freedom to work and move about the classroom.

- The teacher gives the students the responsibility to make the decisions by themselves, in other words to "be their own boss."

- When students are not actively engaged in learning, this teacher is often quick to anger because he/she feels they are giving students freedoms which are being abused.

   This leadership style would be fabulous in a world where all students had the same set of values—honesty, integrity, responsibility, and determination. We would love for every classroom to be totally student centered, where students were always intrinsically motivated. However, this is unrealistic. It is the nature of most teenagers to push the limits as far as they can. Therefore, this laissez-faire, or lax, style of leadership will most likely be a recipe for disaster and anarchy.

"Being friendly with the students is NOT the same thing as being their friend."

Hint:

Do not allow students to address you by your first name, even in fun. Your relationship with students should be a professional one.

Teacher as Balanced Leader

"This leadership approach IS student centered, but recognizes that students need discipline to feel comfortable.

Teens require boundaries to feel at ease."

This leadership style blends both of the other styles to achieve the greatest results. As they say, "Everything in moderation." A teacher using this balanced approach to classroom management will:

· Set limits
· Communicate expectations clearly
· Follow routines and procedures
· Provide students with freedoms and responsibilities
· Offer choice
· Value students
· Invite student involvement on a daily basis

Other Characteristics of a Balanced Leadership Style:

- Is organized in order to maintain a productive classroom.

- Maintains discipline as a key component to this teacher-student relationship.

- Encourages students to be responsible for their own actions and holds them accountable.

- Allows students to be actively involved in the classroom.

- Explains and reinforces clear expectations from the first day of school.

- Consequences are consistent when behavior is inappropriate.

- Students feel valued and motivated.

- Students are given freedoms and choices in order to discuss, move, and work about the classroom freely.

"A well-prepared teacher is a balanced leader!"

Students tend to be much more cooperative with this classroom environment because they feel respected, appreciated, and valued. This leads to students who are intrinsically motivated!

Creating a "Balanced" Classroom Envrionment

As we just discussed, the balanced leadership style results in a balanced classroom which creates a non-threatening environment where students and teachers feel safe. This comfort allows students to be better learners.

In providing a balanced classroom, teachers need to be prepared to accept additional roles of:

- Mediator
- Tutor
- Leader
- Caregiver
- Listener
- Problem solver
- Disciplinarian

"An effective teacher is prepared to fill many roles with grace and flexibility."

Accepting that you have these roles is the key to having positive student relationships. To a new teacher, this may seem like an overwhelming task. How does one manage to perform all of those roles as well as the tasks required of us as teachers. The answer is effective time management and organization.

Classrooms are very complex, busy places! During a typical day we are required to perform many tasks:

- Organize learning activities
- Present lessons
- Prepare materials
- Manage student behavior
- Manage classroom equipment
- Handle administrative/ housekeeping duties
- Beat the Clock!

All of this must be accomplished while being interrupted for various reasons, such as assemblies, intercom announcements, office assistants, helping a sick student or getting a brand new one!

The remainder of this chapter is dedicated to providing strategies for maintaining a balanced and positive classroom environment in the face of these many challenges.

Quick Tips on Successful Classroom Management

If we had to provide a brief overview of our main philosophies on classroom management, this is it!

√ Read up on Brain-based learning. This research clearly shows how a non-threatening environment increases student learning and leads to open communication between teachers and students. See our discussion in the Teaching Strategies Chapter.

√ Distinguish between "Teacher Time" vs. "Student Time." A productive classroom allows for teachers to instruct without interruptions, and then gives students opportunities for debriefing, disscusing and assimilating the new information.

√ When joking with students, be sure to set a limit and end with a phrase such as, "Well, that was fun, but now it's time for us to get back to work. Everyone needs to focus on chapter…"

√ Use eye contact to make sure that everyone has understood the move from "play time" to "work time."

√ You'll find that when your lessons are motivating for students, they beg to stay in the classroom!

√ Post basic classroom procedures so that in the beginning students and parents know what to expect and can become accustomed to your classroom management style.

√ When students are actively participating in classroom activities which are meaningful and motivating, they are too focused to misbehave.

√ Students crave consistency. Your class will run smoothly if students always know what to expect.

√ Consistent behavior builds trust.

√ Trust then builds respect.

√ Frustration builds when students are confused. When frustration builds, behavior breaks down. Don't let this happen to you! Structure your daily routines!

√ Personal choice and group discussions are daily occurrences in a classroom which thrives on student involvement.

Hint:

The more specific directions and expectations are, the better students will understand how to follow them.

Always check for student understanding before releasing students to get started.

Use a key word like "GO!" and do not let students begin the activity until you say your key word.

Key Concepts for Successful Classroom Management

Dealing with your regular classroom duties with efficiency and calmness allows for positive student relationships. Students feel flustered and uneasy when their teacher is in a panicked or unorganized state. Too much unstructured time or too many pauses in instruction result in misbehavior. Also, loss of respect and trust for the teacher can result in additional misconduct. Here are some tips to help you streamline your classroom routines so that you are more prepared.

 **Have Specific Procedures Every Day.**

It is important to have procedures ready for students to follow upon entering the classroom from the very first day. Examples of daily routines which need teacher expectations and procedures:

- What to do before the bell rings
- Checking attendance
- Giving directions
- Collecting classwork and homework
- Distributing materials/ papers
- Student time vs. Teacher time
- Transition times between lessons/activities
- Working on projects
- Reading workshop
- Writing workshop
- Lab time
- Group work
- End of class

"Always remain calm and maintain order."

"A well-prepared teacher trains students on class routines used everyday to build consistency."

"Avoid looking panicked!"

> **Teacher Testimony**
>
> *My first year of teaching I had a horrible feeling at the end of every day! It seemed like chaos as students grabed their backpacks and began shoving everything inside! Some students were asking me questions about homework, while other students were responding to a lesson we had just finished, and most students were excitely chatting with each other. I felt so scattered and disjointed when the bell rang and the students rushed the door. After several weeks of this, I decided to enact an End of Class Routine that we would follow everyday. If the procedure wasn't followed, then students didn't get to leave my classroom. This included cleaning up the room, copying homework into their daily planner, packing up their backpacks, and then writing quitely in their journal until the bell rang. I gave them topics that provided closure to my lesson or that stimulated interest for the next day. When the bell rang, I began dismissing them one student or one row at a time depending on who was the quietest. They put their journals away and left quietly and quickly. I felt so much more collected and relaxed at the end of the day from then on!*

Have an Assignment ready BEFORE the bell rings.

√ Have the chalkboard, an overhead transparency, or your presentation station made out with important information and morning assignments.

√ Students should enter the classroom, begin copying important announcements, and complete the focus assignment found on the board or overhead.

√ Some possible warm up assignments are journal entries, new vocabulary words, grammar practice, math review, and daily geography activities.

√ Warm ups, or focus activities should not last longer than 10 minutes.

√ Students should KNOW every day to come in and get busy with their assignment. This happens through consistency and training from the first day!

- Follow your procedures religiously. You may want to post them so that students can see what to do every day.

- Procedure posters will help students and substitutes throughout the year (Susan Kovalik, 1997).

- Sample procedure posters that you may use can be found in the back of this chapter.

An example opening class procedure

1) Check student mailbox, retrieve graded work and class materials
2) Get class or lab supplies, if necessary
3) Sharpen pencil
4) Copy homework in calendar
5) Complete focus assignment

"A well-prepared teacher has a procedure READY for when students enter the class."

Hint:

If you have a permanent presentation station, simply save the information in a folder to access at the start of each new class!

Here is an example of how you could set up your chalkboard or presentation station before class begins.

Objectives: Date:

Homework: Agenda:
                                         1.
                                         2.
                                         3.
Warm-up Activity: 4.

Teacher Tip: If you are using a thought-provoking introduction and want students to be guided into discovering the objective rather than being told, leave it off the board until after the activity is finished. Then, review the objective with students and write it on the board.

 Type up a sheet with the date, class objectives, class agendy, any project or homework assignments, due dates, and the focus assignment for the day. Be sure you type up one per prep (course taught).

Type up this sheet along with your lesson plans so that everything is ready at the same time. Do not wait until the night before to type up your Beginning of Class information.

Purchase (or ask the school if they have any) copier transparencies. You might also try transparencies for laser or ink jet printers. Copy these typed sheets onto a transparency.

 Place each sheet in the Day of the Week folder with the appropriate lesson plans and other materials.

 This cuts down on having to change board information in between each class period. Simply put the new course transparency on the overhead and you are ready to go. This is perfect for traveling teachers to save time and energy!

"A well-prepared teacher sets up the board for the next day before going home to reduce stress in the morning."

Make your Directions Clear, Detailed and Precise.

When asking students to perform a task—BE SPECIFIC! Tell them exactly what you want them to do.

Example:
"On the following assignment I expect your final product to be typed or neatly written in black ink. I want it to show your best possible effort which means that the information should be correct, it should be neat, and it should be creative. Sloppy and half done papers will not be accepted."

Don't Waste Precious Time

"Become a Master at making effective use of class time and down time."

One important element of being a teacher is multi-tasking. This means that you need to be able to do several things at once. When you are teaching or doing other administrative tasks, you should also be monitoring students and checking their level of comprehension. The following are some examples of how you can effectively manage your time.

When giving a test:

It is not appropriate to sit behind your desk while students are taking a test. You should be monitoring, monitoring, monitoring!

√   Straighten the classroom.
    You need to be walking around monitoring anyway.

√   Prepare responses to student work.

√   Scan over memos from the office and record these items on your desk calendar.

√   Scan over lesson plans to prepare for the next activity.

√   Return graded papers to student mailboxes.

When completing administrative tasks:

Have a daily routine that allows for checking attendance, checking the academic calendar, etc...while students are engaged in another learning activity. The morning/ beginning of class focus activity is the perfect time to take care of your "business".

Checking Attendance (Roll Call)

Try to find the fastest way **WITHOUT** using the students if you can. For the first few days you'll need to call the roll out loud, but then you need to develop a quicker silent method.

√ One easy way to do this is to use a seating chart, check who is missing and record it.

√ Another method which works well with teachers who group students together would be to call out, "Group 1" and have the students tell you who is missing.

√ One last method is to place student journals or folders out for students to pick up when they enter the room. Folders that are left on the table are absent students.

√ With secondary classes, it is not as easy to keep attendance in the gradebook. The school will give you a class attendance sheet for each period that will need to be filled out and placed outside the door for pick up.

√ Any easy way to keep track of attendance is to create a manila folder for each period. Staple the attendance sheet to the right hand side and a seating chart to the left hand side. This way you can easily see who is absent and tardy.

√ If your school uses a specific sheet for reporting absences and tardies, make your own spreadsheet to keep attendance records within your classroom. Use this in your manila folder.

√ Mark absences as an A and tardies as a T. If it is excused, circle the letter.

√ Some schools use an electronic method of reporting absences and tardies. This is done on the computer and should be part of your routine at the start of each class.

The school office will keep track of absences. However, you are ultimately responsible for record keeping in your classroom. It is crucial to keep accurate records, as attendance has legal ramifications.

"You can be held legally responsible for your attendance records, so accuracy is vital!"

Checking Academic Calendars (Daily Planners)

After roll call, you may want to go around the room, while students are still working on their morning activities, to check to see that the homework has been copied down correctly. This gives you an excellent way to say hello to each student personally and check on their well being. It also can be used to your benefit during parent conferences, because it shows that you have taken a proactive role in teaching students to be responsible and reminding them on a daily basis.

Always Prepare Lessons Ahead of Time

Students can immediately tell when the teacher is not in control due to lack of planning. When this happens the class will quickly become rowdy or unmanageable.

√   Stay a little longer after school in order to plan and prepare for the next day. (Use the Day of the Week folders explained in the previous chapter)

√   Before you start an activity, all materials should be organized and ready.

√   Never use class time to prepare for the lesson.

√   Always prepare warm-up assignments and sponge activities ahead. Write them in your lessons and have them typed or on transparencies!

Plan for Transition Times

Don't just let things happen! Take time in your lesson plans to decide what you expect and give appropriate directions to students. This includes transitions between activities and classes. Otherwise chaos can occur. It is helpful to have these procedures or directions written down in the lesson plans or posted in the room so that a substitute will know how your classroom operates.

Between activities

Straighten up	Silent reading	Read Aloud
Logic Puzzles	Thinking Games	Jig-saw puzzle
Work on homework	Study for a test	

Hint:

Daily Planners are an excellent organization tool for students and a great source of two way communication with parents. When checked every day, they are very effective!
Also, saying "Hello" to each and every student is a positive way to start the day!

"Train your students at the beginning of the year regarding procedures for transition times."

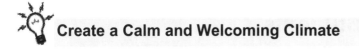
Create a Calm and Welcoming Climate

Maintain your Composure
Create a classroom climate that is calm by not overreacting to situations or problems that arise. Stay alert for behavioral problems and initiate strategies to dissolve the problem before it gets worse.

Avoid Yelling
When you find yourself losing your temper, turn around and count to ten or take several deep breaths while you close your eyes. This will help you remain calm and focused. Yelling only makes things worse. It upsets students and causes them to lose respect for you. Also, increasing the volume does nothing more than add to an already chaotic situation.

Verbalize Directions firmly but quietly OR Use Non-Verbal Cues
Use a quiet signal to help students focus on you while you are giving directions. This allows you to use a quiet and deliberate voice. Do not speak until EVERYONE is silent and looking at you.

Redirect Inapproprate Behavior Immediately
Unnecessary commotion must not rule your classroom. If things get out of control, rely on your non-verbal cues, such as eye contact or a quiet signal, to bring things back to order.

> *"When Students are interested and engaged, behavior problems are at a minimum and positive student - teacher relationships are at a maximum."*

Keep Students Actively Engaged in Learning Activities

"Busy hands are happy hands," our grandmothers always say. Challenge students and keep them involved with lessons by planning meaningful activities that have connections to other subject areas and real life.

Give students project type activities where they must create some sort of a product. This can be as simple as a scavenger hunt of important concepts within a chapter, or as complex as a diorama and oral presentation.

We offer specific strategies for this in the latter half of this book! Please read on!

Organizing Students

Organization is an important life skill that should be taught and reinforced throughout a student's academic career. Spending time on training students in organizational skills through student binders, folders, lockers, and desks is time well spent. Use the beginning of the school year to make student organization a focus, not only during "homeroom" or advisory time, but also in your lessons.

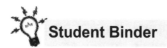 **Student Binder**

It is important that students begin the year in an organized fashion. Teachers can help their students do this by requiring them to set up a binder. Here are a few tips on creating an organized binder:

√   Use tabs to divide sections

√   Students should order their sections according to their schedule.

√   Have students keep graded work in the appropriate subject area.

√   An assignment calendar should be in the very front of the binder.

√   Class or school rules, procedures and syllabus should be placed behind the calendar.

√   Students might keep each course syllabus in the front of that particular class section.

√   Some students may want to keep a smaller 3-ring binder for each class. This will help prepare them for college.

It is important that you check the binders regularly (every six weeks will work). Sometimes it is helpful to take a grade for an organized binder. This will motivate students to continue using it correctly.

"Organization is a key element of Classroom Management "

Organization is a KEY life skill!

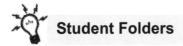 **Student Folders**

A great way to keep students organized is to set up folders for each subject/activity/record keeping area.

Pocket Folders

In addition to the binder, it is helpful for students to keep and use separate pocket folders that STAY in the classroom. Color coding these folders will help with quick and easy access for each activity/ subject area.

Journal
Students place paper in the middle. Then they date and write their daily journal entry. In order not to waste paper, I encourage my students to use up an entire page before beginning a new one. There could be several entries on a page.

Writing Workshop Folder   (Nancie Atwell, 1992)
Students keep notes for Writing Workshop in the middle of the folder, Prewriting/Drafts in front pocket, Works in Progress in back pocket. Final copy will go in the Writing Portfolio. We will discuss Writing Workshop in greater detail in the Reading/ Writing chapter.

Test Taking Skills Folder
Students place paper in the middle to keep notes on test taking strategies covered in class. Practice sheets, scan-trons, and answer keys should be kept in the pockets.

Reading Workshop Folder (Nancie Atwell, 1992)
Students keep a reading log that includes title, author, pages read and a short summary as well as a reading response. Students may also keep their book project work in this folder. We will discuss Reading Workshop in the Reading/Writing chapter.

Student Log
Students use this pocket folder to turn in any major projects. Any data collected and drafts should be placed in the front pocket to show the process of their work. The final copy of the project should be placed in the middle of the folder with any bulky or odd sized papers/products placed in the back pocket.

How could you utilize a pocket folder in your class as a journal or way to keep student work organized?

"Pocket folders are an inexpensive and easy way of keeping students organized in classroom."

Teacher Testimony

It was driving me crazy that my students kept losing their writing samples. We do several drafts on different topics and then towards the end of the semester, I ask the students to pick one draft to turn into a final copy. Half my students couldn't find their previous work! Finally, I got smart and insisted that the students leave their works in the classroom in a writing folder. We are all less frazzled during writing instruction now!

Manila Folders

Writing Portfolio

This manila folder is used to hold student writing pieces. Nancie Atwell, in her book In The Middle , describes an excellent way to set up a writing portfolio. This is a great way to track the progress of a student's writing skills throughout the year. A simple portfolio collects student work to be reviewed at the end of the year. Our Assessment Chapter further discusses and give examples of the use of portfolios.

General Portfolio

This manila folder is used to hold student work of all kinds. Students should have some choice as to the works placed in this folder. Also, when students enter work into their portfolio, they should attach a 3x5 index card with comments about their product. These comments should tell the teacher whether the piece is the student's "best" work, a "work in progress," or a sample to show how they have improved over time (this can include their "worst" work also).

Enrichment Folder

This manila folder is used as a place to hold enrichment work. Students who complete learning center activities on their own can place the products into their thinking folder to be graded for extra credit. In our Teaching Strategies Chapter we discuss how to set up learning centers.

Absent Folder

This manila folder is used to collect work and assignments for students who are absent. Have a student work as a "scribe" to copy down board assignments, homework, notes, and any other important information/ activities done during class on a specific absent form that you use consistently all year. The student should place this form along with any handouts in the absent folder and place it on the absentee's desk. The teacher could be the "scribe" if necessary. This folder is a great way to help students get back on track when they return to school.

Student information

This manila folder is for teacher purposes. As we discussed in an earlier chapter, this is the perfect place to keep student and parent communication records.

> *"A well-prepared teacher brainstorms how to teach students to be organized.*
>
> *Organization is a life skill ."*

> *"Manila folders are of great value for teachers and students. They are economical and can be used in so many ways!"*

Traveling Teachers

Many new secondary teachers begin their career as a "traveling" teacher. Basically this means that the teacher must travel from one classroom to another rather than staying in one room all day to teach. Any school with a large student population and not enough physical classrooms will have one or more "floating," or traveling, teachers. Without a classroom of their own, the traveling teacher must essentially borrow another teacher's room in order to teach his or her class.

It is vital that you develop a good rapport with the teacher who's room you will be sharing. This person will notice whether you are being responsible with their room or not, and they will share that information freely with others in the school. Below are some tips on getting off to a good start:

Before school begins, introduce yourself to each teacher who's classroom you will be using.

- Do not barge into the classroom demanding to have a discussion. Instead, ask if they have a few minutes to talk.

- If they say no, try to determine a time later in the day that you might be able to discuss the situation with them.

- Let this person know that you want to respect their rights and that you want to be sure that you are both on the same page in regards to sharing a classroom.

Determine the following through questions and discussion:

- Is there a place in the room where you can keep supplies or materials for your class?

- Would they mind if you had a small space on the wall or bulletin board to post student work, etc.?

- What supplies/equipment in the classroom are strictly off-limits to both you and your students?

- What supplies/equipment is this person willing to share?

Hint:

If you need special equipment, etc., for a particular class period, talk to the person who is in that room to make arrangements. Do you need to use the computer presentation station each day? Work it out in advance rather than making assumptions!

"Always leave each room exactly as you found it!"

Remember:
No one is required to share anything other than their room space with you and your students. Do not be offended by someone who adamantly refuses to share or help you. It may happen. But it is better that you are aware of that teacher's attitude from the start. Be as friendly as you can and make sure you respect their stuff!

More Tips

• Which classes can you store your own class supplies? Get a crate or other type of storage unit with a lid to hold those materials neatly for each class. Be sure it will fit in the space allotted to you.

√ Will it hold a hanging file folder crate?
√ Will it hold books (textbooks and/or novels)?
√ Will it hold writing, art, and other miscellaneous supplies you might need?
√ Will it hold shoe boxes with office supplies for you and your students?

• Use a tall drawer system with wheels to hold supplies you need for every class. This will be your "Mobile Classroom." Try to find a system with one or more drawers that can hold hanging file folders. These will come in handy to:

√ Keep student folders for those with severe issues
√ Keep enrichment folders for students who finish early
√ Keep idea folders for lesson extensions
√ Keep forms needed during class (detentions, referrals, etc.)
√ Keep Day of the Week folders for each course
√ Keep Lesson plans and attendance folders for each class
√ Keep Substitute folder

• Keep desk type supplies near the top of your unit for easy access. Do Not use the desk supplies of other teachers!

pad of paper	sticky notes	pens/pencils
tape dispenser	scissors	stapler(s)
stapler remover	paper clips	staples
highlighters	markers	calendar/PDA
Computer disks/CD		

• Tack a poster of your expectations to the front of your cart to use as needed with your classes.

• Print out procedures and expectations for each student in each class. Laminate and hole punch to fit in binders. Now you can simply refer students to the front of their binder when necessary. Laminating will keep the pages intact throughout the school year.

Hint:

If the teacher who's room you are sharing is not willing to provide one iota of space, don't give up! Try one of the teachers next door. They may be sympathetic to your plight. You never know until you explain your situation and ask.

Hint:

Rolling drawers are the best way to go because they can hold your materials without spilling the contents everywhere!

Think about how you could use other types of storage containers to help you in your situation.

Other Issues

Students Leaving the Classroom

Students leaving the classroom to go to the bathroom and for other reasons is a huge issue in the upper grades. Why is this? It is neither right nor fair that we subject our students to the embarrassment of requesting permission to answer nature's call. As adults, we would never stand for that kind of treatment. As long as you discuss your expectations at the beginning of the year, bathroom breaks should not be such an issue.

Teacher Tip:
• Create a Sign-Out sheet that includes: date, time out, time in, destination, and reason. Use Excel or some other spreadsheet program to help you make this.

• Explain your bathroom policy the first day of school.

Example:

"I do not expect you to have to ask permission to answer nature's call. However, it is important for your safety and the safety of others that I know where you are at all times and why you are someplace other than my classroom. Here are my expectations if you need to leave the class for any reason:

• Students may leave to use the restroom ONLY during "Your" time which is when you are working on assignments. If I am standing in front of you giving a lesson or instructions, you may not sign out.

• You must fill out the sign-out sheet completely and fill in the "time-in" slot when you return. Bring it to me and you may leave. Only one student may leave for a particular destination at a time. In other words, two of you may not go to the bathroom at the same time. You'll simply have to wait until the other person has returned.

• Your work time is exactly that - yours. However, if you do not complete your assignment during class, it will simply add more to your homework load.

• Take care of your business and get back. If you take longer than 5 minutes, your bathroom privileges will be limited.

"A well-prepared teacher has a policy ready for students leaving the classroom, no matter the reason."

Teaching Assistants

Although middle and high school teachers do not assign class jobs, having a teacher's assistant can be a huge help! Why not let your students help you take care of routine classroom tasks? Also, check with the school office to find out about classroom assistants. Some schools allow students to sign up for one period to be an assistant. If you ask, you might be able to have a student assigned to you for one class period as your dedicated assistant.

The following jobs require an application and letter of interest. These jobs are assigned for an entire semester.

Checkers

At the very beginning of class two students get homework papers from bins, check in grade book that it was turned in (pencil only), make out a list of students who did not turn in assignments and give to the teacher.

> ➔   **Qualifications** - Student must get to class early and finish AM assignments (or warm ups), be responsible, neat, have homework done on time, and upstanding behavior.

Graders

Two students help the teacher grade easier assignments that have a KEY. This can be done when these students finish their class work, or during study period.

> ➔   **Qualifications** - Graders must be responsible, neat, and have upstanding character and behavior.

Filers

Three students help file graded work in student mailboxes. One student helps teacher file materials in folder, notebooks, and student information files.

> ➔   **Qualifications** - Students must be responsible, neat, and have upstanding character and behavior.

Hint:

Giving students different jobs in the classroom makes them feel important and gives them a sense of cohesion in your class.

Assigning jobs to your students also helps with your work load!

Teachers can't do everything – We need help sometimes!

Student Discipline

As we stated earlier in this chapter, student discipline problems will be at a minimum if you keep your students **CHALLENGED** and **BUSY**.

If students are working and having to **think** the entire time they are at school, they will be less likely to misbehave. This does not mean that piling worksheets upon worksheets will keep your students out of trouble. They need meaningful assignments that are motivating as well as challenging.

Activities which are meaningful to students:

- Show connections between content areas
- Require active student participation
- Offer choice for students
- Relate to the real world and real world scenarios
- Require thinking rather than regurgitating information

Many teachers confuse the terms "Classroom Management" and "Classroom Discipline." What do each of these really mean?

Classroom Management - The way you organize and manage your daily classroom events so that no problems occur. This includes:

- Creating a positive classroom climate
- Implementing classroom procedures
- Organizing both the teacher and the students
- Preparing lessons and activities ahead of time

Classroom Discipline - Behavior modification for students who are not meeting classroom expectations. This can include both rewards and consequences for behavior displayed in the classroom.

Do not confuse "Classroom Discipline" with a "well-disciplined class." When your students know exactly what to do and when to do it, and meet the expectations of the teacher each and every day, you have a "well-disciplined class."

When students misbehave and do not meet classroom expectations, you will need some sort of "Classroom Discipline" plan in place to help those students modify their behavior.

"Without effective classroom management on the part of the teacher, you will NEVER have a well-disciplined class!"

"A well-prepared teacher knows the difference between a Well-disciplined Class and Classroom Discipline"

Recipe for a Well-Disciplined Class

√   Teacher who has planned ahead and is well planned

√   Flexibility

√   Established routines and procedures

√   Consistent follow-through

√   Positive attitude

√   Confidence

√   Brain-based classroom
- non-threatening environment
- offers guided choice
- teacher as a learning facilitator
- relates to real world
- motivating
- discovery learning
- students actively engaged

Establishing Expectations and Consequences

"An effective teacher spends time on classroom management and planning so that behavior problems are less likely."

Although we strive to have a well-disciplined class, we still must set expectations for students as well as consequences for not meeting those expectations.

Expectations

It is important that you decide upon five or six rules for your classroom. Your school and/or team may have rules that everyone follows. Be sure to find out what these rules are. Your rules should be clear and concise so that students know what you expect of them.

The rules on the following page set clear expectations for the students in your class.

You must spend time at the beginning of the year training your students in these expectations if you want to have a well-disciplined classroom. Do not stress about taking up class time to teach these expectations. Class time spent the first several weeks of school will ultimately mean more time throughout the year to teach meaningful lessons without disruptions.

Classroom Expectations and School Rules

1. Follow directions given by any adult.
   - Respond each time addressed by a teacher with ma'am or sir
   - Follow directions given the FIRST time given
   - Equal respect for ALL school personnel

2. Be in your assigned seat ready to learn.

3. Have all needed supplies and assignments (paper, pencils, books)
   - Turn in assignments on time
   - Use your time wisely
   - Complete work neatly and carefully

4. Work and move about the building so as not to disturb others. Keep hands, feet and objects to self.
   - Minimum noise level in halls
   - Right of way in halls

5. Show a respectful attitude to everyone.
   - No profanity, inappropriate language, rude gestures, teasing or put-downs.

6. Take care of school property and the property of others.
   - Show respect for building and personal items.

"Rules and Consequences should be clear and concise."

Teacher expectations do not end with classroom rules.

You also need to brainstorm what you expect from your students at ALL times. Take a moment to think about everything that goes in a classroom on a daily basis. Don't assume students will know how, when and where you want homework to be turned in if you don't tell them specifically. If you expect for homework to be put in the tray on your desk - explain this to the students. If you don't explain this, then you will have many students trying to hand you their homework throughout the class period, while you are often in the middle of something else!

Students should be told exactly what you expect from them and then trained in these expectations on a daily basis. Be consistent. Students who know what is expected of them and who know their limits will be less likely to cause problems.

Does the thought of keeping up with student behavior frazzle you?

What is the best way to record and keep track of student conduct? We have provided a variety of ways in the following pages. You can choose one that feels most comfortable to you.

Analogy

Let's put into perspective this idea of explaining our classroom expectations to students. Imagine that you are visiting a foreign country where you have never been before. When you arrive, a list of cultural guidelines and laws are given to you to help you know what is and is not acceptable. You read over these, and feeling confident that you are aware of everything you need to know, you venture out for dinner. Upon arriving at a restaurant, you enter and wait to be seated. The hostess comes and beckons for you to follow her. You calmly follow her to your table. Suddenly she turns around, looks down at your feet and begins to yell at you. You are startled and don't really understand the problem. The hostess is now quickly ushering you out of the restaurant. As you are being pulled back towards the exit, you realize that everyone else is wearing closed toed shoes and you are wearing sandals. It is an unwritten rule, or expectation, that everyone wear socks and shoes inside buildings in this country. Unfortunately, this was not in the list of guidelines, and no one ever told you about this "unwritten rule." Now you are flustered, you feel stupid, and feelings of anger and resentment begin to build because you are being punished for not knowing the expectation.

Hint:

Have a student stand at the front of the classroom and read a paragraph. Then as the student is reading, you walk around the room talking with other students, sharpening your pencil, doing jumping jacks, and acting the way you wouldn't want your students to act while you are presenting a lesson.

Then, have the students explain how difficult it was for her to continue reading with all of the distractions.

Think about these questions:

- How do you expect for papers to be turned in?
- What are your rules regarding neatness?
- Can the students write in print vs. cursive?
- What type of paper do you want students to use?
- Can they use colored ink pens?
- What are your expectations for bathroom breaks ?
- How will students get supplies during class or sharpen pencils?
- What do you expect students to do when they are finished with their work early?
- What are your expectations for students in writing centers, the reading corner, or lab stations?

When going over expectations at the beginning of the year, you want to be sure to:

√ Maintain eye contact with each student - this type of body language helps keep students focused on you

√ Speak slowly and pause after each sentence to emphasize the importance of what you are saying

√ Practice procedures over and over until they are habits!

√ Have discussions with students to explain why these expectations are important to you.

√ Maybe demonstrate some examples of why it would drive you crazy if students...

Getting a Handle on Student Talking

One of the biggest complaints from teachers is the issue of student talking. "They just won't be quiet!" "I constantly have to ask them to be quiet." "They don't listen to my lesson."

What are some things you can do to be prepared to deal with this issue?

Appropriate Talking Times

The first thing you need to ask yourself is *when are they talking?* Are they talking during your instruction, or when you are giving directions? Or, are they talking during a project or work time? There is nothing wrong in allowing students to talk while they are working. Although they may not always be talking about the subject matter, they will stay on task, especially if you are walking around monitoring. Additionally, the more motivating the assignment, the more students will actually be talking about their work.

Human beings are social creatures by nature, and we tend to do a better job when we talk to others. Talking helps us express our thoughts, ideas, and feelings. Students get ideas from one another, judge how well they are doing, and help each other do a good job on their work. Sometimes they are just chatting, but even this helps build a strong community in the classroom.

Talking aloud often allows us to work through a problem, formulate strategies, and organize thoughts. How many times have you found the solution to a problem simply by talking through it? Although some students simply talk to hear themselves speak, if your assignments are both meaningful and motivating, most students will be talking as part of the learning process.

Introduce the concept of "My Time" and "Your time."

Students need to know that there will be opportunities for them to talk and move around. In order to help them understand when it is and is not appropriate, introduce this concept. "My time" is teacher time. This is anytime you are teaching a lesson, giving directions, addressing the class as a whole group, or directly working with a small group. "Your time" is student time. This is anytime students are working independently or in groups (excluding testing situations) on classroom activities. Explain to your class that you know they can be quiet and focused during "My time" because after a few minutes, generally five to fifteen, it will be "Your time" and students can take care of their needs.

Teacher Testimony

In my classroom, I schedule talking pauses after new or important concepts are introduced. This allows my students to discuss their thoughts on the topic with a neighbor. I don't just stop teaching, but instead say something such as, "Now I'd like you to turn to a neighbor and discuss what I just presented to you. Write down any new thoughts and ideas you generate so that you won't forget them. Be prepared to share some of your ideas with the whole class."

Then I give everyone several minutes to talk while I walk around listening and engaging in some of the individual discussions.

I got this idea when I went to a district training for in-service presenters, but now I find that is works beautifully with my students as well!

Introduce this concept at the beginning of the year:

"Whenever I am giving a lesson, directions, am speaking to the class, or am standing in front of the class as a whole, that is MY TIME. During My Time, I expect for students to be silent, looking at me, and listening. You may be taking notes, but you are expected to pay attention to what I am saying. If you are talking to a neighbor, are you paying attention to me? (No) *If you are rummaging around in your backpack, are you paying attention to me?* (No) *Exactly. Now, let's practice what paying attention looks like."*

After practicing a few times on what paying attention looks like, next you might say:

"Now, if I have given you a class or group assignment and have given you time in class to work, that is YOUR TIME. You may get supplies, sharpen your pencil, go to the restroom..."
(These are examples, you DO want to be specific in telling them exactly what they are allowed to do. I let mine get a drink of water or use the restroom if they really need to, because thirsty students and students who need to go to the bathroom won't be thinking about their work - the only things they are thinking about are their bodily needs.)

"When I put up the quiet signal (my hand in the air), or ring the bell (a small dinner bell that I keep in my pocket or on my desk), that is the signal that it is MY TIME again, and I want full attention on me!"

Next, you need to practice this with them several times.

Tell the students to talk and chatter, sing songs, etc.. Then, time them to see how quickly they can come back to order after you signal them. Practicing this is fun for the students, but also allows them to internalize your expectations.

Monitoring and Redirect

When you do allow your students to talk during their work time, be sure you are walking around monitoring their conversations. Although it is okay to get off the assigned topic for a minute or two, too much off task talking is not appropriate. While you monitor, you are in more of a position to redirect student talking quietly, rather than yelling out, "Quiet Down Now!" which is completely ineffective. Instead, walk up behind the student who is taking and say (just to them) something like, "So, tell me what you have done so far? I am taking progress checks." That student is immediately on task and you haven't singled him/her out in front of the class, or yelled at the class as a whole. Standing behind a group of students for several minutes while they are working is also very effective for redirecting off task behavior.

<hr>

Hint:

Keep a clipboard with you as you walk around. On the clipboard, have either index cards or a spreadsheet of student names, so that you can take notes on what is happening: who is on task, who is not, problems, etc...

Later in the chapter we will discuss Clipboard Monitoring.

Remind students that as long as they listen during the lesson, "My Time," that you will let them talk while working, "Your Time."

CONSEQUENCES

When students do not follow the class or school rules, then you must modify their behavior with consequences. Your consequences should be clear and concise, and should be followed consistently. When you do not use the consequences you have set forth, or allow students to persuade you towards leniency, discipline will falter.

Your students will begin to push you more and more until you are frustrated and angry.

The following consequences go along with the Expectations mentioned earlier:

Classroom Consequences

1 demerit = WARNING

2 demerits = Loss of Clasroom Privileges

3 demerits = Detention

4 demerits = Parent Phone Call and Parent/Teacher/Student conference

5 demerits OR a serious offence= OFFICE REFERRAL

"Consistency is vital when working with students!"

These demerits can be marked on a student spreadsheet to help you keep track. Otherwise, it is easy to forget which students received demerits and which ones did not. The behavior spreadsheet should be kept in a separate manila folder (or can be placed behind attendance chart). It should be kept in a place easily accessible by the teacher, but not make public display of student infractions.

Important Teacher Tip:
Writing student names on the chalkboard and placing checks next to the names for misbehavior is not an appropriate way to record behavior problems. Instead, it only serves to embarrass the student. If it doesn't humiliate them, it could have the opposite affect, and the student enjoys the negative attention. Either way, this will generally result in additional rebellious behavior.

Recording Student Discipline Infractions

Remember:

- No student should be allowed to repeat the same misbehavior more than three times in one day (two times in one 50 minute period). More than this should result in an office referral.

- Every day should start "fresh with no mistakes in it."

- Each behavior, whether different or the same, should be recorded

"Make sure that your procedure for marking and recording student behavior is not time consuming or distracting."

Class Rolls

You can mark checks OR the number of the rule not followed in your grade book or on your class roll. You could also make a spreadsheet and attach it to your grade or roll book.

Index Cards

You can mark down the date and the number of the rule not followed on an index card. It is easier and less time consuming to simply write the number of the rule rather than taking the time to make written comments on the card. When you fill the index card, staple another to it. This is helpful when you are contacting parents and want to access a record of student behavior easily.

Clearly State the Expectation

With all of these methods, be sure to clearly state which expectation the student did not meet. Many times students, especially middle school students, whose minds often wander continuously, will not be aware of what they have done.

Teacher Testimony

As a 7th grade English teacher, I have found that it is necessary to tell the student exactly what they have done wrong before applying consequences. At first, if a student spoke out of turn or got out of their seat during my lesson, I would simply stare at them and mark it down in my book. When I showed the student the mark in my book, they were indignant and said that I was being prejudiced or unfair. Finally, I realized that half the time the students didn't even know that they were doing something wrong. From then on I made sure to tell the student exactly what rule they were breaking at the time of the infraction.

Using Rewards

We all know that discipline programs based completely on consequences or punishments are not effective in modifying student behavior. However, there is currently a debate about reward based programs as well. Some researchers contend that rewards can be equally as harmful.

Our belief is that rewards can be used as a motivational tool to help students begin to modify their behavior. As students begin to meet your expectations on a consistent basis, you should rely less and less on rewards as a tool. Remember that students who are actively engaged in their learning do not need outside stimuli such as rewards for motivation. They are motivated by the desire to learn.

For example, in the movie *Dangerous Minds*, Michelle Pfieffer's character walked into an extremely hostile and volatile classroom situation. She wanted to use positive measures to change student attitudes, and began a reward system for classroom participation. As her students began participating more in class and were more engaged, she slowly reduced the number of rewards passed out until finally students were participating because they were truly interested and were intrinsically motivated to learn.

The same should apply to you. If you find yourself in a rough classroom situation where drastic measures are needed, yet you want to foster a positive environment rather than a negative one, a reward based program is the perfect place to begin. As your students' behavior begins to change, you want to wean them off of the rewards until they are participating and behaving because THEY want to, not because you are paying them.

"An effective teacher seeks to modify student behavior by focusing on positives rather than negatives."

Tips:

√ Use sporadically throughout the day, week, month, year

√ Don't rely on rewards in place of good classroom management

√ Work your way towards students who are intrinsically motivated through engaging teaching strategies

√ Be fair in giving out rewards - each student should have an equal chance

> *"You will be surprised at how well your students respond to even the smallest recognition for a job well done."*

Tokens of Appreciation

➔ **Bonus Points**

Use the bonus point coupons in the back of this chapter and add them onto homework/project or test grades. Use coupons in denominations of 1's and 5's.

➔ **Red Tickets**

Buy a roll of red, green, or other brightly colored tickets from a teacher or office supply store. Hand these out for participation, etc. Students write their names on the back and put them into a canister for a weekly drawing.

➔ **Mascot Coupons**

Use school "mascot" coupons, or create your own to give to students for the following: 1st done with morning assignment/ sponge activities, parent signatures on binders, life skills shown in class, or best organized binder.

➔ **Class Leader**

Give this award to the student who has shown the most improvement during the week.

Using Recognition

Students want to be recognized not only for their accomplishments, but also for hard work and improvement. Secondary students are often highly motivated by recognition efforts through a banquet or assembly of some sort.

Provide students with a special certificate noting their accomplishment. Be sure all students have the opportunity to receive recognition

Examples:

Good Citizenship	Top 10 Class Points	Community Service
High Grades	Peer Relationships	Teamwork
Mediation	Teacher Assistant	Effort
Improvement in academics or behavior		

Attitude is Everything!

How true! Attitude IS everything! The attitude you show your students on a day-to-day basis will dictate the type of classroom you have. If you show each and every one of your students respect, then they will show you respect. Intermediate and especially middle school students are highly motivated by the concept of respect. Yet, how do we show our students that we respect them?

Here are some tips:

➜ When a student misbehaves, take them in the hallway and discuss the matter with them privately. Use a tone of voice you would use when speaking with another adult.

➜ Remember that your students will act like adults at times and children at others!

➜ Address your students as Ladies and Gentlemen. You would be surprised at how they will act according to the way you address them. If you insist on calling them boys and girls, OR children, that is exactly the way they will act. Do you enjoy being patronized? Think about it.

➜ Treat them the same way you want to be treated by your peers. Your students will meet the expectations you set for them both mentally and behaviorally.

"Treat your students with respect and you'll find they will respect you in return."

➜ When the class as a whole is being loud, do not yell over them. Simply wait and your silence is more powerful than your screaming. Often a look, or quiet statement of, "I'm waiting," will be enough.

➜ When you are trying to maintain classroom discipline, there are a few things you should definitely not say to your students. These statements are clear indicators that you have lost control.

Things NOT to say:

- I really mean it this time!
- I'm serious!
- I really will... if you don't straighten up!
- How many times do I have to ask you to ...?
- I'm getting angry!
- You better not... or I'll ...!
- Stop it! Stop it! Stop it!
- You make me so mad!

Bag of Tricks

Remember, all communications you make with students must be made thoughtfully with wisdom and discretion. You have to know your students and your limits with each teen. Be aware of your boundaries when using these "tricks". Remember, your ultimate goal is to create a positive classroom environment based on mutual respect. These are quick tips to help you get started in managing classroom behavior.

- **Use a quiet signal when the class is loud or not paying attention.** -Simply raise your hand and wait. At the beginning of the year you need to explain this signal to your class and practice several times. Be consistent in using it. DO NOT raise your voice over the class. EXPECT SILENCE from the class. Wait until EVERYONE is silent. When explaining the quiet signal, you may want to say, "When I hold up my hand like this, I EXPECT everyone to stop what they are doing, get silent, and look at me." Then follow through. You might also use chimes or a small bell as a signal.

- **Code Word** - Discuss with your class a "code" word you can use to signal that you want their attention. Whenever you call out this word, students should stop what they are doing, get silent, and look at you.

- **Stand silently in front of the class and give them "THE LOOK"** (this is discussed later) - If they do not get quiet, simply make a statement such as, "I'm waiting," or, "Excuse me," or ask, "Why am I standing here?" then fall silent again. Students will quickly get the point and quiet down. The more you scream or raise your voice, the louder the class will get.

- **When your students begin acting irresponsibly, take away privileges.** - Explain to them that as long as they act like ladies and gentlemen, you will give them responsibilities. However, if they are going to act immaturely, do not hesitate to take away privileges.

- **Walk around the classroom at all times so that you are in position to get close to a student who is not behaving and can quickly correct behavior.**

- **Give the student a direct look or tap the student's desk with your finger and shake your head that what they are doing is not acceptable.**

- **Sit a problem student close to you**

Teacher Testimony

I once had an Assistant Principal who felt that she was helping me with my classroom discipline by telling me to add to my "Bag of Tricks." I had several problem students that year and needed some advice - Specific Advice! Just some quick tips to use and remember when dealing with problem students would have been so helpful!

- **Write a behavior plan that focuses on rewards rather than punishments**

- **Have a parent conference**

- **Call the parents consistently**

- **Write up behavior in their file for future reference** - Keep all notes written by students and by yourself for documentation purposes.

- **Practice "THE LOOK"** - Think about the one teacher that you didn't dare to cross. How did he/she look at you when you misbehaved? Practice that look. Watch other veteran teachers in your school give "THE LOOK." Once you get good, you can give "THE LOOK" to kids in the mall and have them stop what they are doing - even if you don't know them at all!

- **Practice the "Tone of Voice"** - This is the same as "THE LOOK."

- **Make comments -** A good comment is, "I like how John is reading quietly and not playing around." Then, if you want to, you can give John a Homework pass or small piece of candy.

- **Do not argue with students** - When a student is arguing with you and yelling at you, simply say to them, "I do not have to be treated like this. I am not talking to you right now. When you have calmed down and wish to talk reasonably, then I will discuss it." Then turn around and walk away. You may have to be more aggressive and put your hand out to stop their arguments.

- **Stand your ground** - Remember, you are the adult. Sometimes students who are taller or bigger than you are can be scary. Do not let them feel fear from you. Fear can be sensed and you will be taken advantage of.

- **Take your own time out** - When you feel yourself losing your temper, leave the room and take a quick time out for yourself. It is okay to ask an administrator or an off duty teacher to watch your class while you calm down.

- **Separate the ringleaders** - Find the ringleaders and send them to different classrooms with either current class work, or an assignment which reinforces their understanding of good behavior and the lifeskills.

- **Send a guide** - If you doubt that a student will go where you send them, send a reliable student with them as a guide.

"There are times when it is important to stand your ground, especially on the important issues.

Ask yourself, do I really need to get into a power struggle over this?"

- **Don't get in a power struggle** - Ask yourself – Is it important that I fight this or that I win this battle? Sometimes a power struggle is just not worth it. Refuse to argue or fight, and instead, turn your back to the situation.

- **Use a calm voice at all times** - As soon as you lose your cool, the student has won. If you feel yourself getting upset, simply count to 10. Another good way is to remember - You are the adult and should act maturely.

- **Refuse to yell** - Don't argue with a student and refuse to listen to whining or crying. Repeat that you will be happy to talk to them when they have calmed down.

- **Follow your consequences consistently** - This will really help in the long run and helps build trust between you and your students.

- **Send students to the office ONLY as a LAST RESORT!** - Once students know that you will bow out and let the principal or counselor handle the problem they will push every button you have so that they are sent out of the classroom.

- **Follow through with your stated consequences both written and verbal** - However, think about this — is your problem student TRYING to be sent out of the classroom? Don't give them the satisfaction. Also, think before you blurt out a specific consequence such as, "If you don't stop talking back, I'll _____." Be sure the consequence is one you are willing and able to do.

- **Do not take it personally!** - Students will say lots of things that may hurt your feelings. Don't let it. They may be simply trying to get your goad. Just ignore it and get on with your life.

Teacher Testimony

My first year of teaching I had a seventh period class with 15 boys and 8 girls. Of those 15 boys, 9 of them were placed in the Adaptive Behavior Class for Emotionally Disturbed children. I had one student try to jump out of the window. One brought a gun to school hidden inside of a teddy bear. One student galloped around the room neighing like a horse every day. One student wrote foul language on every book I owned in the classroom. I also had two warring gang members who threatened each other during class. These were sixth graders.
My point? I survived and am still teaching!

Clipboard Monitoring

1. Using a spreadsheet program such as Excel, Lotus, or ClarisWorks, create a spreadsheet. Down the side, allow for student names. Across the top put one rule or work habit in each box. Leave a couple of boxes blank so that you can write in the concept or skill for the day that you want to observe.

Example:

Student Name	1. Stay in Seat	2. On Task During Group work	3. Cooperating wih others	4.
JOHN	1 2 3 4 5	1 2 3 4 5	1 2 3 4 5	1 2 3 4 5
ASHLEY	1 2 3 4 5	1 2 3 4 5	1 2 3 4 5	1 2 3 4 5

2. Use a system of numbers to help you keep track of infractions. Make sure there is enough space for comments as well if necessary.
   With rules, each number represents the number of infractions
   With concepts/skills, you write the skills in the blank columns and underneath, each number represents the level of mastery
   5 = Excellent, 4 = Good, 3=Fair, 2=Poor, 1=No Mastery

3. Place a week's worth of spreadsheet forms on the clipboard so that you won't have to remember each morning to put a new sheet up.

4. Make enough copies for several weeks. There should be one spreadsheet per day. Label the date at the top of the spreadsheet before using it so that you'll know which day it refers to.

5. Be sure to use the clipboard to record good behavior and to make comments about students who go above and beyond what is expected of them. This will help you when it is time to write progress reports or report card comments. It will also help you if you ever have to recommend a student for an honors position or award.

6. File these sheets in a three-ring binder in chronological order. Use tabbed dividers to separate each six weeks or grading period. Why a binder? Well, a binder keeps all of the papers together in one place with no fear of losing them. Also, it is easier to flip through pages in a binder than it is in a manila folder.

7. Be sure to document behavior disruptions, etc...in the student's folder at the end of the week so that you won't have to bring a ton of extra papers to a parent conference. If you are in a huge hurry, you might just make a copy of the form to put in the students folder. Just be sure to blank out other student names before putting it in a particular students folder.

          © 2003 Survival Kit for New Secondary Teachers

DATE:_____   CLASS:_____

STUDENT NAMES	1.	2.	3.	4.	5.

Opening Class Procedure

1. **Check Student Box**
    -Get graded papers and put in Binder
    -Get necessary folder(s)

2. **Get supplies ready for class**
    -Sharpen pencil
    -Get book for class

3. **Copy homework into Academic Calendar**

4. **Complete Focus Assignment**

5. **Be ready to share**

Writing & Reading Workshop Procedures

1. Get your writing folder, reading folder, and novel from your mailbox.

2. Be ready to take notes.

3. When writing, write quietly for the entire 20 minutes.
   - -respect each other's need for quiet
   - -conference outside or in centers
   - -respect each other as authors

4. When reading, quietly get your book and reading folder, and find a place to read.
   - -read silently
   - -respect each other's need for silence

5. When time is up, record what you have done in your reading log.
   - -date
   - -author's name
   - -title of book
   - -number of pages read
   - -a short summary OR complete the reading response on the board.

6. Put folders and book back in your mailbox.

End of Class Procedure

1. Put away all materials neatly and clean your table.

2. Take out Journal/Log folder.

3. Open your Academic Calendar.
>   **-check that all homework is written down correctly**
>   **-add any new assignments**

4. Complete End of Class Journal Assignment posted.

6. Wait to be dismissed.

Classroom Management

Your assignment is to define each of the following words. You must copy the ENTIRE definition!

Respect -

Responsibility -

Integrity -

Discipline -

Cooperation -

Effort -

Honesty -

Perseverance -

Friendship -

Authority -

Attention -

Quiet -

Work -

Organization -

Flexibility -

Initiative -

BEHAVIOR MODIFICATION PLAN

EXPECTATIONS	MONDAY	TUESDAY	WEDNESDAY	THURSDAY	FRIDAY
1.					
2.					
3.					
4.					
5.					

- -

Cut along the line.

Instructions: Work with the student and/or parent to determine five behaviors you expect the student to perform. Some examples include: stay in seat, use a respectful tone of voice, keep hands to self, take turns when speaking, etc. Then, each day a student exhibits one of these behaviors, place a sticker or initial the box for that day. Reward the student on a weekly basis.

For example:
     5 stickers = a special job to do (erase board, line leader, run an errand, etc.)
   10 stickers = a homework pass
   15 stickers = special lunch with the teacher
   20 stickers = computer time/ library time

NOTICE OF CONCERN

Date_____   Student's Name_____

Student's ID Number_____   Grade_____

Subject_____ Teacher_____

Counselor_____

To Parent/ Guardian

_____   This notice is sent to advise you that your child is having academic difficulties.

_____   This Notice is sent to advise you that your child is at risk for failure.

_____   This Notice is sent to advise you that your child's behavioral conduct may result in disciplinary actions.

_____   Student cannot participate in extracurricular activities due to failure.

Tutorial help: **M   T   W   Th   F   S**   Time:_____

Academic Difficulties

Failure to complete assignments   Failure to make up work/ tests   Excessive absences

Failure to bring materials to class   Poor quality of work   Excessive tardies

Poor test(s) results   Failure to follow directions   Lack of effort

Other_____

Behavioral Misconduct

Talks excessively   Ignores correction   Disruptive

Distracts other students   Displays negative attitude   Displays disrespect

Other_____

Parent/ Guardian is requested to have a conference with the teacher at one of the conference periods indicated below:

CONFERENCE TIME: 1st Choice _____   2nd Choice _____

Please Sign and Return

Parent / Guardian Signature_____   Date _____

We Missed You!

Name _____

Date of Absence _____

You missed these cool activities in class today!	**Important Assignments**
You missed the following Quiz/ test on:	**Journal topic/ Warm up assignment** **Other**

© 2003 Survival Kit for New Secondary Teachers

CONCLUSION

As we prepare to take on the many roles of teaching, we must keep in mind the end result. If we desire a well-disciplined class which is learner centered, it is vital to train our students in our expectations and procedures. Proactive, not reactive, strategies are required to maintain a classroom where students know what is expected of them at all times. Remember, adolescents need boundaries and structure in order to feel safe in their environment. Although they will test and strain these boundaries, children ultimately want to know that they cannot be broken.

When there is consistency in the classroom, trust is built between all members. Where there is trust, respect follows. If we want our students to respect us, then we must respect them as well. This includes setting expectations and being consistent in our requirements. When everything changes from day to day, students never know what to expect and as a result become excitable, unruly, and sometimes angry.

Good classroom management takes time and effort. It is not easy being consistent and it is not easy always enforcing the expectations set. However, without consistency behavior breaks down and learning does not occur. Thus, effective learning on the part of the student is the result of dedication, preparation, and planning on the part of the teacher.

Additional Resources

Choice Theory in the Classroom
by William Glasser, M.D.

Discipline without Stress, Punishments, or Rewards
by Dr. Marvin Marshall

Discipline with Love and Logic
by Jim Fay and Dave Funk

The Bully Free Classroom: Over 100 Tips and Strategies for Teachers K-8
by Allan Beane

Questions for Reflection

1) How would you describe yourself as a leader? How do you think this will translate in the classroom? Will your style of leadership invoke positive or negative reactions from students?

2) How would you compare the terms of Classroom Discipline and Classroom Management? Which is more important for the overall development of a positive classroom environment? Why?

3) How can you justify using class time to train students on classroom management procedures and practice classroom expectations when these activities may take away class time spent on curriculum?

4) Why is it so important that you know what your expectations and daily classroom procedures are before school starts?

5) Debate the pros and cons of using rewards in the classroom. Support your reasons.

Suggested Activites

1) Brainstorm and type out a list of classroom procedures you will want to use with your students at various times during the day. Think about the beginning of class, end of the day, transition times, etc.

2) Compose a list of expectations for your students that goes beyond common sense classroom rules. Think about your "pet peeves", important life-skills, and daily tasks.
For example:
- How will papers be turned in? Where?
- How will you handle student supplies?
- Do you expect ink or pencil? Do you care if it is purple or green ink?
- How will you handle bathroom breaks?
- Do you expect honesty & integrity in the classroom? personal best? cooperation?

Start a list now and keep adding to it through your student teaching and/or first year. You'll know you've got an expectation when you say to yourself, "My students will never...," or "I'll have my students do ..."

3) Plan how you will organize student work. Will you use spiral notebooks, pocket folders, or a 3- ring binder? How will you label each section of a binder or notebook? Where will students keep their unfinished work? What do you expect students to keep in their binder?

          © 2003 Survival Kit for New Secondary Teachers

Notes/ Reflection on Chapter

Lesson Plans

> ## My planning book is empty and I'm not sure where to begin.
>
> ## What do I do?

While we all learn about lesson plans in our teacher education courses, for some reason it all goes out the door when faced with a blank page for the first time. What do I teach? Where do I start? How do I organize it? All of these questions run through our head as we stare at either a blank piece of paper or a blank plan book. This chapter will give you several tips for writing lesson plans and will provide a couple of templates to help you get started.

Type out your lesson plans on regular paper

Teacher stores and schools will often sell/give teachers a plan book. While these books are nice, they do not give you enough room to adequately plan. The most you can fit into those squares is a brief outline of your plans. While this seems easy enough, it will cause you more grief later on.

Type out detailed lesson plans

Your lesson plans need to be detailed so that you will have a smooth, well organized day. This also helps when you have a substitute. With plan books teachers have to rewrite more detailed lesson plans for a substitute to follow. You will save hours by having it already done.

Although it may be a pain to write out detailed lesson plans, it is worth the effort! You will feel more prepared, relaxed and confident each day rather than stressing out over last minute unplanned activities and time fillers. We cannot emphasize enough how vital it is to overplan each lesson! You can always cut an activity, but it is hard to come up with one spur of the moment.

Benefits of having detailed lesson plans:

- Serve as a way to keep teachers focused and on target with objectives.
- Students see the teacher as well-prepared and organized.
- Principals and other staff members view the teacher as efficient and effective.
- Teachers have a smooth flowing day.

> *"A well-planned teacher has a focus activity ready for students to complete as soon as they enter the classroom."*

As we stated in the previous chapter on classroom management, students can immediately tell when the teacher is not in control due to lack of planning. This often causes behavior in the classroom to break down. Each class period should be planned out from bell to bell. What is the focus activity? What will you do first, second, third? What will the students do first, second, third? Every moment should be planned.

Focus Assignment

When students first enter the classroom, they need a focus activity of some sort to help them calm down and get ready to start class. This must be done every single day and for every class period (when changing classes) in order to maintain consistency. When used here and there, students never know what to expect. This adversely affects their behavior. The focus assignment is sometimes called a "bell-ringer", "warm-up", or "sponge" activity.

Types of focus activities:

- Write in journals
- Creative writing activity
- Calendar questions
- Sentence corrections
- Simple review activity
- Geography questions
- Name the state, scientist, explorer
- Math problems
- Review questions from previous day's lesson
- Vocabulary
- Pop-quiz
- Bulletin board activities—current events, calendar, vocabulary, authors, birthdays, etc.
- Daily Oral Language/ Geography/ Math/ Science
- Quote of the Day

Teacher Testimony

My students all copy their homework into an academic calendar as soon as they walk into my class. Then, while they are all working on their warm-up activity, I go around and check their calendars. I initial each entry that has been copied down correctly. This gives me a chance to say hello to each student and see how everyone is feeling. I can actually diffuse any problems right from the start of class!

While students are completing their focus activity quietly at their desks, you can use that time to call roll, visit with individual students, and take care of other housekeeping items.

Some quick sponge activities can also be used for transitions when students are finished early.

 **Objectives**

What do you want students to be able to do by the end of the lesson/day? Your objectives should be written in a manner that can be evaluated.

For example: Students will be able to identify the main theme in the novel, Great Expectations.

You don't want to write objectives that are hard for you to measure student achievement or knowledge.

For example: Students will understand the theme of a story.

First of all, this objective is not specific enough, and secondly, how will you measure student understanding?

 **Procedures**

What will you do during class time to achieve your objectives? This may include direct instruction, individual practice, group practice or application, enrichment, and possibly even assessment. Your procedures should reflect effective teaching practices such as varying learning activities, making connections to the real-world, application of learning, etc. We discuss these issues further in later chapters.

After writing out your procedures, ask yourself if the activities are:

- Mostly teacher-centered or student-centered
- Varied for different learning styles
- Actively engaging for students
- Helping students meet the objective(s)

> *"A well-planned teacher varies learning activities to help students meet a specific objective."*

Example:

Objective: To be able to identify the effects of wind erosion.

Procedures:
1) Student groups make predictions about the effects of the wind erosion experiment and record in lab journal
2) Student groups follow lab instructions for erosion experiment. Record in lab journal.
3) Students make observations about the effects of erosion and record in lab journal.
4) Groups share their observations
5) Lesson - Students take notes about wind erosion.
6) Students view photos of various regions in the US and identify effects of wind erosion in each photo.
7) Students work in pairs to compare/contrast the effects of water erosion(previous lesson) and wind erosion. (if time) (extension activity)

Closure

Closure to a lesson is one of those elements that is so important and yet so misunderstood. In our lives we often talk about needing some closure before moving onto something new. It is the same with lessons. If a teacher spends time and effort teaching a topic, and then immediately switches to a new topic or dismisses students without any kind of a closure, there is a sense of being left in the lurch. We all need a conclusion or summary of some sort before moving on. Here are some tips for providing closure:

- Students should be actively involved
- Question students about the lesson/ what they learned
- Students reflect in their journal about the lesson and share
- Ask students how this lesson/topic relates to the real world or to them personally
- Use a visual object and/or catch-phrase to sum up the lesson

Materials

It is equally important to plan for all of the materials you will need for the lesson and activities. Be very specific and include the textbook, student notebooks, etc.. This will help you know to remind students to bring a particular item(s) that they may not use every single day. Planning out materials also helps you stay organized in gathering what you need before you teach a particular lesson.

Assessment

When you plan, you need to know how you will assess student mastery of the objective(s). In order for an assessment to be valid, it must test what the students have learned. Before you plan a lesson, think about how you plan to assess the objective. Will you use a paper/pencil test? Will you use a class activity? Will you use a project or group assignment? Will you require students to recite information or apply it?

Once you've decided how you plan to assess students, then you can check your lesson and activities to be sure that they appropriately prepare students for the assessment. For example, when looking at the sample objective and lesson on the previous page, you might decide that an appropriate assessment would be for students to identify the effects of wind erosion on a particular region. This type of assessment would be valid since students learned and applied the information in a similar manner.

"It is important to plan a closure activity and an assessment when writing lesson plans."

Tips for Planning

Organize your plans on disk.

If you are using a computer, organize your plans into folders for each six weeks or units. Then, further organize each six weeks into folders for each week. This way you can place typed handouts, tests, newsletters, etc. into the folder with your plans.

Example:

Disk: McDonald American Lit

1st Six Weeks (Folder)
           -August 6-10 (Folder)
                -lesson plans (file)
                -vocabulary test (file)
                -reading assignment (file)
                -parent newsletter (file)
                -novel pages (file)

Have a chosen planning day.

Choose one day out of the week to write your plans. Wednesday is usually a good day and will give you time to gather materials for the next week. Also, many principals request copies of lesson plans on Fridays. If something unexpected happens on Wednesday, then you still have one day to get them finished. Be consistent with this schedule and plan your time accordingly.

Use a template when planning.

Using a template will help you work out your lesson plans with ease. If you save one week's plans on a disk, you can simply copy them onto a new file and change as necessary. *See sample templates in the back of the chapter.*

"A well-planned teacher sets aside one day each week to stay after school and plan lessons for the following week."

Steps of Lesson Planning

These steps are for teachers who are beginning the year with no idea of where to start. For those of you who already know WHAT you are going to teach, look at the templates provided later in the chapter.

1.) What are you required to teach? Look at a scope and sequence or overview of state required essential elements for your subject and/or grade level. *(Use State Department of Education Webpages)*

2.) How can you organize that material into units? Try to make these units meaningful to students. For example, a unit on Nouns is not going to motivate any of your students, but a Mystery unit might.

3.) Write an overview for your first six weeks on a calendar. This does not need to be detailed, but should give you an overall picture of what you will cover during that grading period. If you teach several courses, make a calendar for each course taught. This will be extremely helpful to refer to when you sit down to write daily lesson plans.

"An effective teacher works hard to make lessons meaningful to students."

4.) Write lesson plans for the first week. In the beginning you may want to go one day at a time unless your principal requires you to turn in your weekly plans. Use the following format:
- **Date**
- **Objectives** - what do you want the students to know or be able to do?
- **Materials** - what do you need to accomplish this?
- **Procedures** - what are you going to do 1st, 2nd, 3rd, etc.?
- **Assessment** - how are you going to know you met your objectives? This may not occur for several days or weeks into the grading period, but you need to know what you are going to do.

The following three pages show examples and templates for planning. A sample calendar and daily lesson plan is included.

Here is a sample *calendar* with a six weeks overview. A sample lesson plan is provided for the day shaded below. A blank template of each will be in the back of this chapter.

Monday	Tuesday	Wednesday	Thursday	Friday
Introduction Name Game Journal Entry Procedures Expecations	Student Info. Get-to-know Activity Assignment #2	Organizing for class Get-to-know Assignment #3	Set up writing folders Assignment #4	Pop Quiz over procedures & expectations Assignment #5
Writing Steps Writing Process Prewriting 1	Pre-writing 2 Link to Week 1 Assignments Hot Topics	Lifemap Using Real-life experiences for writing Prewriting 3	Writing Modes Prewriting 4	Genre Overview Prewriting 5
Mystery & Horror Genre Practice	Sci Fi & Fantasy Genre Practice	Adventure & Historical Fiction Genre Practice	Autobiography & Biography Genre Practice	Round Table sharing of writing sample
Drafting stories - choose 1 genre or previous pre-writing to start first story	Drafting Stories Draft #2	Drafting Stories Draft #3	Drafting Stories Draft #4	Choose 1 story to take to Final Copy - Round Robin Sharing for feedback
Peer Response - instructions & model with the class	Peer Response - Groups of 3	Revision - peer and teacher feedback	Revision - peer and teacher feedback	2nd Draft -- must be completed by Monday
Peer & Teacher Feedback on 2nd Drafts Edit stories	2nd Revision of papers Must be ready by Wednesday	Proofread/ Last Edit -- Peer & teacher feedback if necessary	Final Copy due in class today	Exam on writin gprocess, writing modes, and genres

"An outline in calendar format is an excellent way to see the flow of learning concepts throughout a grading period.

Use pencil to easily switch concepts and activity ideas as needed."

Sample Lesson Plan - 9th Grade Creative Writing

Objectives: To be able to compose a narrative using real life experiences
To be able to design a life-map of important events

Materials: Real Life story (from my life), object to go with the story, large white paper, markers, crayons, color pencils, large sheets of paper for each student

Homework: Write a draft of a story based on real life experiences

Focus Activity: Read the news article about the ozone layer on the overhead (or the handout) and relate the events in that story to your life. How is this affecting your life, or how might it affect your life in the future?

Procedures:

9:00-9:05   Student enter and work on focus assignment. Teacher checks attendance and visits with each student around the room, checking homework calendars

9:05-9:10   Share a few journal entries as a class.

9:10-9:25   Lesson - Real Life Writing

a) read own real life story to the students, "My Golden Puppy"

b) discuss - what made this story enjoyable? Did you think it was good? Why or why not? What about it was fun or interesting? Move into class discussion about how real life experiences can make a better story because we are able to add more details. We are writing about what we know.

c) show students the object related to the story and explain that the story was based on a real life experience.

9:25-9:45   a) Pass out large sheets of paper.

b) Explain to students that we will be writing and illustrating a life map which will help us remember important events in our lives.

c) Students create their own life-map.

9:45-9:50   Closure - Students write on index cards -- why should we use experiences & knowledge from our own lives in our writing? Pass in cards/ Clean up to leave.

Blank Template

Date:

Objectives: To be able to
To be able to
To be able to

Materials:

Homework:

Focus Activity:

Procedures:

1.)

2.)

3.)

4.)

5.)

6.)

7.)

8.)

Closure Activity:

Assessment:

© 2003 Survival Kit for New Secondary Teachers

Homework

Homework for tonight is...Groan, whine, whimper! These are often the responses from our class as we dole out their duties for the evening. Why do we put ourselves through the aggravation of assigning homework only to hear loud protests? Often we only receive a half-hearted effort, if it gets completed at all. Is homework really necessary?

Over the past century our society has gone from the belief that homework is essentially bad to the belief that homework is good and back again. In their book, who's teaching your children, Vivian Troen and Katherine Boles trace this transition from the 1900's to recent times. It seems we have come full circle.

Although ten years ago the consensus was that homework was good, Troen & Boles point out that "parental backlash against the ever-growing burden of homework is clearly spreading nationwide." Additionally, current research shows that homework given in sixth grade and increased through high school is beneficial. (p. 125-126)

When students complete assignments in the classroom, the following holds true:

- Teacher can supervise student work

- Students get immediate feedback on their efforts

- Teacher can correct misunderstandings and incorrect answers immediately

- Students do not repeat wrong information over and over which must then be unlearned during class

- Teacher can assess student learning/ acquisition of skills while monitoring students

As such, student practice of skills/knowledge during class time is a much more effective measure of assessment and/or extension of learning than sending it home where it may or may not be completed by the student.

For the reasons stated above, it is important to keep homework as a tool for practice and review of skills/concepts learned in class rather than as an assessment tool.

"What is the goal of your homework assignments?"

Assigning homework in moderation can be useful to instill values of self-discipline and responsibility in older students. Homework is effective in helping to build a work ethic in our students. However, it must be done in moderation!

Teachers should remember that when homework is assigned, one student could easily spend hours on the same assignment that takes another student just 15 minutes to complete. Why do we need to assign 25 math problems when 5 will show us whether or not students can apply the concept?

Keep in mind the following factors which influence a teen's ability to complete homework:

- A chaotic home environment with many children - the student may have adult responsibilities within the home.

- Students who are without parental supervision for most of the time after school hours.

- Students living in poverty who may not have a place to complete homework nor the supplies needed.

- Students who might work after school.

- Busy family and extra-curricular lives including sports, church, clubs, community service activities, and family events.

Must Teach Organization Skills

It is vital that you teach students how to keep themselves organized when assigning homework on a regular basis. It is difficult for many students to keep up with homework assignments for several classes along with the materials needed to complete those assignments.

- Keep an "Unfinished" or "Homework" section in the binder where students can place work to be done for each class. You might encourage students to keep a pocket tab in that section to hold loose handouts.

- Train students to keep materials, handouts, and work completed in a specific section of their 3-ring binder for each subject area.

- Train students to use an academic calendar to copy down homework for each class. Check that this information has been copied down correctly and initial it each day.

"It is vital to teach students organization skills to keep track of assignments and due dates."

Write out Homework Procedures

Procedures are important to help students and parents know what you expect in regards to homework assignments. Type out your homework procedures and expectations to give to students and parents. One copy should go in the student's binder and the other should be posted on the refrigerator at home. *(An example can be found in the next chapter.)*

• What homework stays the same each night or each week?

• Do you expect parents to sign the academic calendar once a week?

• When and where do you expect assignments to be turned in?

• What is your policy for absences and late-work? How long do students have to turn in the assignment? How will their grade be affected?

Tips

-Offer positive feedback for students who turn in their work on time.

-Allow students two days for every one day absent to make up their work. Remember, they are now having to complete double the assignments, so cut them a little slack.

-Take off points each day an assignment is late. I usually take off 5 points for each day. Be sure to clearly explain your policy for latework.

-Remind students of missing assignments each day. Many will forget that they owe you the work.

-Provide before or after-school time to make up missing work or to complete homework with you available for supervision and help.

-Set aside one place in the classroom where assignments are turned in to be graded. Keep this the same all year to cut down on confusion.

-Have parents sign the Homework Procedures/ Policy form to be placed in the students' binders.

"Having homework procedures/ policy typed out helps both students and parents know what is expected."

 **Grading Homework**

Remember that homework should only be used to instill the values of self-discipline and responsibility within our students. Additionally, homework serves as a time for students to practice new skills/concepts taught. One fifty minute period is often not long enough to effectively practice and master certain skills. Obviously practice at home must be mandatory!

As we discussed earlier, homework is not a valid assessment tool for student learning since there are so many unknown variables which can influence completion of the assignment. That being the case, homework assignments can sometimes be graded with a system of checks for the level of completion. Additionally, be sure to weigh in-class assignments and other assessments of learning heavier when calculating overall averages.

Example:

(√)   (homework completed)
(√−)   (homework partially completed)

These types of grades might count towards a participation grade, but individually should not account for much of the student's overall average. In-class assignments and assessments should make up the majority of the student's grade in order to accurately reflect learning.

"Be sure to check your district or school policy on grading homework before developing your own."

OVERVIEW

When thinking about homework, keep the following in mind:

- Do more work during class time.

- When assigning homework to older students, take into consideration outside factors affecting completion of work.

- Make homework assignments meaningful.

- Do not use homework as a final assessment of student learning.

Teacher Observations

Every new teacher will have a formal evaluation sometime during the year. In some school districts and states, teachers are evaluated anywhere from one to four times. Although this is an intimidating procedure, teachers can really use this as an opportunity to show the exciting things they are doing in their classroom. This is also an excellent time to find out what YOU can do to become a better teacher.

When your first observation comes calling don't panic. It is normal to feel nervous, but there are some simple ways to make sure that you have a successful observation.

TIPS

- Make sure that your lesson plans are detailed so that you feel organized and in control.

- Have ALL materials ready and easily accessible for your lesson.

- Have a clean desk since most principals will sit there during the observation. (hint: they rarely look in your drawers so you may want to open them and shove everything in)

- Warn the students that the principal will be there to observe the class. Discuss how they should behave while visitors are in the room (since the principal technically is a visitor). Go over class rules and your expectations for student behavior. **Do not tell them that YOU are being observed to encourage positive behavior on the part of the students.**

"A well-prepared teacher uses detailed lesson plans to stay organized throughout the day."

- Make an extra copy of your lesson plans for the principal to take.

- You may have a pre-conference to discuss any out of the ordinary situations that may occur in your classroom. This is a great time to give a copy of lesson plans and discuss how your classroom works. A forewarned principal is often more lenient.

- If there is a problem student, the principal may like to see a behavior plan or other disciplinary forms.

OTHER TIPS:

- Be prepared

- Be early

- Stay calm - you are not going to get fired today!

- Pretend that this is someone just visiting your classroom

- Have the principal come into your classroom casually several times before your formal observation. This will help you get used to having them there.

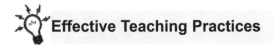 **Effective Teaching Practices**

There are some effective teaching practices that your principal will be looking for throughout their observation of your lesson. We must stress to you that these are strategies you should be implementing from day one in the classroom! Plan out your strategies and routines in detail so that they will become everyday occurances rather than a "show" put on for your formal observation.

➜ **Greet your students in a pleasant way.**

"Good morning John, how are you feeling today? We missed you on Monday."

➜ **Have a sponge activity for students that leads into your lesson. Make this a fun/ exciting/ interesting activity**
    -fun facts
    -math puzzle
    -journal

Teacher Testimony

As a student teacher I was anxious about the state teacher assessment tool, and wanted to be sure that I was adequately prepared for my first observation. I asked the assistant principal, whom I had worked with on several occassions, if she would mind observing me. She was happy to oblige and I learned a lot from that first observation. I was still nervous, but it helped that I knew it would not count against me.

Also, during my first year, I asked the assistant principal in my new school if she would visit my room frequently. This helped me get used to having her in the classroom, and as a result I was less nervous.

➔ **State your objectives for the day and go over the agenda.**
"Today we are going to…"
"You should be able to…"

➔ **Is your class organized?**

Do your students know what to do and when to do it?

Teacher Tip:

- Have a quiet sponge activity that students are working on while you take care of roll, etc.

- State your objective/ agenda first, then do a fun introductory activity.

➔ **Give positive, yet specific feedback.**

"Thank you Julie. I really like the way you described the haunted house using excellent adjectives!"

"A well-prepared teacher develops good teaching habits from the first day of school."

➔ **Be sure to walk around the room and monitor student behavior and participation.**

➔ **Before students work in cooperative groups, ask students what the rules are for group work.**

➔ **Re-direct students when they are misbehaving. A simple tap on the desk or look will often take care of the problem.**

➔ **Vary your activities through the lesson. Don't lecture the whole time. Make sure students participate.**

    ex: - introduction
           - take notes
           - practice individually
           - group activity
           - closure/summary

More Teaching Strategies

→ **Give plenty of wait time when asking questions.**

-Count to at least 15 slowly when waiting for student response.

→ **Make sure your information is accurate. Check your spelling and pronunciation of words.**

→ **Make sure students are on task the entire time.**

→ **Be cheerful and vivacious when teaching - principals do not like boring blah teachers.**

→ **Dress to impress!**

Do not expect your students to respond positively to changes made in your teaching strategies and style for a single observation.

If you try to do something different from what you normally do in the classroom on a daily basis simply to impress your principal, you will most likely do more harm to your observation than good.

You should be consistent with your teaching style every single day. Do not put on a "show" for your observation. These are effective teaching strategies you should be doing from the first day of school!

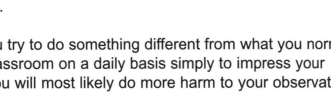

Hint:

Don't throw a curve ball at your students by implementing a new procedure they are not familiar with simply to impress your principal.

It will back-fire on you.

CONCLUSION

Detailed lesson planning is one of the major keys to a successful classroom. Without it teachers are unprepared and unorganized which causes students to be unruly and disruptive. Rather than broad topics in a small box, lesson planning encompasses so much more. It involves thinking through objectives carefully, developing engaging activities to motivate students and enhance the lesson, and creating meaningful assessments of knowlege learned. To use an analogy, lesson planning is the jar that contains our methods for teaching students. When used properly, everything flows out smoothly into each container. Without it, our ideas and strategies have no guidance and spill hapazardly around the room.

Additional Resources

Daily Planning for Today's Classroom: A Guide to Writing Lesson and Activity Plans
by Kay Price and Karna Nelson

The End of Homework: How Homework Disrupts Families, Overburdens Children, and Limits Learning
by E. Kralovec and J. Buell

Questions for Reflection

1) Why do you think it is important to write out detailed lesson plans for each day instead of simply writing "fractions" in the planning book?

2) Do you feel it is important to have a focus assignment for every single class? Why or Why Not?

3) What is your opinion of giving students time in class to do assignments rather than as homework?

4) How can you prepare yourself and your class for a formal teacher observation?

Suggested Activites

1) Following the guidelines within this chapter, create your own lesson plan template on the computer to use for your classes. Organize a disk or CD with folders for each six weeks of this or an upcoming school year. Inside those create folders for each week (ie - August 5) to hold lesson plans. Create a separate folder to hold your template.

2) Brainstorm your homework procedures/policies and type out for students & parents.

3) Brainstorm a list of possible warm-up activities (focus assignment for beginning of class) for each subject you teach. Type them and place them in a manila folder labeled "Warm-Ups" to use when needed.

The First Day

The first day of school is the most important of the entire year. You can make or break your classroom environment on this day. The climate of the classroom should be one of mutual respect and understanding between the teacher and students. You want the students to go home with a feeling that the year will be interesting as well as challenging, but also have a clear sense of your expectations. This chapter will contain several tips for getting off to a good start as well as examples of how to run your first day.

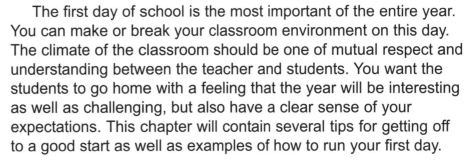 **What to expect**

The first day of school will be hectic, even chaotic in a way, but your goal is to have "organized chaos" through planning. Be prepared for lots of things happening in your classroom all at once:

- Parents and students who are lost and may be asking you for directions to another class.
- Administrators and other school staff popping in to ask you questions, informing you of new procedures, or getting a head count.
- New students arriving who are not on your class list.
- Students seeing friends and buzzing with excitement.

This chapter should be used in combination with the Before School Starts chapter and the Classroom Management chapter. It is vital to have classroom organization and structure set up before students ever arrive. You want to be prepared with classroom routines and procedures, so you can begin training students from the first day.

The first day of school is starting soon!

Where do I begin?

© 2003 Survival Kit for New Secondary Teachers: McDonald and Hershman

> *"A well-prepared teacher knows how they plan to seat students on the first day of school."*

> *"Welcome students to your class with a note at each seat along with a peppermint or pencil."*

Prepare seating assignments and/or have grouping arrangements ready.

Being prepared with a way to seat students as they arrive shows planning and organization on your part. It sends a positive message to students that you know what you are doing and that you have certain expectations from the start.

Some teachers plan out where they want each student to sit. The draw-back to this method is that there will be students who do not show up, and others who arrive although not on your class list. What will you do if a student does not have a seat prepared for him/her? This could cause hurt feelings.

We prefer to sit students randomly during the first week or so of school. This will give you a good idea of who should and should not be sitting next to each other as you develop your class seating chart. Additionally, it is easier to have a general note of welcome ready at each spot which will be appropriate for all circumstances. Some strategies are listed below.

- Cut up and laminate several different colored squares. Each color should represent either a table or a row of desks. Have enough of each color squares for the seats at that table, or in that row. Tape one colored square to each table or on the first seat of each row. When students enter the classroom, greet them and have them pull a square from a bag or basket. They then locate a seat for that color. This is an organized way of seating students, yet it is random and does allow for some choice. It is also less time consuming as students enter the room.

- If you are working with tables or groups of four, another fun way to seat students randomly is to use the four suites of playing cards, or numbers. This works the same as the colored squares.

- Expect for extra students to show up that are not on your class roll. Be ready for this scenario when you are planning your seating arrangements. Have extras for everything you do on the first day. Also, you may have students who do not show up that day, and may or may not show up later. Just be prepared for this.

- Be prepared for chaos the first several days as student schedules change, new students enroll, and students away on extended vacations return.

Do EVERYTHING in PENCIL the first couple of weeks of school!

There is nothing more annoying than getting all of your student records, grade book, etc. looking very nice and neat only to have a student drop your course or enroll late!

Be prepared for a lot of extra paperwork for add/drop schedule changes, student lockers, special services forms, attendance forms, etc. Keep it all organized in an accordion-style folder with each pocket clearly labeled. If you have a form to fill out and return, do so immediately rather than letting it pile up on your desk.

 Have a short, fun, and easy assignment ready for students as soon as they walk in the classroom.

- **Journal topic** - Write a fun and interesting journal topic on the board or overhead and have students write and illustrate.

- **Student fun facts sheet**

- **Brain Teaser or Challenge** is a fun way to start of every class, not just the first day. It is fun to do, yet it also stimulates the brain into thinking mode.

- **A Quick Quiz** to assess what students already know. This activity can be used to help you assess student prior knowledge.

Have all lesson plans and materials ready for the day. Don't forget to use your Day of the Week Folders!

Know where you want students to put their supplies.

- You can ask students to hold on to their supplies until later in the day/class. Just make sure to decide this in advance so that you are consistent.

- You should have a supply list for your class ready before school starts. If you haven't already sent one out, be sure ot do so on the first day.

> *"A well-prepared teacher has an assignment ready for students to begin as soon as they enter the class."*

Hint:

You want to have students busy and engaged while you take care of housekeeping duties. Otherwise you will get off to a bad start.

Planning for the First Day - What do I do?

√ **Be sure to alternate your class time between formal procedures, expectations, and fun team building or ice breaker type of activities.**

√ **When presenting your teacher introduction, be energetic, but not too informal or familiar with students. Show them your firm side, so they do not get the impression that you are ALL about fun and games.**

~ While you want your students to like you, you do not want to be their best buddy!

~ This is a good time to discuss your personal standards. "I believe in doing your personal best." "Character counts!" "Honesty and integrity are traits that I value highly."

~ Decide for yourself how much information you want to reveal to the students before the first day. The students may ask you questions that you are not prepared to answer. Practice how you will respond to inappropriate questioning.

~ Do not tell the students that this is your first year teaching. The students will immediately feel an upper hand! Tell them that you have taught __ grade in the past and that you look forward to this year as being one of the best.

√ **Have a poster or overhead that lists the class/school schedule and explain it.**

Students like to know what to expect in the flow of the day. This will deter them from asking you throughout the whole class, "When is lunch?" or "What's next?" Additionally, if you get questions such as these, it takes less class time to say, "Look at the schedule."

Be sure to write your the class agenda on the board for students to follow.

Teacher Testimony

"My first year of teaching I didn't realize how much my tone of voice influenced the way students responded to me. Although I had gone over the class rules with them several times throughout the year and trained them in my procedures, I was still having trouble with certain students ignoring my directions or acting familiar with me. Then I heard myself on a recording, and realized that when I speak I have a very soft and timid sounding voice. No wonder they weren't taking me seriously. That summer I practiced using a more forceful voice. I used the tape recorder to help me analyze my voice, and could really tell a difference by the end of the summer. The next year I felt that my students showed me more respect because my tone of voice demanded it."

√ **When presenting rules and consequences speak clearly and firmly.**

- Your tone of voice and attitude are crucial at this point.

- Pause after every expectation/rule, and look each student directly in the eye. Do not go on to the next expectation until you have looked at each and every student. This sends the message that these expecations are not to be taken lightly.

- You need to set distinct expectations and leave no questions about discipline unanswered.

  - Make sure your rules and consequences posters are displayed where all students can see them. Also, make sure the writing is large enough to read from anywhere in the classroom. Most districts have a media center where you can take your typed up rules and consequences to be enlarged to poster size and laminated.

  - It is important to have the students complete an activity where they will demonstrate knowledge and understanding of each rule and consequence.

    For example:
    Have students brainstorm and chart behaviors falling under each rule/expectation.

    Copying the rules generally doesn't help student internalize the information.

We discussed setting expectations for students in detail within the Student Discipline section of the Classroom Management chapter. Take some time to review that information and apply it to your first day of school lessons.

BRIEF OVERVIEW:

- Take time to train students in expectations and procedures.
- Expectations are not just class rules, but also life-skills to be exhibited in the classroom
- Demonstrate the "why" behind different expectations for visual learners
- Introduce the concept of "My time" vs. "Your time"

Hint:

Pausing after an important statement sends a powerful message to students that they had better pay attention to what you are saying. Direct eye contact completes that feeling of seriousness. You'll find that if you pause long enough, everyone will lift his or her head to look at you. In a world where we are bombarded by noise, silence gathers attention.

- Throughout the first week of school you want to have several team building and ice-breaker activities. These should be structured and organized activities, not a free for all. Make sure to have clear instructions for each activity.

- Have the students fill out a student information sheet with all necessary information. A sample is included in the back of this chapter.

- Students feel appreciative when you display their work. Have them do activities on the first day that you can hang up in the classroom or hallway right away. This is a great way to show the students that you value them and their work.

- Go over your procedures and expectations with the students. It is helpful to provide them with a copy to take home! This will include homework expectations, daily assignments, quizzes and testing information.

Hint:

Displaying student work on the very first day really goes a long way to showing students that they are valued. While this may not seem like much to you, our students want to know that we value the work they do in the classroom.

On the following page is an example of a list of procedures for an English class. Notice how EVERYTHING is listed so that students and parents know exactly what is expected each day. Parents can put a copy on the refrigerator.

In addition, your syllabus should outline as many assignments and projects ahead of time with due dates. This will help prepare students for the eventuality of college and/ or vocational school

---

English 101

8/14-8/18	Introductions, Creative writing assignments, Expectations, Class procedures, Get-to-know activities
8/18	Test over expectations; Round Robin sharing of writing
8/21-8/25	Writing process, Pre-writing, Real life writing
8/25	Pop-quiz; Round Robin sharing
8/28-9/1	Genre studies - Mystery, Horror, Science Fiction, Biography, Fairy Tale, Historical Fiction
9/1	Pop-quiz; Round Robin sharing

PROCEDURES & HOMEWORK

"It is a good idea to have your homework procedures and policy typed up and ready to send home with students."

MONDAY

Homework: Write 1-2 page original draft
Vocabulary paragraph – Due Thursday
Other homework written in calendar

TUESDAY

Homework: Testing skills practice
Read for 20 minutes and write a response in log
Other homework written in calendar

WEDNESDAY

Testing skills practice due from previous week

Homework: Write 1-2 page original draft
Other homework written in calendar

THURSDAY

Vocabulary homework due

Homework: Read for 20 minutes and write a response in log
Study for pop quiz
Study for vocabulary test
Other homework written in calendar
Parents check over and sign student binder

FRIDAY

Pop-Quiz
Vocabulary test
Teacher checks binder – parent signature and Reading
Response log
Round Robin Sharing of Stories written in class and at home

Hint:

Depending on how you plan to implement homework, your policy and procedures page may not be as lengthy as this sample.

A plan such as this one does help everybody remember what is expected each day.

Checklist for the First Day

Use this checklist to make sure you are ready to start your first day!

_____ I know how I am going to seat my students when they first walk in the door.

_____ I know how I am going to greet students when they arrive to the classroom.

_____ I have a short note welcoming my students on each desk. (Remember, you don't have to write names on these notes)

_____ My board/overhead/presentation station is set up with the date, my name, an agenda for the class/day, and opening assignment instructions.

_____ My lesson plans are written out in detail and are where I can get to them easily.

_____ I have a syllabus ready to hand to students.

_____ My class list(s) are with my lesson plans.

_____ My attendance sheet(s) are with my lesson plans.

_____ I know what students are going to do with their supplies when they bring them to me.

_____ I need the following materials for today:

_____ The materials are out and ready for students to use.

Sample Lesson Plan (One 50 minute Prep/Course)

Objectives: To be able to know everybody's name
To be able to understand the classroom policies and procedures
To be able to share orally

Homework: Create a mind-map or web of the expectations discussed in class. Be prepared to share.

Materials: white paper, index cards, classroom policies and procedures

Procedures:

5 min.   Housekeeping - Students complete information cards - include name, address, phone number, parent's names & phone numbers (if different), birth date, class schedule
While students are working you should – call roll, and do other opening day procedures

5 min.   Teacher introductions

10 min.   Name game – students get in a circle. 1st person says name, 2nd repeats name & says own name. Go around the circle. Teacher should be last and should say everyone's name.

20 min.   Classroom expectations and procedures

10 min.   Closure - Emphasize importance of working together to learn. I am your guide. What you put into your learning/this class is what you will get out of it. Etc. Journal -- What are your goals for this course? What expectations do you have from me as the instructor?

The first few days should be spent getting to know students and training in classroom procedures/expectations.

If you have Blocked scheduling and have 90 minutes with each class, you will want to alternate between going over classroom procedures/expectations and fun activities.

For example, you might add the following before the closure:

15 min.   Student pairs develop a mind-map of the expectations discussed.

10 min.   Student pairs group together and share mind-maps. How are they similar? How are they different? Can you see the thought patterns of other students? What does this tell us about working together in groups as opposed to working individually?

10 min.   Share results as a class. Why is it important to know expectations up front?

         © 2003 Survival Kit for New Secondary Teachers

Get-to-Know Activities

Here are some activities you can do during the first few days/ weeks of school:

♦ **Name Game**

Students get in a circle. 1st person says name, 2nd repeats name & says own name. Go around the circle. Teacher should be last and should say everyone's name.

♦ **Scavenger Hunt for Signatures**

Students use the sheet found in the back of this chapter and walk around the room trying to find other students to fit each description. When they have found someone, they need to get that person's signature in the box.

♦ **Back to School Bingo**

Similar to Scavenger Hunt. See the sheet in the back of this chapter.

♦ **M & M Game**

Pass around a large jar/ can filled with M&M's. Instruct students to take some as it comes around. Then, after everyone has taken some M&M's, they must tell one fact about themselves for each M&M they have BEFORE they eat any!

♦ **Partner Interviews**

Students pair up, or are paired up with someone they do not know. With the class as a whole, brainstorm five or six questions to ask. Students then interview each other using index cards. When everyone is finished, each person must stand up and introduce their partner to the rest of the class and share the interesting new facts they learned about their partner. This activity is often used in middle schools.

◆ Groups Activity

Have each student brainstorm for 2 to 3 minutes and list the different groups they belong to. These groups include any and every way that students could categorize themselves. For example, they might be:

-daughters   -African American   -Texan
-sons   -student   -football player
-pianist   -babysitter   -shopper
-Christian   -sister   -friend

Be sure you give examples of the groups you belong to in order to help students begin their brainstorming.

Once everyone has their list, go around the room and allow each person to introduce him or herself and share the groups they belong to. Ask students to listen for commonalities in the lists.

This is an excellent activity to jumpstart a discussion about tolerance of others, accepting differences, and focusing on our similarities as ties to friendship. It is also a great way to help us identify different strengths and talents among our students.

◆ Setting Goals

Setting goals is another important activity that can and should be done during the first week of school. Have students think for a few minutes and jot down their goal for the class or for themselves for the year.

Go around the room and have each person share their goal(s) with the rest of the class. Compile these into a list of Learning Goals for that class.

This can also be used as a "get-to-know" activity, or it can be done individually with just the teacher as the audience.

Use the goals set by students to help you get to know them better as well as to set goals for your teaching throughout the semester and/or year. Post these goals immediately, or at the very least type them up so that each student can have their own copy.

"The first few weeks of school you will need to spend time developing a cohesive class, where students know and respect each other."

Team Building Activities

If You Were …

In this activity the students all answer the questions and then share them with the class. This is a great way to get to know each students' personality!

Sample questions:

➔ If you were a car, what kind of car would you be?
➔ What kind of animal are you like when you are angry?
➔ If you were a bug, what kind of bug would you be?
➔ Name something that always makes you smile.
➔ If you could be like any other person, who would it be?

Assumption Game

Students work together as a class to try to figure out "what happened" or "why" by asking yes or no questions.

For example,
"A man on his way home saw the masked man coming towards him so he turned and ran. Why?"

Students might ask, "Was the first man scared of the other man?" You have to answer yes or no. "No" answers are just as helpful as "Yes" answers. For example, if the answer is, "No, the man is NOT scared" then students do not need to ask if he is a burglar, etc. There is no limit to questions unless you want to set one.

(The answer to the example is that it is a baseball game. The man is running to home plate and the catcher is coming towards him with the ball.)

You can make them up yourself, or have students create them and share.

** This is a great activity to develop critical thinking skills. You can get these kinds of scenarios in books with logic games. One website that has logic puzzles and situation games is Braingle - www.braingle.com/Situation.html

"Check to see if there is a Ropes Course near you.

This is an excellent opportunity for teambuilding with your students!"

Team Draw Activity

- Break students into groups of four.

- Have each student select a different colored marker or overhead pen.

- Give each team one transparency or large sheet of white paper.

- Students are to draw a team picture without talking.

- Each student must use only the marker they have chosen and may not switch colors. Set a time limit for this activity. Five minutes is a good limit. Directions for students are in the back of this chapter.

This activity is designed to show students the importance of EVERYONE working together and communicating with each other. You will notice that some colors are used more than others. Lead students to the idea of team roles. There are leaders and followers in every team. Who are your leaders? Which colors were not used at all or were used very little? These are students who need to be encouraged by the group to participate.

Design Team Activity

Break students into groups of four. Choose what you want students to design according to your unit or theme. Our theme was space, so we had students design their ideal spaceship or space station. It is nice to offer students a choice of two or three designs. Another idea might be to design the perfect classroom, cafeteria, gym or playground. Students need to work together as a team on this project. Make sure you give them lots of time to brainstorm, sketch and do a final copy.

"Help students get to know their group members by doing different Team Building Activities."

People Scavenger Hunt

Find someone in the classroom for each phrase below and have them sign on the line. You may use each person's name only twice.

New to this school this year _____

Has on something red _____

Has an older brother _____

Has a younger sister _____

Was born in September _____

Read a book this summer _____

Has a dog for a pet _____

Went swimming this summer _____

Has blue eyes _____

Can play a musical instrument _____

Walks to school _____

Went on a vacation trip this summer _____

Has visited a foreign country _____

Has visited at least five different states _____

Has exactly seventeen letters in entire name _____

Is the youngest in their family _____

Knows how many centimeters are in a meter _____

Has brown hair _____

Is an only child _____

Desert Survival

You are on an airplane that is forced down in the Sahara Desert in North Africa. The plane is off course. It was traveling at 200 miles per hour and lost radio contact 5 hours ago. All passengers are okay. There is no guarantee of a rescue, nor of continued survival. It is a 3 day journey north, to a city.

As a group, you must choose the items to take with you. Only 7 of the 20 items can be chosen to help your group survive the desert trek.

Your group must be ready to tell why the seven items were chosen.

Desert Survival Box

a hand mirror
a parachute
a pencil
1 book of matches
2 cans of coke
scissors
an electric fan
1 tube of toothpaste
a 10 dollar bill
1 school math book

a long sleeve jacket
an umbrella
a safety pin
T.V. guide
nail clippers
a compass
a portable radio
1 jar of spinach
a hunting bow and 1 arrow
1 box of saltine crackers

© 2003 Survival Kit for New Secondary Teachers

All About _____

My Favorites

Sport: _____

Kind of Book: _____

T.V. show: _____

Color: _____

Movie: _____

My Interests

Hobbies: _____

Places I've traveled: _____

_____

Future occupation: _____

My Wishes

Where I'd like to travel: _____

_____

My one wish for me: _____

_____

My one wish for the world: _____

_____

Welcome!

Dear Parents:

Hello! I am looking forward to having your teen in my course this semester. I feel confident that we will have a terrific year full of learning. I believe that it is important to teach students HOW to learn so that they can become life-long learners.

Communication is very important to me, so please feel free to ask any questions and express any concerns or ideas you may have. Your teen's education and well being is my #1 priority this year. I want to work together with parents and students to make this year a success for all of us!

Sincerely,

- -

Name of student _____

Name of parent/ parents _____

Daytime phone _____

Evening phone _____

Explain any special interests, sports activities, and hobbies he/she has:

List any allergies the student has toward foods, or other products:

List any medications the student is currently taking:

Are there any special notes or comments you would like to make?

© 2003 Survival Kit for New Secondary Teachers

Student Information Sheet

Name _____

Address _____   Phone_____

_____

Mother's Name: _____   Work phone_____

Father's Name: _____   Work phone_____

Guardian's Name: _____   Work phone_____

Brothers or Sisters:_____   Age _____

_____   Age_____

_____   Age _____

Your Birthdate: _____

Age, as of today:_____

What is your favorite...

    Sport:_____   Food: _____

    Book: _____   Movie:_____

    T.V. show:_____   Subject:_____

In my spare time I like to: _____

_____

I collect: _____

I enjoy playing: _____

I like to read: _____

Do you have any special talents and interests? If so, what are they?

_____

_____

_____

Back to School BINGO

Try to find classmates to initial each square. Try to get five in a row (across, down, or diagonal). If you want a REAL CHALLENGE, try filling the whole box!

Read more than five books this summer.	Moved into a new house this summer.	Flew on an airplane this summer.	Has traveled to a foreign country.	Has visited five or more states.
Likes to play soccer.	Has a younger sister.	Has visited Washington, D.C.	Has a dog as a pet.	Plays more than one sport.
Is wearing a watch.	Has exactly 15 letters in their full name.	FREE	Has a four digit house number.	Has blue eyes.
Has a bike.	Earned perfect attendance last year.	Will celebrate their birthday this month.	Has relatives in other states.	Can play a musical instrument.
All of their grandparents are still alive.	Has relatives in other countries.	Has an unusual pet.	Made Honor Roll last year.	Was born in June.

© 2003 Survival Kit for New Secondary Teachers

Back to School BINGO

Try to find classmates to initial each square. Try to get five in a row (across, down, or diagonal). If you want a REAL CHALLENGE, try filling the whole box!

Instructions for Team Draw Activity

In your teams, have each person select a marker. Using only your own color and with no oral communication, create a team picture on your blank paper.

Once your illustration is complete, discuss your handiwork and give it a title.

Star Activity

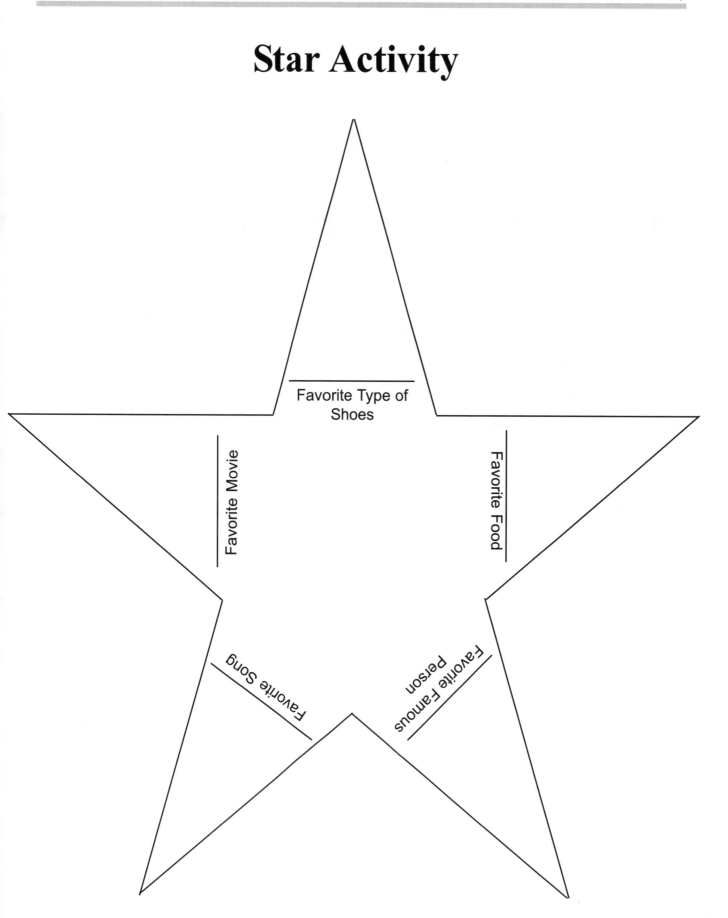

Favorite Type of Shoes

Favorite Movie

Favorite Food

Favorite Song

Favorite Famous Person

CONCLUSION

Although the first day of school is often hectic, it is vital that you set the proper tone. If students see you flustered and unorganized, they will store that picture of you in their heads for the rest of the year. Following expectations and staying organized will not be a priority to your students because of it. However, if students see before them an organized teacher who knows exactly what will happen first, second, and third, they will be more likely to develop into a well-disciplined class.

Remember that your tone of voice and posture affect how students view you as a teacher. Be firm when going over expectations, but also let students see your unique personality. Take the time to get to know your students and to train them in what you expect to happen within the classroom. In essence, the first day is a time for you to "set the stage" for the rest of the school year.

Questions for Reflection

1) Why is the first day of school so important?

2) How do you think having a poster clearly visible with the daily schedule listed will help you? Why should you go over this schedule at the start of class?

3) Why do you think it is important to alternate between giving information about class rules and procedures, and fun get-to-know or team building activities?

Suggested Activites

1) Decide how you will sit students randomly. Create the squares, shapes, cards, or other objects you plan to use. Laminate these and place them in a ziplock bag for use on the first day of school. (Pre-service teachers may want to keep these in their 3-ring binder along with other classroom materials)

2) Brainstorm three different activities that you might ask students to complete as soon as they walk into the classroom on the first day of school. Be sure that each activity is age-appropriate and can be completed individually by each student with little to no help from the teacher.

3) Write out detailed lesson plans for the first two days of school. Be sure to include the objectives, materials, and procedures. Under procedures, list each item along with the directions or your comments/reminders in an outline format. When you get your daily/class schedule, you will be able to plug those items into different time slots. See our sample plans in this chapter and the Lesson Planning chapter.

NOTES/REFLECTION:

Parent Communication

> I know I need to talk to parents, but I don't know how!
>
> What do I do?

The concept of parents as partners is not a new one, and we don't believe it is one that teachers disagree with in general. Rather, it is difficult to know when and how a positive partnership can begin with parents. Many teachers, especially new teachers, may feel insecure or awkward when communicating with parents and thus try to get away with as little interaction as possible. This attitude of minimal contact is one that will ultimately hurt the student.

As educators, we have a responsibility to involve parents because of their fundamental rights. However, it is also to our great advantage as well as the student's to involve parents. Recent research documented by Fuller and Olsen in their book, Home-School Relations: Working Successfully with Parents and Families, shows that family involvement has a profound effect on student success in both academic achievement and behavior. Students who have highly involved parents are more likely to be well-adjusted and successful than those whose parents are not involved in their school life.

Key to Success: *Act Early and Often!*

School + Parents = Success

What happens when parents get involved in their child's education? Grades go up and behavior improves, too! Parent involvement does make a difference.

Source: U.S. Department of Education

Starting Off On the Right Foot

- Before school even begins, start communication with your students and their families by sending introductory postcards or notes. The students enjoy getting these postcards, and start the year off with a positive attitude toward their teacher! The parents think that you are really special and organized, just because you did that simple task!

For an example of a welcome note, see the Before School Starts chapter.

- Call the parents *within* the first two weeks of school. Call early, before **you have** to call with bad news on some students! Always have positive and encouraging things to say about their teen! Tell the parents you are looking forward to a great year. Ask them if they have any questions or comments. (They are usually so excited and shocked that you called that they rarely have any serious or in-depth questions.) Tell them that you want to have open communication lines with them and you hope you can depend on their support! This gets the year off to a wonderful beginning, and you'll have future successful phone calls (even if there is a problem to report)!

Sample Phone Call

Hello, Mr./Mrs. _____

I am looking forward to having _____ in my class this year. He/she seems to really _____ (positive comment). We are going to be doing some interesting learning activities this year that I think _____ will enjoy.

If the child is already exhibiting negative behavior, this is the prime place to mention it.
(See the list of ways to discuss behavior problems, so that parents are not defensive or offended, later in the chapter.)   [I did want you to know that I have noticed _____'s tendency to _____. Have you had experience with this in previous years or have anything to add about this type of behavior? I know that together we will be able to solve this problem and make this a successful year for _____.]

I wanted to let you know that I am hoping for open lines of communication between us, so if you have any questions or concerns, please do not hesitate to call me right away. My planning/ team time is from _____ to _____ every day. Before we hang up, do you have any questions or comments for me right now? It was great talking with you and I look forward to working with you and _____ throughout this year.

Hint:

Ask your mentor if you can listen in on some of his/her parent phone calls to hear first hand how they handle different types of situations.

You might also ask them to listen to your conversations in order to offer constructive feedback on ways you can improve.

Hint:

If you are concerned that certain parents may not be receiving the progress report from their teenager, mail it home with return receipt. The parent must sign for the letter and you will get a receipt in return showing their signature. Keep this in your files for future reference.

Keeping Parents Up-to-Speed

In order to help their teen, parents need to have the whole picture of what is going on in school. Their only reliable link to this information is you, the teacher. How can you relate to parents what is going on in the classroom? Here are a few you can try:

- Positive Notes
- Academic Calendars
- Progress Reports
- Newsletters

Positive Notes

Send short notes of a "job well done" home with the student. This only takes a few seconds on the part of the teacher, but can make a world of difference for the student and parent. Students feel appreciated and rewarded. Parents feel proud, happy, and thankful that the teacher is dedicated and paying attention.

Yes, older students benefit from this type of attention. Many businesses have started using this type of praise and motivation with their employees to raise morale and satisfaction with their job. It is well-known that people like to be appreciated. Our students are no different.

Progress Reports

Another great way of informing parents about a student's progress prior to report cards is the progress report. Most schools require you to send one of these home at the mid-term period for students who are failing. Other schools require progress reports to be sent home for everyone regardless of their grades. Some schools don't require them at all! Whatever the school requirements, we suggest that you send home a report at least once before the report card. The more reports you can send home, the better, especially for students who are in danger of failing.

We know that this may seem like a tremendous amount of work to keep up with, especially to new teachers who are already overwhelmed. However, we also know from personal experience that sending out progress reports will save you the grief and hassle of dealing with angry parents.

Academic Calendars

An academic/homework calendar can work as a wonderful two-way communication between you and the parents. Having the students fill out their own calendar each day is also an excellent way for them to be held accountable for their class and homework assignments. This calendar should be kept in the front of each student's binder.

➔ Plan class time each day to write in homework assignments, upcoming events, etc. into the calendar.

➔ Be consistent in your use of the calendar. This will be helpful during parent conferences.

> **For example,** *a parent may be upset because he/she "wasn't aware" of the assignments due, simply say, "Did you check the academic calendar? All of our assignments are written there and initialed by me each day for accuracy."*

➔ This is a life-skill you are teaching. Be systematic about it.

➔ Leave 5 minutes at the start of class or before the end of class for students to copy assignments.

➔ Require parents to read and sign the calendar at least once a week. Check that they have signed it.

➔ Encourage parents to make their own comments in the calendar as a way to communicate with you.

➔ Check calendars at the start of each class. Be sure you read the comments so that you can respond appropriately and in a timely manner.

➔ Assist special needs students with filling in the calendar. You might assign a "buddy" to help them copy the information as needed.

➔ Remind parents that the academic calendar is a tool to help them monitor their teen's homework and other assignments such as projects and tests. There is no excuse for either parents or students to say they were not aware of an assignment/test when the calendar is used properly.

"Using an academic calendar is one of the quickest ways to initiate non-threatening two-way communication with parents."

Newsletters

In our classrooms, we send home a weekly newsletter. If this is your very first year of teaching maybe a bi-monthly or monthly newsletter would be more manageable for you. A newsletter is an excellent way of keeping your parents informed of:

- Classroom activities
- Units/themes of study
- Upcoming events and field trips
- Important due dates for projects and tests
- Keep them up-to-speed on the latest learning strategies
- Give parents tips on creating a good learning/study environment at home

Tips for Helping Parents Create Good Study Habits at Home

A few of our families come from backgrounds where they did not grow up with good study skills, and don't know how to help their children establish them. As educators, we can do a lot to help parents. By giving tips, advice, and strategies in quick increments that are not too overwhelming for parents to absorb and enact into their daily lives, we are educating parents and making our jobs as teachers easier.

Here are some tips you can include in your newsletters to "train" parents on how to create good and effective study habits for their teenager. Be sure to only put one or two tips per newsletter in order to keep parents from being overwhelmed. Feel free to rephrase these in your own style.

Stress to your teen that you are a team player in their school life. Your role is to help them be better students. It is important for your children that you create an environment where they can study and do homework with few interruptions and distractions.

Schedule a time to complete homework when it is appropriate for both your teen and the rest of the family. Routines are important as adolescents feel more balanced and comfortable when they know what to do each day. Don't expect them to sit and work quietly on homework during a chaotic time in the house.

Plan a "calm," "settle down," or "quiet time" for the family every day. Parents can be reading, folding laundry, working on the computer, etc., but the TV and phone should be off limits during this time. This will send the message that we all need time in a quiet environment.

Hint:

Create a newsletter template on the computer that you can use over and over. Simply cut out the parts that no longer apply and insert the new events and information.

Use the information you receive at staff developments to keep parents up-to-date on the latest teaching and learning strategies. Explain in plain language to help parents better understand *why* you are using these "new-fangled" ways of teaching.

Send a copy to your principal, assistant principal, counselor, and department/ grade-level chair so that everyone is on the same page.

More Tips for Parents to Include in your Newsletter

Help your teen set up an area where he/she can study. This does not necessarily have to be their bedroom. Some adolescents do better when Mom or Dad are nearby and would work well at the kitchen table. If younger siblings offer too much distraction, send them to their room or another room for "quiet time".Decide upon one location and consistently use it as a place to work and study.

Don't complain about homework in front of the student. If you have a comment or concern about homework or academic requirements, please call the teacher later. You have a huge impact on how your teenagers view school and their teacher; don't let it be a negative one. You may be undermining the ability of the teacher to do his/herjob.

Parents need to keep in mind the goal of homework. It is an opportunity for older students to have additional practice in skills learned throughout the day as well as a discipline building activity. Homework gives your teenagers the opportunity to work independently, develop responsibility and self-discipline.

Don't do the homework for your teen. Some parents may get carried away and want to do the project so that it is "done right." Doing the work for him/her may hamper their comprehension of the material and interfere in the teacher's reasoning behind the assignment. Offer your help as a guide and advisor. Ask questions that will help the student come to their own conclusions about the assignment. If your teen is having extreme difficulties, call the teacher and ask for extra tutoring before or after school.

Make sure that your family is eating well. Just like our cars cannot run without fuel, the human brain cannot run without food. Even just one missed meal can affect an adolescent's behavior and learning. Please make sure that everyone comes to school well-fed and fueled up for the day.

Other Study Tips:

• Parents should check each evening that the homework listed in the calendar has been completed.

• Help student put completed work into appropriate section of binder or "finished" side of folder.

• Check off each assignment in the calendar as it is completed.

• Have snacks readily available to help keep the brain going during work time.

PARENT NEWSLETTER
September 1, 20__

THIS MONTH

We begin our economics unit this month and will be studying different money systems, the exchange rate, the stock exchange, and real life finances including balancing a check book and keeping a budget.

THANK YOU'S

Thank you to all the parents who volunteered to go on our field trip to the Museum of Natural Science and History. We appreciate your support.

MAJOR DUE DATES

September 22, 20__   Life Finance Project Due
September 29, 20__   Economics Test

WISH LIST

If anyone has experience with the stock market, budgeting, accounting, or economics itself, we are in need of several guest speakers and/or materials to enhance student learning during this unit. Please contact me at 555-456-7890 as soon as possible to discuss ways you can help us learn about world economics! Thanks!

LEARNING/ TESTING STRATEGIES

Recent research shows us that real world experiences help students retain information and skills better than lectures and rote drill. Take time this month to share how you handle your budget and checking account with your teen. This might also be a great time to open a bank account in the student's name so that they can begin to learn the skills of balancing an account and setting a budget for their own extra expenses. Another real world experience that will enrich your teen's learning this month is to check out the stock reports in the newspaper. Pick one or two favorite stocks and follow them each day.

"An effective teacher communicates with parents consistently throughout the year so that everyone is on the same page."

Calling Parents

We would love to go through the whole year with no discipline problems or lack of study habits on the part of our students, but this is an unrealistic dream. There comes a time in every first year teacher's life when a problem with a student arises, and must be handled with a parent phone call. Don't procrastinate, but call immediately! Follow these steps for a successful parent phone call.

STEPS

- Decide in advance what is to be discussed. Write it down in bulleted format as a reminder.

- Gather information and documentation to support your purpose for calling. (Grades, behavior records, health records, notes from the parents, student work can all be helpful.) You should already have a folder for each student with this information included.

- **Begin with a positive comment before stating anything else!**

- Always tell the parent that you and the family need to work together as a team for the best interests of their child. Tell the parent that he/she is the *most important person in that teen's life*, and it is in the teenager's best interest if the parent and teacher work together.

- State your reason for calling in specific terms:
  - I need your help in…
  - Let's work together to solve this problem I am seeing, which is….

- When appropriate, offer the parent assistance in discipline strategies, and/or helping their teen.

  → Checking their homework assignment calendar every night and checking for completed homework

  → Instituting a behavior checklist at home and school

"A well-prepared teacher thinks through a parent phone call before making it and has student information easily accessible."

- Offer a consequence when possible for the behavior if not improved (detention, poor grades, office referral, etc.).

    "If _____ (student's name) does not _____, I will have no choice but to _____. Please let's see if we can't try to solve this problem as soon as possible, so we can move on with a terrific year.

- Before hanging up, summarize the conversation and reiterate any agreement that you came to. End the conversation on a positive note by trying to mention something the student did well that week!

- Always follow up a parent phone call with a note acknowledging your conversation, reiterating any solution strategies, and thanking them for their time and support.

- **Keep diligent records of EVERY parent phone call**! See sample of phone conference document at the end of the chapter.

    - You may want to keep a copy of the phone record in your student information folder, OR you can keep index cards on each student.

    - **index cards** - Set up a 5 x 7 index card for each student. Include the student's name, address, birthdate, parent's names, and phone numbers. Under this information, keep a record of parent contacts with dates and comments. Whenever you are ready to make a phone call, simply pull the index card and take it with you.

Simon, Paul 2211 St. Andrews Place Wonderful, CA 34598	5th Period 11/07/88
Martha Simon (H) 456-9089 (W) 329-0897	
Peter Simon (H) 456-9089 (w) 289-7658	
2/1/03	called re: no homework — spoke with mom, she
	will begin checking academic calendar & will
	sign every night. I will check in the morning
	that it was signed.

Hint:

WARNING:

When using e-mail to communicate with parents, DO NOT discuss personal or confidential information about their child, even if they request it. Instead, in your e-mail, ask that parents call you, or to check the note you sent home. E-mails are not secure, and can be intercepted and read by other people which violates the Privacy Act.

Hint:

Using index cards is an easy way to keep student information and parent phone records in one place.

Another way is to use manila folders and staple a parent phone log on the inside.

Assertive Phrases

Some of these assertive phrases may be inappropriate if used unwisely or without discretion.

All communications you make with parents, both oral and written, must be made with wisdom and careful consideration.

- I am very concerned for your teen's well being, and I wanted to make you aware of what I am noticing.

- I understand your point and/or feelings…how can we work together to solve this problem?

- It is in your teen's best interest that we work together to solve this problem.

- Your teenager needs your help.

- I need your support.

- You are an important influence on your teen. Your involvement is crucial for his or her success.

- When students do not follow the rules/expecations, it is their responsibility to pay the consequences.

- If this problem isn't solved now, it could lead to greater problems later on.

- I need you to take stronger disciplinary action at home.

- I want to help your teenager improve, but we need to work together, not against each other.

- We need to talk together face to face in order to determine the best way to help your teen. When can we meet?

Remember, your goal is not to get into a battle with the parents, to make them angry, or to sound superior to them – you just want them to realize that you need their help and support!

Hint:

When talking with angry or frustrated parents, the best course of action is to let them vent their emotions at the beginning of the conversation. Take notes so that you can verify their concerns after they are finished. Next, explain that you want what is best for the student and that your job is to help their teen do well in school, not fail. Ask the parent if that is their goal as well. If they answer yes, then say, "We want the same thing for (the student), so how can we work together to help him/her?"

Communicating with Parents

There are some words and phrases that will not elicit a good response from parents – Try using statements that are less threatening instead.

Before using a strong or harsh word, rethink that expression and state your case in a more pleasant way.

Remember, not only are you trying to help the student, but you are also a representative of your school and district. It is imperative that you be professional in all communications with parents and other community members.

"An effective teacher understands that each student is very special to their parents. Thus, they use diplomacy at all times."

Negative Phrases	More appropriate Phrases
Poor study habits	Not meeting her potential
Dirty/ Smelly	Is not using proper hygiene
Irresponsible	Can learn to make better choices
Wastes time	Needs to use time wisely
Rude or mean	Inconsiderate of others
Lazy	Capable of more when he tries
	Not meeting his potential
Troublemaker	Disturbs the class
Cheats	Depends on others to do his work
Sloppy	Should try to be neater
Selfish	Does not like to share
Steals	Takes objects without permission
Stubborn	Insists on having her own way
Uncooperative	Difficulty in working with others
Obnoxious	Tries to get constant attention

Using the wrong phrase with parents can really bomb!

The Parent-Teacher Conference

Many teachers and parents worry about conferences. This shows in the fact that so many parents never show up for a scheduled parent-teacher conference.

- Teaches may feel nervous or fearful. This is normal, no matter how effective of a teacher you are!

- Parents often feel uncertain and have mixed emotions about meeting with their teen's teacher.

- Parents may want to please the teacher and make a good impression, but also want to express their concerns or frustrations.

- Many parents have a hard time saying what they really think and are timid, but some parents are extremely defensive and overbearing.

- A good start to every conference is a warm and welcoming greeting along with a smile!

- Whatever the type of parent that a teacher may be dealing with, teachers should always have the same goal in mind.

- The objective of every conference should be to develop a working partnership with the parents, so that the student's best interests and learning is everyone's focus.

- You want to put the parents at ease by letting them know that your only goal for the conference is to build a positive relationship with them in order to benefit their teenager.

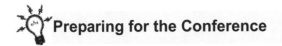 **Preparing for the Conference**

- Decide in advance the purpose of the conference. Make notes to yourself of what is to be discussed.

- Learn about the home environment as much as possible to avoid uncomfortable topics or saying the wrong thing. If the student's father is dead, you don't want to ask, "Where is Suzy's dad today?"

- Collect information and documentation on the student, such as grades, your grade book, student work, behavior records, tardy slips, absent notes, and health records. You should have a student folder with all of this information together, but you may not want to bring everything you have compiled on this student over the year. Be selective, only bring what is necessary and could be helpful during the conference. Planning is a huge part of preparing for a conference!

- Be organized with materials ready before the parents arrive.

- Prepare a plan or agenda for the parents to follow along. It takes pressure off of the parents if they know what to expect. The parents and teacher can make notations on the agenda. Write down any plans that were decided upon. See the sample agenda prepared for you at the end of the chapter.

- Some teachers meet in their own classrooms, others arrange to meet in the library, principal's office, or school conference room.

- Parents have busy lives, too! Send home a reminder note to parents with the date, time and location of the conference. You may want to have a tear-off portion of the note where parents can jot down questions and concerns they'd like to discuss with you, and send it back to school with their teen, so that you can be even more prepared!

"Teachers look professional and organized when ready with student records and an agenda for the conference."

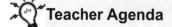 **Teacher Agenda**

1. Greeting – Smile and welcome the Parents. Introduce yourself if this is your first meeting. Thank the parents for coming.

2. Start with a positive or encouraging comment about their teen.

3. Explain the objective and purposes of the conference, and why you felt it necessary to meet in person. (You can better share work samples, etc…) Provide the parents with their own copy of the conference schedule/ agenda.

4. Ask the parent for their observations and/ or feelings about their child.

5. Provide your observations and concerns. Be specific on how you feel the student could make improvements.

6. Review the documentation that you have gathered for the conference.
    Student work samples
    Grade book
    Discipline/Behavioral Reports
    Any special education forms or referrals
    Scores and reports from standardized testing
    Any input provided by other teachers that work with this
        student

7. Ask for parental input, questions, and/or concerns.

8. Discuss ideas and develop a strategy for student improvement. Write down any plans on the agenda.

9. Plan a timetable for expectations of improvements made, and plan for a follow-up conference to discuss the results of the first conference.

10. Closure - Summarize the conversation and reiterate any agreement that you came to.

11. Thank the parents again for their cooperation and try to end on a positive note.

"Make sure you state facts and have documentation to back up your statements."

After the Parent Arrives:

Having a successful conference can be an obtainable goal. Here are some suggestions for after the parent arrives.

- Start with a friendly greeting and a smile. Thank the parents for making the effort to come, and show a pleasant, relaxed attitude. Try to put them at ease and make them feel welcome.

- Begin with a positive statement about their child!
    For example:
    "I am delighted to have Suzy in my classroom. She is a joy."

- Ask how the parent is thinking and feeling about their teen's behavior, progress, and/or grades. It helps you to understand the student's behavior if the parents' attitudes are known.

- Share observations about the student. Ask for parent observations and compare with yours.

- Listen to what the parents say and respond to their comments. You do not have to control every discussion.

- Discuss ways both you and the parents can help the student to improve.

- Make sure to have documentation in order to demonstrate your concerns. If the student has been having problems with grades, show the parent some of the student's work (or lack thereof), or maybe show them a negative pattern that is forming in your grade book. Do not make generalized statements,
    "State the facts, Ma'am!"

- Do not interrupt the parents while they are speaking. This often makes them feel defensive. Wait until they are finished speaking before you begin.

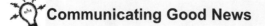

Communicating Good News

Some students are just SO wonderful that there really is no need for a discipline related student or parent conference EVER. However, you still want to stay in communication with the parents and let them know of their teen's progress. Parents of good students really want to know how their teen is doing. The following is a sample letter that you could send home to mom and dad at various points throughout the year.

"Don't forget to report the good news too!"

November 25, 20___

Dear Mr. and Mrs. Parent,

I am pleased to inform you that Joy continues to be a well behaved and dedicated student. It is certainly a pleasure to work with someone who consistently follows the rules and cooperates with both adults and other students. Joy demonstrates a high level of effort in her class work, and shows a positive attitude toward learning.

If you have any questions and feel the need to further communicate with me regarding Joy's school work, please don't hesitate to call or schedule a conference. Otherwise, I just wanted to let you know how proud I am of Joy's progress this year. I appreciate all of your work in helping Joy become a responsible student. Thank you!

Sincerely,

Mr./ Mrs. Teacher

Middle School Teachers and Student Conferences

Often Middle Schools work in Teams who will use their team planning time to conduct student or parent/student conferences. These steps for conferencing will work well for students as well as parents. Also, the previous agenda will work for student conferences. It is important when working with older students to give them input in a parent/ teacher conference. This builds their self-esteem and will motivate them to change their behavior. Simple threats of conferencing with parents DO NOT motivate older students.

"A behavior plan often works well with older students!"

Working up a Behavior Plan

In our section on student discipline we have included a sample behavior plan. This plan is often helpful to bring to a conference, or to complete during the course of a conference when deciding upon a plan of action.

> **Remember:**
> - Behavior plans are a means to correcting student behavior, not punishment.
>
> - Students and parents will be motivated to follow this plan if they are allowed to participate in the creation of it.

Open House

Most schools have an open house within the first month of school. This is a great opportunity for you to meet, greet, and welcome your students' families into your classroom.

For teachers, this seems to be an exhausting process, since you have taught all day long, and then have to return to the school that evening for a few more hours. We wouldlike you to have a good attitude toward open house, since it will be inevitable. It can really help make your year a great one, if you know some of the secrets. On the following page we have listed a few tips.

Open House Tips

- Do not hold parent-teacher conferences during open house! Conferences should be done privately, not when other parents and students are wandering around. If parents press you about answering specific questions, ask them if they would like to schedule a conference and write it down on your calendar that night to show them you are serious about conferencing with them. Explain that you cannot discuss specific aspects of their child's behavior and/or grades while other people are around.

- Some parents may ask general questions about their child, **for example:** *"How is Suzy doing so far?"*

You could answer that question by giving one specific comment such as, *"She is a joy to have in class, and very energetic. Be sure to take a look at Suzy's work displayed in her portfolio."*
If you really need to talk further with the parents, or you can see that they truly want to talk about their child, go ahead and schedule a date and time to meet.

- Plan to have between ten and twenty solid minutes to inform parents of your classroom policies and expectations. You may want to explain your education philosophy at that time so that they have a better understanding of how you teach. A planned activity is not necessary. However, you do not want to talk AT your parents. Make your speech fun and interesting, as well as informative.

- A secondary open house is often scheduled so that parents follow their child's schedule. Each session lasts no longer than 20 minutes. You will have one or two sessions with no parents due to your planning and/or team time. Use this time to catch up on grading papers since the night will be very long!

- Have student work displayed around the room and in the hallways for parents to admire. Unlike elementary school, it is impossible to display student work on their desk, as you have 150 students.

- At various times during the year, the school may hold additional open houses which are geared toward parent conferences. Have your grade book and the most recent graded assignment with you. Be prepared for a long line of parents. Keep your comments short and precise.

Parent-Teacher Conference Plan

Please feel free to make any notations on the agenda.

1. Objective and/or purposes of conference

2. Parents share any observations of the student they feel are important and that relate to student work and behavior at school.

3. Teachers provide observations, review documentation and share any concerns.

4. Parents and teachers discuss possible strategies for improvement.

5. Parents and teachers decide on a plan of action.

6. Closure

Parent Phone Record

Student's Name_____

Date Call Completed _____

Subject (s)_____

Parent's Name _____

Telephone Numbers (Home) _____ **(Work)**_____

Purpose of Call _____

_____

Matters Discussed:_____

_____

_____

_____

_____

Plan of Action:

_____

_____

_____

_____

_____

Conference Request Form

Date _____

Student's Name _____

Teacher(s) _____

Dear Parent(s): _____

It is important that we have a conference regarding your child's:

_____ATTENDANCE   _____WORK HABITS

_____BEHAVIOR   _____OTHER

This conference has been scheduled for :

Date: _____ Time: _____

Location: _____

If you have any questions, or need to schedule for a different time, please call me at

_____

_____ I will be at the conference. My questions and/ or concerns are:

_____

_____

_____ I cannot make this scheduled conference. A better time would be:

_____

Parent Name: _____

Parent Notification of Student Conference

Date_____

Dear_____ ,

    This note is to let you know that my teacher and I have had a conference and we have decided that I need to improve in the areas checked below. If I improve my behavior, it will not be necessary to schedule a parent conference at this time.

_____ Poor attitude

_____ Showing respect for other students

_____ Showing respect for adults

_____ Knowing when to talk and when to listen

_____ Staying in my seat

_____ Behavior in the halls

_____ Behavior in the restroom

_____ Courtesy when teacher is talking with a visitor

_____ Good manners in the cafeteria

_____ Following guidelines of lunchroom behavior

_____ Getting assignments in on time

_____ Using time wisely

_____ Good sportsmanship
                         _____Playground   _____P.E. _____Classroom

Please sign to show that we have discussed this note. This will be in your classroom file.

Student_____

Teacher_____   Parent _____

Missing Assignments

Name: _____

Assignments: **Original Due Date:**

_____

_____

_____

_____

_____

_____

_____

_____

_____

_____

_____

_____

Parent Signature: _____

Parent Communication

DATE: _____

SUBJECT: _____

Today, _____

       _____ **was tardy to class.**

       _____ **was unprepared for class.**

          _____ **no pen/pencil**

          _____ **no notebook**

          _____ **no textbook**

      _____ **did not have his/her assignment or homework**

          _____ **ASSIGNMENT/HOMEWORK** _____

          _____

      _____ **Other** _____

          _____

This is the second occurrence of this problem. If the problem persists, I will call you. Please sign this note and return it to school tomorrow. Thanks for your cooperation.

Sincerely,

Teacher

PARENT SIGNATURE: _____

CONCLUSION

In reading this chapter, we can see that parent involvement is vital to student success. Research shows us that students who have actively involved parents are higher achievers in school. They cause fewer behavior problems and are more engaged in school activities. It is vital to develop a working partnership with parents throughout the school year. This cannot occur without some time and effort on the part of the teacher.

Be sure to call parents regularly from the first week of school and throughout the year. Ask parents to offer their perspective. After all, they know their child much better at this point than you do! Keep parents informed of what is happening in the classroom. Regularly ask for volunteers to work with student groups, or utilize parents as guest speakers. Whatever tools you use, be sure to keep up constant communication with parents to help ensure student success.

Additional Resources

ABC's of Effective Parent Communication
by Dyan Hershman and Emma McDonald

Home-School Relations: Working Successfully with Parents and Families
By M. L. Fuller and G. Olsen

How to Deal with Parents Who are Angry, Troubled, Afraid, or Just Plain Crazy
by Elaine McEwan

Questions for Reflection

1) Why should we strive to have positive relationships with parents?

2) Why is it so important to keep parents informed about what is happening in the classroom?

3) What are several ways to keep parents informed about classroom events and activities?

4) How do you plan to implement two-way communication between you and parents throughout the school year?

5) How will you use the academic calendar as part of your classroom?

Suggested Activites

1) Design a template for your classroom newsletter to send home to parents.

2) Create a series of paragraphs explaining current teaching strategies used in the classroom. Be sure to use plain language. Explain what the teaching strategy is and why it helps students learn better. Each strategy should be explained in one to two paragraphs that can be implemented into your parent newsletter.

3) Design a series of note-cards or postcards on the computer with "Thumbs Up" sayings or other statements of positive feedback. Print and copy on colorful cardstock paper. Cut into individual cards and file into manila folders. Now you are ready to pull out a note, sign it, and give it to a student.

4) Begin brainstorming a wish list of items you would like to have in your classroom. This should be everything you want in your ideal classroom. When you enter your own classroom, check off those items that you already have available. Now you have a list ready to offer parents.

Notes/ Reflections on Chapter

Reading and Writing Across the Curriculum

How can I teach and/or implement essential reading and writing skills in my class?

The skills of reading and writing are such an important part of every classroom. Whether you teach the actual subjects of English and Reading or not, these skills are vital in all aspects of learning and life. Without the ability to read and write, students cannot function effeciently and successfully in the world, not to mention those oh-so-important standardized tests.

While most of us will admit to the importance of these skills, there are many teachers who feel that the teaching and practicing of reading and writing is solely the domain of the Language Arts teacher. This is absolutely not true. With the current crisis in student achievement and the recent *Leave No Child Behind Act*, more than ever it is important for every teacher in the school to incorporate reading and writing skills in the classroom and across subject areas.

The goal of this chapter is to help prepare all teachers to be able to implement these vital skills in their classroom. The majority of ideas presented in this chapter can and should be utilized by all teachers, no matter what subject is taught. We owe it to our students to help them become better readers and writers. So, now, how can we prepare ourselves to either teach reading and writing, or integrate these skills into our lessons?

Set up a Classroom Library

- Choose one corner of your room to be dedicated to reading. It doesn't have to be huge, just a space big enough for two or three kids to sit comfortably. However, if you have a nice big room, make your corner as big as you like!

- Partition it off a little from the rest of the room to make it seem like a special quiet place.

- Books and other types of reading material are an important part of a reading corner and should include non-fiction as well as fiction. Be sure materials is available for a wide variety of reading levels.

What should be included?

- How-To books
- Fun Facts books
- Magazines
- Newspapers

- Historical Fiction
- Non-fiction books related to subject
- Student publications
- Poetry books

> "A well-prepared teacher has a variety of reading material for student use in the classroom."

Hint: Magazines, How-To books, and other non-fiction books provide great sources of information for in-class research.

There are several wonderful books put out by Scholastic and other educational publishers on Science, Social Studies, and other subject area topics. Check out Scholastic's webpage: http://click.scholastic.com/teacherstore/ or Amazon.com: http://www.amazon.com to browse for good non-fiction books to include in your reading area.

- Bookshelves will serve two purposes:
    - They hold books
    - They make great partitions

- Make the corner seem inviting to students.
    - Add pillows and a beanbag
    - Add chairs or even a small couch (if your room is big enough for that)
    - Add small lamps or floor lamps. This will give your students the impression of a cozy reading place. Not everyone has room for these nice extras, but if you do - go for it!
    - Put down carpet squares if your room isn't carpeted.

> "Make your reading area a place where students feel calm and comfortable."

Teacher Testimony

I really wanted to set my classroom library apart from the rest of the room, so I pulled in a comfy overstuffed chair, bean bags, colorful carpet squares, big pillows, and a floor lamp. There was no window near my corner, so I created a window out of butcher paper and "hung" curtains to make it seem homey. I also stuck a big palm tree way in the back of the corner. All of my students enjoyed that corner and I often used it for more than just reading.

Getting the Materials

You may say, okay that sounds fine and good, but where do I get this stuff, and how do I get it without spending money I don't have? Here are some tips:

 Gathering Books

√   **Hold a book drive.**
- Make it a contest between either your students or your classes.

- Send home a letter to the parents explaining what you are doing and why you are doing it.

- Ask for both fiction and non-fiction reading material.

- When students bring in their books, have them write "Donated By:" and their name on the front cover.

- Another option is to create book plates using large labels on the computer. You can print these with the student information or have students write their information in the appropriate places. This helps make your students feel like an important part of your classroom library.

√   **Book Clubs**

- The Scholastic book club often sends out their magazine to teachers. If you do not receive any within the first month of school, go online to their websites and request the TAB magazine for grades 7 and up. Encourage your students to order.

  - **Free Books.** Oftentimes the book clubs will offer free books for every so many dollars spent. Let students help you choose some for the classroom library.

  - **Bonus Points.** When students order, you get bonus points. You can use these bonus points to get books for your classroom library.

  - **Teacher Specials.** Book clubs also offer teacher specials where you can get packages of books for lower prices. Take advantage of these deals!

Hint:

It is important to check each book donated for appropriateness and unwanted marks.

Teacher Testimony
One year I got several adult books that were not appropriate for middle school students to read. Also, a few of the books had bad language written either on the cover or on the inside pages. I'm glad I checked before placing them on my reading shelves!

"Don't forget about Public Library Sales and Garage Sales for low-cost books!"

Use of the Reading Area

1.) Rotation

Have a rotation schedule for students to follow when deciding who gets to sit in the reading corner. Otherwise, you are going to have chaos on your hands with everybody fighting or racing to sit in the corner. (Even the big kids do this!) Alphabetical or table groups is the easiest way to arrange a schedule.

2.) First come, first serve

This is a very dangerous way to decide who sits in the corner because everyone will race to get there first.

3.) Reward system

Reward students who have good grades, good behavior, or who have improved by allowing them to sit in the reading corner. Be careful with this method and watch for inadequacies. Some students may never get to use the reading corner if you use it in this manner.

"I'm not a Reading teacher, so why should I have a reading area?"

- Quiet time area
- Student research
- Access to books
- Enrichment of content
- A place for students who are finished early to read

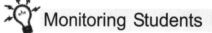

Monitoring Students

1.) Clipboard

Walk around and use the clipboard to help with observations. Keep notes on who is doing what during reading time. For more on this technique, see the Assessment and Classroom Management chapters.

2.) Reading Logs and Responses

Have students keep a reading log with daily responses to their reading. Students should record the title of the book, author, and number of pages read each day before completing their response. A page of reading response questions is included in the back of this chapter.

Teacher Testimony

One way I use my reading area is as a quiet place where angry or frustrated students can calm down. I explain to my students that when we are having a horrible day, for whatever reason, it keeps us from learning properly. I encourage them to let me know when they need to cool down, and I send them to "Australia" which is my classroom library with a palm tree in it. With all of the emotional issues teenagers face, it is nice to have a quiet place for them to use when they need to shill out for a while. It may seem a waste of time to some, but I can see the difference in my student's attitudes and behavior when they rejoin the class.

Hint:

Use Bloom's Keywords to help you develop reading responses on a variety of levels.

Implementing Literature Circles/ Literature Groups

Setting up literature groups can be very confusing and hard to manage. How can we effectively prepare to implement literature groups in our classroom? Below are several different strategies and tips to help you get started.

1.) Assign a group of 4 or 5 students to a particular book.

These groups are often heterogeneous, containing students at a variety of reading levels. You can have the students choose their own book to read as a group, or they can choose a book from several that you have picked out, or you can choose the book you expect them to read. The novel read in literature group can relate to a topic studied in Science or Social Studies, or might be a particular genre that you are studying.

- Each group either reads the book together aloud in class or assigns particular chapters to be read each evening. Then, during class time, students discuss the chapter.

- It is important that you provide students with guiding questions to use during discussion. Each person should record the answers to discussion questions.

- Another option is to provide statements about characters or events within the story for students to either prove or disprove. Have students go around the circle and either agree or disagree with the statement. Require students to state their reasons and provide specific quotes or events from the story to support their position.

Example: *The Count of Monte Cristo is a true villian.*
Do you agree or disagree with this statement?
(Using The Count of Monte Cristo)

Hint:

As we stated earlier, it is vital that you remind students of class procedures, your expectations, and how to work together as a group every time. This should be done before students get together in their groups. When you begin to see student discussions that do not meet your expectations, model exactly what you want to see.

> *"A well-prepared teacher plans out a routine and procedures for literature group time."*

What activities can I use to jumpstart discussion or enrich student learning?

- Students create a storyboard that shows the major events/themes happening within that chapter.

- Students create a timeline that shows the major events happening within that chapter

- Students keep an index card for each character. As they read, students are to write down different traits for each character. This could be extended to include relationships between that character and others as well as any changes that occur to the character over the course of the story.

- Use agree/disagree statements to jumpstart discussion. Students must support their opinion with reasons and with quotes or events from the story.

Internet application

When students come across a concept that is new (they have no prior knowledge about a concept (ex: sailing terms, rabbits vs. hares, a particular culture, etc.), utilize the internet to help extend their knowledge.

- Help students make a list of keywords related to the concept for an internet search (ex: schooner, rigging, etc.).

- The group can use the classroom computer to search for information.

- Students can print out information and share their new knowledge with the rest of the class (mini-research).

Hint:

Two great search engines for kids are Google (www.google.com) and Ask Jeeves (www.askjeeves.com). Students can type in a variety of combinations of their keywords until they are able to locate relevant information.

Whole Class Reading Strategies

There are several different methods for reading a passage as a whole class. These can be used in any subject area.

Choral Reading

Students all read together out loud. A variation on this is to assign each student a different sentence. Have each student read their sentence in turn. Another way to do this is to break the students into groups and have assign each group a different passage to read aloud. Lastly, you could assign half the class to read every other paragraph.

Oral Reading

Students take turns reading aloud. The following techniques are fun to use:

- **Popcorn reading** requires students to read anywhere from two to 8 sentences aloud. When they are finished, they call on another student to pick up where they left off. If the student does not know where they are in the passage, they must stand up for their reading portion.

- **Pass the Ball** reading is where a student has a squishy ball or wadded up piece of paper. When they are through reading their paragraph, they "toss" the ball lightly to a student of their choice to continue the reading.

Reader's Theater

A technique where students sit in the front of the room and are each assigned a character. One student is the narrator. While reading a story, each student reads the dialogue spoken by their character and the narrator reads the rest of it. You could also assign several narrators.

- **Variation:** Break students into groups. Assign each group a section of the textbook chapter or novel chapter. Student groups take the text and turn it into a script to be read the following day. Make copies of the scripts, assign parts, and begin reading.

Hint:

Reader's theater is just one way you can integrate the required curriculum element of theater into your classes.

Creating a script from a textbook chapter to read aloud in class is another way this skill can be integrated.

A third strategy is to have students act out the main events or main idea of the passage they are reading.

Once again, these ideas are not just for Language Arts classes. How can you integrate theater into other subject areas?

Individual Reading Time

This may be called Silent Reading time, D.E.A.R. (Drop Everything and Read), or another name by your school and district. The idea is for students to quietly find a place in the room to read on their own to encourage the enjoyment of reading. Students often enjoy this time, especially if you dim the lights and play some soft piano or classical music. Allow your students to sit anywhere they want so that they will be comfortable and motivated to read.

Writing Activities with Reading Passages

Use writing activities to enhance reading. Whether you teach Language Arts or another subject area, reading and writing go hand in hand. We often write about the things we read and we read what someone has written. It is hard to keep the two separate. Here are some ways you can use writing activities to enhance student reading in your class.

Reading Logs

Have students keep a daily record of what they read in and out of class. You could also give students an easy to fill out log sheet to help you keep track of what they are reading and how much they are reading.

Genres

Teach students the different genres and have them write their own stories using the critical attributes of mystery, horror, science fiction, fantasy, fairy tales, adventure, fables, historical fiction, or biography.

Dialectic Journals

A professor at Emory University in Atlanta, Georgia used to make her students keep dialectic journals to enforce "active" reading. Students fold their paper in half and draw a line down the middle. On one side they write any words or quotes from their book that captured their attention. On the other side, students write what they were thinking while they read that word or passage. This helps them track their train of thought through reading. A sample dialectic journal is provided in the back of this chapter.

"A well-prepared teacher brainstorms ways to incorporate writing activities to enhance student reading in class."

Reading Responses

Have a question ready for students to answer about their reading for the day. Students can record this in a journal of some sort. Collect these responses every week or every couple of weeks so that you can record participation grades for your individual reading time.

The reading response journal/log is also a perfect opportunity for students to practice various reading skills. Instead of always asking for a summary of the pages read, you could have students do one or more of the following:

- Create a storyboard showing at least 4 major events (events which impact the outcome of the story or impact other characters) from the pages read.

- Create an illustrated timeline showing at least 4 major events from the pages read.

- What were the pages mostly about? What are some specific details that support this main idea? Support the main idea with words, phrases, and actions from the story. Write down the page numbers where you found these details.

- Describe two or three different cause & effect patterns within the pages you read.

- Write down 2 fact statements and 2 opinion statements from your reading.

- What do you think will happen next in the novel? Why? Support your reasons with quotes from the book. Include page numbers.

- What events in the story caused your character to react in an unusual manner? What events in this part of your reading have caused an unusual reaction? If none, why?

- What events are affecting your character, and in what way is the character affected?

- Compare and contrast the reactions of 2 different characters to the same event, or compare and contrast 2 characters from your story.

See pages 194, 216, and 218 for additional ideas.

Hint:

Use the reading skills listed in the next couple of pages to create your own responses.

Also, using Bloom's Keywords make creating reading responses a piece of cake!

"This type of assessment helps prepare students for state tests such as the TAKS (Texas Assessment of Knowledge and Skills)."

Graphic Organizers

After reading a passage, novel, or non-fiction book/textbook in class, have students fill in a graphic organizer. Graphic organizers are great to reinforce main idea, sequencing, compare/contrast, fact/non-fact, and many other skills.

Additionally, if you decide that you want to extend the reading into an essay or other written product, a graphic organizer is a great pre-writing activity. Several different types of graphic organizers are available in the back of this chapter to help you get started.

Webbing

Students draw a circle in the middle of their paper and write the title of the book in that circle. Then, they draw other circles off of the main one for each chapter, and write the main idea for one chapter in each of the smaller circles.

Mind Mapping

This is exactly the same as webbing, except that students use pictures/illustrations instead of words.

Listing

Students can draw boxes down their paper, or number their paper 1-10. Have them put events from the book in order within the boxes.

Table

Students make a chart out of their paper by drawing a line across the top and one down the middle of their paper (forms a T-chart). Students can use this kind of a table for comparing/contrasting, advantages/disadvantages, pros/cons, or fact/non-fact.

Venn Diagram

The Venn Diagram is a great way to organize compare/contrast information. Students draw two overlapping circles (a small portion is overlapping). In one circle write traits of one object. In the other circle write traits of the second object. In the overlapping section (middle), write traits that the two objects have in common.

"Graphic organizers are a great way to reinforce reading skills."

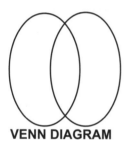

VENN DIAGRAM

"Graphic organizers can be used to organize information from non-fiction reading in other subject areas."

Reading Skills to be Taught and Practiced

The following are reading skills that should be taught in reading and practiced in every single class. If you do not specifically teach reading, it still should be relatively easy to integrate either a review or use of these skills in your class. The best way to help your students recognize that they use these skills on a daily basis is to use the vocabulary and point them out in your own lessons.

Examples:
"What was the sequence of events that caused the Civil War?"
"We just identified a cause and effect. That is an important reading skill."

- Identify main idea
- Summarize a passage
- Distinguish fact from non-fact
- Sequence events
- Identify supporting details in a passage
- Determine word meaning (vocabulary)
- Determine cause & effect relationships
- Compare and contrast ideas
- Make observations and analyze issues within a passage
- Locate specific information in a passage
- Use graphic sources to help interpret reading
- Make generalizations and draw conclusions from a passage
- Identify purpose of a text
- Making predictions

As you read these objectives, ask yourself, how many of these am I already doing without being aware of it? How many Science and Social Studies teachers, for instance, require students to locate facts from the textbook? Sequencing is another commonly used skill in Math, Science, Social Studies, Music, Art, and PE classes.

"Well," you may ask, "since I'm already reinforcing many of these skills in the classroom, what more is there?" Awareness on the part of the teacher is the first step. However, we must also make our students aware that these skills are not just practiced in their Language Arts class, but that they can be applied in all areas - academic and real life.

Example:
A Science teacher has a lesson on electricity. Before the textbook reading, the teacher introduces important vocabulary terms. At this time it would be very easy to incorporate a short discussion on how the prefix or suffix of a word gives a "clue" as to the meaning of the word. This little bit of "reading instruction" doesn't take long, but now two reading skills have been emphasized in a science class. To take it a step further, the teacher could also point out how using prefixes and suffixes help determine word meaning in everything they read from technical VCR manuals to advertisements. In the course of a few minutes within a lesson, the Science teacher has reinforced reading skills, applied it to their curriculum, and applied it to the real world!

Hint:

When planning out lessons, think about ways you will incorporate vocabulary, textbook reading, and reading from other sources to enhance student learning. As you write your objectives, be sure to include the reading objectives that will be used in the lesson.

Example:
Students will be able to identify key vocabulary terms within the text.

"A well-prepared teacher helps make his/her students fluent readers through integration of reading skills."

Ideas and Strategies

Below are some practical ways you can incorporate reading strategies into your classroom, no matter what subject you teach. Think about how you can use the different activities within your specific curriculum.

Vocabulary

Introduce vocabulary terms before beginning a unit or lesson. Discuss how the root word, prefix, or suffix offers a "clue" to the meaning of the word.

Activity:

Have students guess the meaning of a list of words on a sheet of paper. Next to their guess, ask them to write down the "clue" that helped them determine the meaning. Next, pass around a handout that gives students the correct definition of each word along with the "clue" or "clues." Allow students to share their meaning and "clue" for each word, then share the actual definitions. To add an element of fun to the activity, offer peppermints or red tickets (incentives) for students who get the definition correct. You could also offer a prize to the student with the most creative definition, logical reasoning, or creative "clues" for each word. This will encourage students to take risks in guessing the meaning and show them that you reward effort as much as correctness.

Activity:

Create a word-wall for important terms. You can keep the word wall up all year, or change it for each unit of study. Another option is to create portable word walls for each unit using tri-fold display boards. These can be moved around the room easily or folded up and put away when not needed. Upper-level teachers may have one board for each class they teach. A permanent word wall might include terms that are needed all year while portable word walls would show the important terms for a specific unit.

A word wall is easy to create. Simply divide a section of your classroom wall or the display board into rows and columns to show each letter of the alphabet. You might need several rows to accommodate all 26 letters. Then, using Velcro or sticky-tape, place a laminated card with each letter in the appropriate column/row. As new terms are introduced, write them on laminated construction paper or cardstock and stick them under the appropriate letter. Another option is for students to keep a vocabulary notebook with a "word-wall" of their own inside.

Instead of organizing by alphabet, your word wall could be organized by themes of study.

"If every teacher in the school makes an effort to point out and reinforce the reading skills used in their class, the effects will multiply and we will see a surge in fluent readers!"

Reading a Textbook

Use reading objectives to help focus the purpose of student reading.

Activity:
(Locating information from a non-fiction reading)

Create a scavenger hunt of questions for students to answer when reading through a chapter or subchapter of a textbook. Students can work in groups or pairs, reading aloud (quietly) and helping each other locate the answers, or they can work individually. A scavenger hunt is also a fun homework assigment.

An alternate idea: Have students read through a subchapter or section of the chapter as a group. In pairs, or individually, students create their own scavenger hunt questions. Compile the questions for the entire class to complete. The Scavenger Hunt activity also works well for a take-home assessment activity.

Activity: (Sequencing)

There are several good sequencing activities that you can use in the classroom. We discussed a few earlier in this chapter in regards to reading groups. Additionally, when learning a scientific procedure or math equation, students can write out the steps to completing the procedure/solving the problem. Another idea is to then write a "How To" essay explaining the specific steps.

When reading about a historical era or events, students can create an illustrated timeline to show the correct sequencing of events. Another fun way to present a sequence is through a storyboard.

After students read a chapter about a scientific procedure, math equation, or historical time period, give students (or student groups) an envelope with the events, steps, etc. typed on slips of paper. Have students close their books and put the events/steps in correct order. Students can paste or tape their strips on colorful construction paper or on butcher paper as a class.

Activity: (Fact/Non-fact)

After students read a chapter or section in their textbook, have students create two to four statements. Two of the statements should be true and two should be false, but not outrageous. For example: a) Whales are mammals (T/F). b)Whales are related to fish (T/F). Students will have to have paid attention both to write the statements and to answer them correctly. Encourage students to try to "trip up" the rest of the class with their statements. This will motivate them to read and listen more carefully.

Activity: Word of the Day

Write a word of the day on the board for students to read and memorize. Before reading the chapter, say the word aloud with the class. Have the class say the word aloud together. Instruct students to keep an eye out for this important word during reading.

"Use a variety of reading techniques. Students get bored doing the same thing every day."

Hint:

When presenting a new activity, have students do the work as a class the first time to model and answer any questions they may have. In the future, allow them to work in groups, then in pairs, and then individually.

This gives students the opportunity to help each other and learn from one another before applying what they have learned on their own.

"A little thought and creativity can go a long way towards integrating Reading and Writing strategies in other subject areas."

Sample Lesson

The following is a sample lesson written by a P.E. teacher to integrate Reading and Writing skills into his class.

Objectives:
- Students will be able to use note-taking skills to read and research about Olympic Athletes.
- Students will be able to use reading strategies of selecting main idea, sequencing, and finding supporting details throughout note-taking.
- Students will be able to identify steps to becoming an Olympic athlete.
- Students will be able to write a formal business letter

Materials:

Video clips of Olympic Athletes, TV and VCR, Books and other print resources (magazines, etc.) on Olympic athletes and the Olympic games, Computers with Internet and CD-Rom Access, Encyclopedias, Paragraph on transparency to use to teach note-taking skills, clear transparencies to practice note-taking format, Index Cards, Transparency of proper business letter format for example of letter writing, paper and pencils (students)

Anticipatory Set/ Attention Getter:

1. Show the students video clip, "Highlights" of Olympic athletes. Most of the footage is of athletes participating in Olympic games. Some are performing their sport during the Games throughout the ages, some are in training, some are receiving medals, and others are in commercials for Nike, Gatorade, etc.

2. Discuss and brainstorm with students the following:
"What does it take to become an Olympic Athlete?"

Begin a K-W-L chart to record "What we know" about becoming an Olympic athlete. examples (hard work, dedication, ability, money, etc.)

Thank you to Juddson Smith, P.E. Coach, Plano ISD, for sharing this lesson plan with us!

Continuing Instructional Procedures:

3. Review the KWL chart. Have students brainstorm questions to put in the "Want to Know" section. **Examples:** *How do they get to the game? How do they get the money to train?*

4. Explain objectives to students - to research information and take notes on how they might become an Olympic athlete, then to write a formal business letter requesting help in their steps to obtaining their goal - a Gold Medal!

5. Mini-lesson on Note-taking *(see pages in Survival Kit for New Teachers)*
      -give specific notes on note-taking
      -practice with transparency of paragraph
      -show students how to use the index-card with title, author, and page
       number(s) of source at the top and notes in the middle.

6. Students begin researching information individually and in groups on how a person becomes an Olympic athlete. Students should be recording the source information and taking notes on index cards.

Closure for Day: Have students tell me different steps for taking notes from a source. Ask students to tell one new thing they learned about the Olympics today.

Homework: Tonight think about which Olympic Sport you would like to participate in. Pretend you have mastered the sport and are ready to go to the Olympics. We will use this in tomorrow's lesson.

(continued lesson on Day 2)

Anticipatory Set (Day 2)

1. Read a silly (appropriate) letter from "Letters from a Nut" or a silly letter asking for donations. Ask students - How do you think a business would respond to this letter? If you were in charge of donating money, would you give this person any?

Procedures

2. Put transparency of proper letter on overhead. Discuss with students. Identify the parts of the letter (heading, body, closing) and go over expectations for activity (what I expect your letter to look like)

3. Students write 1st draft of letters.

Check for Understanding

-Monitor student work as they are researching and observe. Help as needed.
-Ask students to share their information periodically while monitoring.
-Monitor students while writing letters. Help as needed.
-Have students read letters aloud before writing final draft. Student correct errors as heard.

Closure

Have students each go to the chart and fill in one item they learned about becoming an Olympic Athlete. Read them and discuss.

Assessment of Learning:

-Collect notes taken during research -- did students follow the correct format? Evaluate student understanding of Main Idea and Supporting Details (TAKS skills) through notes.

-Use Rubric to grade the final draft of student letters. Grade content, correct knowledge, creativity, and neatness.

> *"A well-prepared teacher reads the novel before planning lessons in order to integrate their own experiences and knowledge into the discussion."*

> *"Lesson planning for novel studies is more effective when the teacher has done some prior reading and research."*

Reading Novels in Class

It is very hard for students to sit still during an entire 50 or 90 minute class either reading or listening to someone else read. To keep students engaged during the entire class, alternate between reading, discussion, and written activities.

You may be tempted to either read the assigned novel every day or play a CD of the novel being read aloud. Not only is this incredibly boring, but it is not engaging students actively. It is important to stop at various times throughout the reading to check for understanding, discuss unfamiliar vocabulary, and relate the story to the students' lives.

Whenever teaching a novel, be sure to read it ahead of time and think about ways you can relate it to the students.

√ Look up information on the internet about the time period when the novel is set to look for fun or interesting facts.

√ Compare and contrast the life and times of the character with that of the students.

√ Bring in maps to integrate Geography skills and to help students determine location in relation to where they live.

√ Look up information on the author to help students understand why he/she may have written the book

> ***Example:*** *Charles Dickens lived during the Industrial Revolution. He often wrote about the poor living conditions of the time through fictional stories. What kind of story plot might your students use?*

√ How can you integrate information learned in other subject areas?

> ***Example:*** *My Brother Sam is Dead is set during the American Revolution. This is a perfect opportunity for integrating a little history into the lesson.*

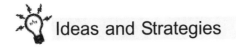 Ideas and Strategies

Activities done throughout the reading are more effective as teaching tools than when given after students finish reading the novel. Below are some different activities to use while reading.

Activity: Paper Bags

Use plain brown lunch sacks for this activity. Have students draw an image from the chapter or pages read that stood out in their mind (ex: the deep red brick house was imposing and seemed to Jack that it was frowning slightly at him). The image could also be a scene from the book, the setting, or a character from the novel or story. If you are reading a textbook, the image might be a famous person or event described in the passage, or a rendering of the concept being described in a textbook or non-fiction reading.

Students put other information inside the bag. Activities might include:

- main idea of the chapter/novel
- outline of the problem and solution
- timeline or storyboard of events
- explanation of skill or concept
- real world application of skill/concept

- vocabulary words
- drawing of plot events
- character cards with basic information
- description of the procedure or events

You can also create additional activities using the Bloom's Keywords in the back of this chapter.

Activity: Venn Diagram

Use this graphic organizer to compare/contrast different characters, events, etc. within the story. Require students to support this information from the text, referencing page numbers. (ex: Where exactly does the book say or show that the Count of Monte Cristo is generous? -using The Count of Monte Cristo

Activity: Letter Writing

Integrate two different skills with the letter writing activity. Have students write either an informal or formal letter to a character from the novel (or a person from the textbook) explaining his/her predictions about upcoming events or the outcome of the story. Students could also use the letter to draw conclusions about the novel or about characters within the novel. A letter is a fantastic forum for applying any of the reading skills mentioned earlier in this chapter.

Activity: News Articles

Apply student comprehension of the novel or textbook reading through a news article. Have students use the reporter's method of the 5 W's (who, what, where ,when, why) and 1 H (how) in analyzing the novel. Turn these "facts" into a news story complete with headline. This is a great activity for both novels and in-class textbook reading.

 Hint:

Running out of ideas? Take a look at the Motivating Students chapter later in this book. Could you adapt any of those ideas to use as an activity with your reading assignment?

Using Journals in All Classes

Journaling is not an activity set aside just for English teachers. The journal is one of the best ways to assess student learning after a lesson as well as a great way to provide one-on-one feedback for each student. Here are a few tips to help you implement journals in your classroom.

Provide Structure

Students need structure to feel comfortable with any assignment. This includes the journal. Simply asking students to "write down what you've learned today" won't work. An unstructured journal topic such as this leaves students feeling flustered and abandoned. They will spend the entire five minutes asking themselves and you, "what are you looking for? what should I write? How much is too much or too little? Where do I begin?" After a few seconds their brains overload and they go into self-preservation mode. This turns into the usual answer of "I don't know" or "Lots of stuff."

Instead, when planning your lessons, use your objectives or key elements to form your journal topic. The topic question or statement should directly relate to your lesson and should be easy to answer within a five minute time limit.

Examples:
- Explain briefly how you would figure the sales price of a $20 pair of jeans with a 15% discount. (used after a percentage lesson)

- What affect did the environment have on where early people settled and the type of home they built?

- What are the three branches of government and which is your favorite? Explain your reasons.

Have Expectations

Students also need to know what you expect of them. Have your expectations written out in detail for the journals. Think about the following questions as you decide.

- What is your goal for the journal each day?   What is the purpose?
- How much do you expect students to write?
- What kind of grade will they receive for their journal?
- What do you expect in terms of spelling, grammar, etc.?

Example:
I expect my students to write at least five sentences each day. Their journal entry must stay on topic and answer the question posed. I expect complete sentences and correct spelling. The journal is a way for me to check student learning each day and is also a way for me to talk with each student individually. If a student has something to say to me that they don't want to voice out loud, they may write it in their journal AFTER they have answered the question, OR before class the next day. Students will be given a participation grade for the journal once a week.

"A well-prepared teacher knows exactly how he/she plans to use journal writing and plans accordingly."

Have a Procedure

It is important that you have a journaling procedure for your class. Students need to know exactly what to do for this type of assignment.

Example: (used at the end of class)
- Put away all materials
- Clean area around desk
- Take out journal
- Write journal entry silently until bell rings

You must get your journal from the table before class starts each day.

Grading

Don't freak out about grading journals every day with a specific number grade. The participation grade doesn't need to be more than a check, check-plus, check-minus, minus, or a "0". It is quick to give out and easy to record. However, it does show students that you are reading their journal and that they are being held accountable.

At the end of the week or every couple of weeks, review their journal entries as a whole and determine a letter grade at that time, as needed.

Provide Feedback

Students really want to hear what you have to say. They look for your feedback every day. Be sure you have one or two things to say to each student in their journal. It doesn't need to be much, but at least once a week be sure that you offer detailed comments in their journal.

Don't be afraid to use your pen and correct mistakes. If no one ever corrects student mistakes, how will they learn? If you see a grammar or spelling error, correct that as well. The more students are held accountable for their writing skills, the more they will improve. An employer in the real world will judge every piece of writing received from an employee, even informal notes.

Use this as one-on-one time. Have you noticed something particular about one student? Take some time to write them a note and ask about the situation, or just let them know you are available to talk if they need it. The journal can serve more than just one purpose, and students really respond to the teachers who take time to learn more about them as a person.

Teacher Testimony
I used spiral notebooks for my student journals and kept each class' in a plastic crate. At the beginning of each class period, I pulled out the journals for students to grab as they entered the room. This was one way I checked for student absences. I looked to see which journals were still up front, checked to see whether the students were actually in class and marked the rest as absent. It worked pretty well and took less time than calling the roll.

"Your attitude affects whether or not journals will be a valuable teaching tool in your classroom."

"Help students become familiar with the format of your State's assessment tool. Format your formal tests to look and act like the 'real deal'."

Evaluating Student Reading

Now that you have your students reading and practicing vital reading skills, how are you going to evaluate what they know and don't know about the book/information they read? Whether your students read individually or as a class, you must determine three things:

1) Did they read? How much are they reading?
2) Did they understand what they read?
3) Can they think critically about their reading?

The following assessments will help you answer those three questions:

1.) Novel Study

Create a book study with several assignments designed to test various reading skills. For example, you might ask students to write a one page summary, create a diorama of the setting, make character trading cards, or write a poem about the main character. It is important to give students choice, so out of five activities, require students to complete three or four. It is also important that you give the book study to students up front so that they know what will be required of them when they finish reading the book. Two sample book study activities are included in the back of this chapter. Also, using the Bloom's Keywords found in the back of this chapter will help make Book Study activities easy to create.

2.) Dialectic Journals

Collect your students' dialectic journals and grade them. This is an excellent assessment tool since the students must write down their own thoughts and feelings about the story. It will give you a good indication of whether or not they understood what they were reading.

3.) Reading Responses

Collect the reading responses every two or three weeks for grading purposes. These will show you what your students are getting out of their reading time.

5.) Formal Tests

You can give a formal test to see which reading skills students have mastered. Set up your formal tests so that they are similar to your State mandated test. This will provide your students with additional practice in that particular format. The more familiar students are with the format of a high-stakes test, the better they will perform.

Hint:

Want to assess how much students are reading? Collect the reading logs to determine how much each student is reading during class and at home.

Writing Instruction

In this section, we are going to discuss the different writing modes and give you some ideas on how to use these modes in your class. For more detailed instruction on the Writing Workshop method, read Nancie Atwell's book *In The Middle*. It will give you a structured program for teaching writing. Our goal is not to teach you how to be a writing instructor, but to give you some more ideas on writing in your class.

The Writing Process

The writing process is the series of steps that a person uses when they write. Using these steps can help students to think more about their writing rather than just slopping something on paper. It also teaches them that writing is a process that takes time!

STEPS

1. Pre-writing:
    Putting thoughts on paper informally. Students can use: jot list, brainstorming, webbing, journals, free-writing.

2. 1st Draft:
    This is also known as the rough draft. Students put earlier thoughts into paragraph form.

3. Peer Response:
    Students read their papers aloud to a partner. The partner makes notes on the following questions: What did you like about the paper? What questions do you have?

4. Revision:
    Students Add details, Remove extra words and phrases, Move words and phrases around and Substitute blah words for exciting ones (ARMS).

5. 2nd Draft:
    Students write a neat copy of their paper.

6. Proofread:
    Look for and correct grammar and spelling mistakes.

Hint:

Post the basic writing process steps on a poster where it can be clearly seen by all students.

"Teaching students the writing process makes them think more about their writing."

Idea

- Create a spreadsheet with student names down the side (one per class) and writing process steps across the top.

- As students work through the steps of the writing process, put a check mark next to their name..

- Students may move between steps 2 through 4 several times before getting to the last step of Final Copy. Each time a student enters a step, keep track with a number.

- This offers the teacher a quick way to check on student progress as well as to redirect students who may be off task. Keep your clipboard with you at all times while using the Writing Workshop.

- You may even want to leave a spot open to record the title/theme/ mode of the piece each student is writing.

> *"A well-prepared teacher knows how he/she plans to monitor individual student progress when using the Writing or Reading Workshop method."*

Writing Modes

- **PERSUASIVE/DESCRIPTIVE** - (a.k.a. persuasive essay)
  Students must make a choice and convince an audience with reasons.

- **INFORMATIVE/CLASSIFICATORY** - (a.k.a. compare/contrast essay)
  Students must discuss likenesses and differences between two objects, persons, or ideas.

- **INFORMATIVE/DESCRIPTIVE** - (a.k.a. descriptive essay)
  Students must describe an object, picture, or event for an audience.

- **INFORMATIVE/NARRATIVE** - (a.k.a. how to essay)
  Students must write a sequence of steps on how to do something for an audience.

COMPARE/CONTRAST MODE

Ideas for Practice Essays

- Tell how your shirt is different from your partner's.

- Tell how you and your mom think alike and how you think differently. (Let students choose another topic or suggest something like musical tastes — that should keep them going for a bit!)

- Tell how subtraction and division are alike and different.

- Tell how one problem solving technique is different from another.

- Tell how SimCity and SimAnt are alike and different.

- Tell how flowers and trees are alike and different.

- Compare and contrast the respiratory and circulatory systems.

- Compare and contrast sailboats with ocean cruisers.

- Compare and contrast the British soldiers and the Colonists soldiers.

- Tell how the hero and villain in your story are alike and different.

- A fun way to organize a compare/contrast essay is to use colored index cards. Use yellow, green and blue index cards. Write information about one object on the yellow cards. Write information about the other object on the blue cards. Write their shared characteristics on the green cards. This provides excellent visual organization.

WHAT DO I LOOK FOR IN A COMPARISON/CONTRAST PAPER?

- Topic sentence that tells what is being compared and contrasted.

- Classificatory vocabulary (on one side, however, on the other side, unlike, like, similar to, different from)

- Transition words (first, second, third, instead)

- Expanded sentences (She was pretty and she was smart)

- Interesting adjectives (can you picture the difference between the two objects?)

- Advanced vocabulary (did the student think of using a thesaurus?)

- Adverbs (usually and especially are common here)

- Specific examples to support thoughts

"You can compare and contrast anything!"

Hint:

When doing a Compare/Contrast essay with a novel or when using sources for information, be sure that your students support their statements with a citation of the page (page #) or source (book, page #).

We need to teach our students from the very beginning how to support their opinions with information from the story.

PERSUASIVE MODE

Ideas for Practice Essays

"Use Mini-persuasive writings to help students practice giving SOLID REASONS for their position!"

- Should girls be allowed to play on the football team?

- Should students wear uniforms to school?

- Should students be allowed to use a calculator on math tests?

- Should students provide their own art supplies?

- Any concerns in the local or global community such as rainforests, oil spills, garbage dumps, cold war, etc.

- Any concerns in the school

- Mini-persuasive writings - Why I should be allowed to go to the bathroom, or, to see a principal or another teacher, or, why I shouldn't have to do homework.

This is the hardest purpose/mode for students and the one they are not given enough practice with. Mini-persuasive writings may help students be able to give solid reasons for choices.

WHAT DO I LOOK FOR IN A PERSUASIVE PAPER?

Hint:

Give a checklist to students that shows what elements you expect to see in their persuasive essay.

Students need to know what is expected of them.

Also, you can use the checklist to help you with the grading process.

- Position Statement

- Introduction

- Three clearly stated reasons

- Specific examples under each reason

- Elaboration phrases (as well as, one example, for instance, additionally)

- Persuasive vocabulary (obviously, clearly, noticeably, stands to reason, unmistakably, evidently, glaringly, plainly, needs no explanation)

- Transition words (therefore, in conclusion, for example, nevertheless, another)

- Interesting adjectives

- Specific verbs

A graphic organizer and grading checklist are included in the back of this chapter.

DESCRIPTIVE MODE

Ideas for Practice Essays

- Use objects from a particular time in history.

- Use objects from a particular area in science.

- Use geometric figures

- Historical or famous people

- Characters from a book

- A day in their life or in someone else's life

- An embarrassing event

- An alternative setting for a book

WHAT DO I LOOK FOR IN A DESCRIPTIVE PAPER?

- A topic sentence that tells the reader what is being described.

- Location words (up, down, below, above, next to, left, right, behind, in front of, beside, around)

- Time words (first, second, then, next, after that, finally)

- Interesting adjectives (radiant, sparkling, streaming, graceful, tinkling, delicate, gentle, ridged, cuddly, glistening)

- Interesting verbs

- Specific examples - elaboration

- Use of the 5 senses (touch, taste, smell, sight, sound)

- Comparisons to other objects (closer to, farther from, bigger than, smaller than, brighter than)

- Use of adverbs (slowly, quickly, intently, softly)

"Use these fun description activities to motivate your students!"

- Give students peanuts or apples and have them describe theirs so that another person can pick it out. Take up the essays and pass them back randomly. Who can choose the correct peanut or apple from the description?

- Put an unknown object in a bag and have students describe it by touch only. Who came the closest? Why?

- Put students together. Students should be sitting with their backs to each other. One partner reads their description of an object and the other partner draws the picture of the object.

Bloom's Taxonomy Keywords

We want to encourage higher level thinking skills in all areas of our classroom. What better way than to use the Bloom's keywords to help develop reading discussion questions, reading responses, and writing activities. Use the keywords below to create responses on a variety of reading responses.

KNOWLEDGE
define
list
identify
describe
match
located

COMPREHENSION
explain
summarize
interpret
rewrite
convert
give examples

APPLICATION
demonstrate
show
operate
construct
apply
illustrate

ANALYSIS
compare
contrast
distinguish
deduct
infer
categorize

SYNTHESIS
create
suppose
design
compose
combine
rearrange

EVALUATION
judge
appraise
debate
criticize
support

"Increase critical thinking skills by utilizing higher levels of Bloom's Taxonomy when creating reading responses."

Sample Questions: Count of Monte Cristo

- Identify the main character(s).
- Describe the mood of the story.
- Explain why the Count is helping Morrel.
- Give examples of how Danglars betrayed Edmond Dantes.
- Illustrate Faria's plan of escape from Chateau d'If.
- Compare Edmond Dantes to the Count of Monte Cristo.
- Predict what you think will happen to the Count now that his revenge has ended.
- Compose a letter to Mercedes from Edmond while in prison.
- Suppose Dantes escaped prison without knowing the events which lead to his arrest. Create an outline of events that might have happened were this true.
- Is Faria a helpful character? In a paragraph, criticize his actions.
- Should the Count have taken vengeance on Danglars and the others? Why or why not? Support your reasons.

WRITING PROCESS NOTES

The Writing Process

1) **Pre-writing** - Gather ideas for a story or essay

2) **Rough Draft** - Write ideas into a story or essay (sloppy copy)

3) **Peer Response** - A friend/ partner reads the story and responds to it

4) **Revise** - Change the story to make it better

5) **2nd Draft** - rewrite the story neater

6) **Revise again** - Check the story for spelling and grammar mistakes

7) **Final Draft** - Proofread the story and write/ type a final neat copy

3 Kinds of Writing

Real - You choose who you write, what you write, and how you write.

Quasi-real - You get to choose either what you write or how you write, and the teacher chooses the other.
Used to enhance knowledge of specific modes of writing.

Practice - You get no choice.
The teacher chooses what and how you write for practice purposes.

PRE-WRITING NOTES

Pre-writing - the process of gathering ideas

There are 5 types of pre-writing:

Freewriting - write without stopping - don't worry about spelling or
punctuation, just write!!!!

Jot list - list everything that comes to your mind about a topic

Webbing - use your topic and write down all ideas in a web

Mindmapping - just like a web except that you draw pictures instead of
writing the ideas

Looping - after freewriting, pick ONE important idea, circle it and use it to
start the next freewriting exercise

GLOBAL RESPONSE

WRITER/ READER

- Read your own story out loud to one or two partners.

- Speak clearly

- You may correct mistakes you see as you read your story.

- While you read your story, your partners should be taking notes by filling out the following form:

    I think this story is about _____.

    What I especially liked was _____.

    I was wondering _____.

- Write down ALL comments made by the listeners on the margins of your story.

- Underline things the listener especially liked.

- Write down all questions in the margins.

LISTENERS

- Listen to the story carefully

- While you are listening, jot down specific words, phrases, or other things that you liked or were confused about. Write down questions about the story.

- After the writer has finished reading the story, tell him/her your comments out loud. DO NOT simply GIVE the writer your sheet - tell him/her what you thought about the story.

When the first person is finished reading and all comments have been made and written down, it is the next person's turn.

(Adapted from Global Response presented duringSpring Branch Writing Project, 1993)

REVISING A STORY

A - Add details to your story --use a caret ^ to add words

R - Remove words, phrases, or sentences that are not needed
strike out words ~~words~~ you don't need

M - Move words, phrases, sentences, or paragraphs around --
circle (you want) words or phrases to move

S - Substitute exciting words for boring, blah words --
Cross out the word and write the change on top

         evil
ex: ~~bad~~

· Try to answer any questions asked by other students or the teacher

· You may need to revise your writing piece more than once.

· A revised paper should look messy with arrows, carets, circles, etc.

CRITICAL ATTRIBUTES OF FANTASY

I. CHARACTERS

- Imaginary creatures – fairies, elves, dwarves, dragons

- Royalty – kings, queens, princesses, princes

- People with powers – wizards, witches, etc.

II. SETTING

- An imaginary world

- Medieval times – castles, primitive setting

III. PLOT

- Usually good vs. evil

- Has lots of magic

- Seems innocent

CRITICAL ATTRIBUTES OF SCIENCE FICTION

I. CHARACTERS

- Regular people

- Spacers – pilots, captains of space ships, people who live in space, etc.

- Aliens

- Robots

II. SETTING

- Space – on a ship, moon, or other planet colony, or space station

- Future

- Other planets in space

III. PLOT

- Usually good vs. evil

- Take over by aliens or robots

- High technology

- Can be the plot of another genre – ex: adventure or mystery

CRITICAL ATTRIBUTES OF MYSTERY

I. CHARACTERS

- Detective(s)

- victim

- Suspects – family members, servants, business associates, friends, strangers

- Police or inspectors

II. SETTING

- anywhere

III. PLOT

- Usually a crime of some sort – murder, theft, missing person, kidnapping

- Clues given throughout the story to help the reader

- Always a motive behind every suspect

  MOTIVE = a reason to commit the crime

- Suspenseful – never really know who did it until the very end

© 2003 Survival Kit for New Secondary Teachers

CRITICAL ATTRIBUTES OF HORROR

I. CHARACTERS

- Evil person – madman, wicked scientist, etc.

- Ghosts, monsters

- Good person – hero or heroine

II. SETTING

- Old houses – haunted or otherwise occupied

- Laboratories

- Dark – late at night and early morning

- Deserted towns

III. PLOT

- Usually good vs. evil

- Suspenseful – sudden twists in the plot

- Often scary

- Gruesome details – blood, gore, people dying

- Twilight zone

- Evil supernatural events occur

CRITICAL ATTRIBUTES OF ADVENTURE

I. CHARACTERS

- Pirates

- Thrill seekers

- Ordinary people

- Police, firemen, emergency technicians

II. SETTING

- Nature or wilderness

- Large city

- Lots of traveling between places

III. PLOT

- action

- Sport or adventure of some sort – something bad happens

- Survival

- Rescue

CRITICAL ATTRIBUTES OF HISTORICAL FICTION

I. CHARACTERS

- Famous people from history

- A friend of the famous person

- People from the future

- Relative of the famous person

II. SETTING

- A famous event or place from history

III. PLOT

- An event from history or events from history

- Usually told from a different point of view

- Based on partial truth

AUTOBIOGRAPHY/ BIOGRAPHY NOTES

Autobiography – A story about someone's life written by that person

Biography – A story about someone's life written by another person

I. CHARACTERS

- The person about whom the book is written

- People associated with that person

II. SETTING

- Wherever that character lived, worked, and traveled

III. PLOT

- There is usually not ONE problem and solution

- Sometimes there is not any problem and solution

- The story is about the person's life and the events that happened to him/ her

© 2003 Survival Kit for New Secondary Teachers

Graphic Organizer for Persuasive Essay

Position Statement:	
Reason 1:	**Elaboration:**
Reason 2:	**Elaboration:**
Reason 3:	**Elaboration:**
Conclusion: (Restate your opinion and three reasons)	

ELABORATION: Each point should be elaborated with either:
    -a story illustrating a specific example   -a quote   -statistics/data

GRADING CHECKLIST FOR PERSUASIVE ESSAY

Does the paper have:

_____ **Position statement**

_____ **Introduction**

_____ **Three clearly stated reasons**

_____ **Specific examples under each reason**

_____ **Elaborative phrases** (as well as, one example, for instance, additionally)

_____ **Persuasive vocabulary** (obviously, plead, visible, distinct, confidence, sincerely)

_____ **Transition words** (therefore, in conclusion, for example, nevertheless, another)

_____ **Interesting adjectives**

_____ **Specific verbs**

Other comments:

© 2003 Survival Kit for New Secondary Teachers

Graphic Organizer for Comparison/ Contrast Essay

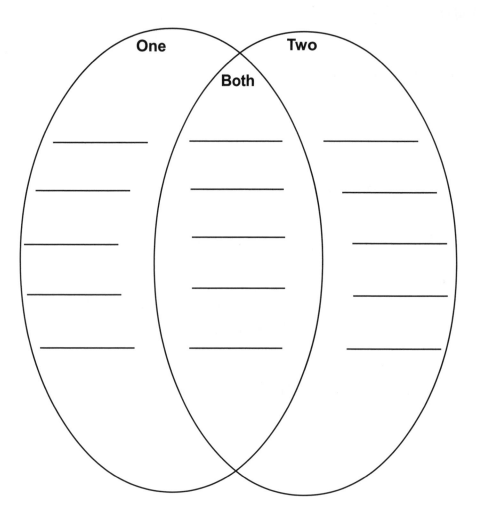

Be sure that you have an equal number of entries for each side so that your essay will not be lopsided. Also, don't forget to write in the page numbers from your text/story where you found words or events to support these characteristics.

GRADING CHECKLIST FOR COMPARISON/ CONTRAST ESSAY

Does the paper have:

_____ **Topic sentence that tells what is being compared and contrasted — specifically**

_____ **Classificatory vocabulary** (Merits, favorable, fitness, drawbacks, advisable, etc.)

_____ **Transition words** (one, second, third, instead, finally)

_____ **Expanded sentences** (complex or compound)

_____ **Interesting adjectives** (Can you picture the difference?)

_____ **Advanced vocabulary** (Did the student think of using a thesaurus?)

_____ **Adverbs** (Usually and especially are common here)

_____ **Specific examples to support thoughts** (Passing the test takes studying or great amounts of luck!)

Other comments:

GRAPHIC ORGANIZER FOR DESCRIPTIVE ESSAY

Object 1:	Adjectives:	Location:

Object 2:	Adjectives:	Location:

Object 3:	Adjectives:	Location:

GRADING CHECKLIST FOR DESCRIPTIVE ESSAY

Does the paper have:

_____ **Topic sentence that tells what is being described**

_____ **Location words** (up, down, below, above, next to, left, right, behind, in front of, beside, around.)

_____ **Interesting adjectives** (radiant, sparkling, streaming, graceful, tinkling, delicate, gentle, ridged, cuddly, glistening)

_____ **Interesting verbs**

_____ **Specific examples – elaboration**

_____ **Use of the 5 senses** (Did they describe how it smells, looks, feels, tastes, sounds?)

_____ **Comparisons to other objects** (Is it larger or smaller, thinner or fatter than something?)

_____ **Use of adverbs**

Other comments;

GRAPHIC ORGANIZER FOR
HOW TO ESSAY

INTRODUCTION

STEP ONE:

STEP TWO:

STEP THREE:

STEP FOUR:

STEP FIVE:

STEP SIX:

STEP SEVEN:

CONCLUSION:

GRADING CHECKLIST FOR HOW TO ESSAY

Does the paper have:

_____ **Topic sentence that tells what is being done or made**

_____ **Creative adverbs** (usually ends in –ly.)

_____ **Specific examples** (materials, techniques)

_____ **Interesting adjectives** (Describe persons, places or things — can you see it?)

_____ **Interesting verbs** (Not run — sprinted!)

_____ **Phrases and clauses** (Begin with which, that or who)

_____ **Other interesting vocabulary** (Use content specific vocabulary and avoid "baby talk")

_____ **Time order words** (First, second, next, then, last)

Other comments:

Beginning Book Study

Each six weeks you will be required to complete a book study. During this book study you will read a novel of at least 100 pages and complete the activities below. This project is due _____ . If you read more than one novel of 100 pages or more, you may choose one of the books to use when completing the activities below.

1) Illustrate a scene from your book on the front of a lunch sack (paper bag) with the title and author's name.

2) Write a summary of your book. Make sure you include the title, author's name, and the number of pages you read. The summary should be at least one page long. Remember, a summary includes the main idea with some details from the book.

3) If you could give this book a different title, what would it be? Write your title for the book and why you think it should be named that on a slip of paper and put it in your bag.

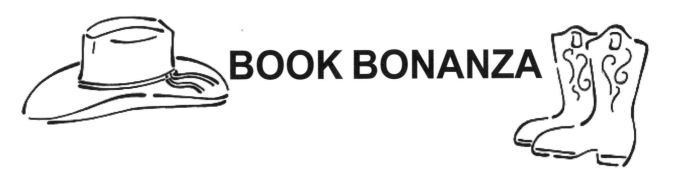

BOOK BONANZA

During this unit, you are to read a novel. After you have finished the novel, you will be responsible for completing the following activities.

This book study is due _____ .

1) Write a summary of your book. Make sure you include the title, author's name, and the number of pages read. Remember, a summary is the main idea and some details. Focus on major events which affect the characters and/or story.

2) Choose five new and interesting words from your book. Create a small vocabulary book. On each page, write the word in bold letter, the definition, your own sentence using the word correctly, and draw a picture of the word in a way that helps you visualize what it means. Try to think of creative ways to make your book!

3) Create a map of the important locations in your novel. Use a key with symbols to explain your map.

4) Project: Choose one of the following, or have your own idea approved by me.
- a.) create a game based on your novel
- b.) write a play script based on a scene in your novel
- c.) make a mobile depicting the characters and setting
- d.) act out a scene from your novel
- e.) write a song based on your novel
- f.) _____

_____

© 2003 Survival Kit for New Secondary Teachers

Reading Responses

- What made you like/dislike the main character?

- What animal is the main character mostly like? Why?

- Choose one of the characters to invite to a party. Which one did you choose and why?

- Would you be friends with the main character? Why or why not.

- Describe the tone of the story.

- Describe the mood of the story.

- How does the weather in the setting affect the story?

- What would happen to the story if the setting were 1000 years into the future?

- What would happen to the story if the setting were 250 years in the past?

- How might the setting be different if this were a different genre?

- If you were the main character's brother or sister, what advice would you give him/her?

- How might you describe the main character to a friend in a letter?

- What problem did the main character face? How would you have solved it differently?

- Which planet is the main character most like? Why?

- Which character would you like to be? Why?

- If you were one of the characters in this story, how would your life be different from the way it is now?

- Describe the relationship the main character has with the other characters in the book.

- Write about one funny thing that happens in the story.

- How would you end the book differently?

- What happened in the story that made you feel angry? Why?

- Write about one sad thing that happens in the story.

DIALECTIC JOURNAL

STUDENT RESPONSE

I would be mad if my mom ignored me all the time. This woman sounds totally selfish! I guess as long as they could sew and talk, it didn't matter if they knew anything else. What a waste.

She sounds like an 18th Century version of a couch potato. How boring to sit all day without TV. How did they do it? I don't think I could just sew all day long. I bet she gets fat because she sits all day.

I totally can't imagine sitting around basically doing nothing. Did all women do this?

No brain and no beauty? How did she ever get married in the first place?

QUOTE FROM BOOK

"To the education of her daughters, Lady Bertram paid not the smallest attention. She had no time for such cares." (*Mansfield Park*, p. 17)

"She was a woman who spent her days in sitting nicely dressed on a sofa, doing some long piece of needlework…" (*Mansfield Park*, p. 17)

"…of little use and no beauty…" (*Mansfield Park*, p. 17)

Responding to Our Reading

After reading the chosen fiction or non-fiction selection/ chapter, use the following discussion/question starters to further enhance student learning. Be sure that you use at least one starter from each level listed below to ensure the students are using higher level thinking skills. These starters can be written on a transparency for students to respond to their reading or for a group discussion.

KNOWLEDGE
Define words from the reading that were unfamiliar to you.
Identify three major events, concepts, or characters presented in the reading.
Describe the setting of the story or event, OR describe the concept from the reading selection.
Locate three facts/details from the passage read. Locate a place from the reading on a map.

COMPREHENSION
Retell the event/story/concept from the reading.
Summarize what you just read with the main idea and some supporting details.
Give examples of...
Explain how...

APPLICATION
Predict what will happen...
Demonstrate how...
Construct a model of..., character traits of...
Apply this reading to your own life.

ANALYSIS
Compare and Contrast ...
Make a T chart and categorize elements from the reading
What can we infer from this reading? about this character?
Distinguish one aspect of the character, event, concept from another

SYNTHESIS
Compose a letter...
Design your own...
Create a new product that solves a problem from the reading
Suppose you were in the situation we just read about, how would you react?

EVALUATION
Debate two sides of the issue/event in your reading
Appraise the usefulness of a concept/issue/event from your reading
Criticize a decision made by a historical figure or character from the reading
What is your opinion? Support it with details from the reading

Conclusion

Reading and Writing are not just skills that have importance in English and Literature courses. They are skills that impact student lives daily and must be practiced in ALL subject areas. The more students practice reading and writing, the more proficient they will become. This is especially true of those learning the language. The more we encourage the use of reading and writing skills in all of our classes, the more our students will begin to see the importance of the written language in their lives. Many students feel that reading and formal writing are only important for their Language Arts classes. It is up to us to show them that even architects, scientists, and mathematicians must be able to write formal papers and understand what their colleagues have written in journal articles and other types of reading text. The best way we can do this is by pointing out how we use reading and writing in our specific subject area as well as applying those important skills within our course requirements. It is not necessary for every teacher to teach the elements of literature and writing, but it is vital for every teacher to model the importance of reading and writing skills within their content area. Simply pointing out the reading skill being used to determine meaning and writing daily journals will do much to increase student proficiency. Just think what can be accomplished when students are actively reading and writing in each and every class!

Additional Resources

In the Middle: Writing, Reading, and Learning with Adolescents by Nancie Atwell

Classrooms that Work: They can All Read and Write by Patricia Cunningham and R.L. Allington

Nonfiction Matters: Reading, Writing, and Research in Grades 3-8 by Stephanie Harvey

Questions for Reflection

1) Why is it important for specific reading and writing skills to be integrated in all curriculum areas?

2) What purposes can a reading corner serve in other subject area classrooms?

3) Do you foresee e-books and/or the computer as part of your reading area in the future? Why or why not?

4) How do you plan to ingetrate writing activities that encourage higher-level thinking skills into your lessons? Brainstorm specific examples.

5) When reading a required textbook chapter, how might you incorporate various reading objectives? Why is this important?

          © 2003 Survival Kit for New Secondary Teachers

Suggested Activites

1) Develop a plan for creating your own classroom library. Think about the following aspects:
   - a) What types of reading materials will you include?
   - b) How do you plan to obtain this reading material?
   - c) What method(s) will you use to determine who gets to use the reading corner?

2) Using a reading currently used in your classroom or student teaching, create a series of reading responses using Bloom's Keywords.

3) Give three examples of writing activities that can be used in any subject area and explain the purpose of each.
   example: *Dialectic journal with textbook reading encourages active reading.*

4) Write out your expectations and procedures for journaling in your classroom. (See pages 61-62)

Notes/ Reflection on Chapter:

Brain-Based Classroom

Creating a learning environment where students are motivated to learn and collaborate with one another should be our ultimate goal. How can we accomplish this?

- We need a solid base of knowledge and understanding of the actual content we teach.

- We need an understanding of human nature.

- We need an understanding of how the brain learns best.

1.) Knowing Our Content

Why? Well, the more knowledge we have about a particular event, concept, or skill, the better we are able to teach it. The wealth of information stored away in our brains through study and experiences makes it possible for us to expand upon the basic information presented to students in textbooks.

Could we teach a subject straight from the textbook and cover the required objectives? Probably. Would it be considered effective teaching that will follow the students throughout their lives? No way. Knowing your subject materials brings with it the confidence that you know what you're talking about. You'll be able to share stories and fun facts that add depth to student learning. And, you'll be better prepared to help students apply this learning to their lives and the world around them.

I want to have a brain-based classroom!

Where do I start?

Example: A class is reading a chapter in Social Studies about the early United States government and the first president.

Teacher A:

After students read the chapter, the teacher discusses the information from the text and assigns a worksheet with various questions to assess comprehension of material read.

Teacher B:

While students read the chapter, the teacher stops at various points to check for understanding. When students read about the first president, the teacher pulls out two wooden squares the size of teeth and passes them around the class. When students ask about the squares, she tells them, "How do you think George Washington may have used these?" Students brainstorm and they discuss the possible uses. The teacher then goes on to tell them that George Washington actually wore wooden teeth. Students are then encouraged to look on the internet for other interesting facts about the U.S. founding fathers or early presidents.

Which lesson do you think students will remember and retain?

Hint:

Kids Discover Magazine is an amazing source of interesting information, fun facts, and great photos on a variety of topics including Science concepts, Famous People, Historical Events, Current Events, and World Cultures. Check the school library to see if they subscribe to this magazine.

"Other types of professionals must stay well-informed of content for their field as well as current practices, and so must we!"

Look at the example for Teacher A. Did this person discuss the history of U.S. government? Yes. Did they cover a required objective? Yes. Will the students remember this information? Most likely not.

Look at the example for Teacher B. Do you think that using the fun fact and concrete object of "wooden teeth" grabbed student attention? Definitely! Additionally, the extension activity is motivating for students and encourages further thinking on their part. This type of lesson is likely to be remembered by students for years to come.

Taking information about a famous person and relating it to students' lives helps make that person real to them. Getting students actively engaged in a discussion about the pros and cons of wooden teeth will stick in their mind and will stay with them longer than a two sentence or two paragraph statement about George Washington from the textbook.

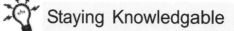

Staying Knowledgable

How can I be sure that I am able to extend and enrich student knowledge on topics/concepts that I don't know much about or understand?

1) Read and Keep Reading

-biographies   -science journals such as Discover
-historical events   -non-fiction books

Non-fiction books and magazines can be very interesting and sometimes fun to read. Remember, the more you read, the more you know!

2) Research

√ As you do your lesson planning, write down key words from the textbook and/or other resources from which you plan to teach

√ Use those keywords to do an internet search for information - type in "fun facts" along with the keyword(s) to see what comes up in your search.

√ How is this skill/concept applied in the real world?

> **Example of real-world application:**
> Last year my husband and I were remodeling our bathroom when he found that he needed to enclose a vent at an angle. Neither of us knew how to figure out the measurements to cut the 4 X 4 board. So, I turned to the internet, went to Ask Jeeves (http://www.askjeeves.com) and typed in "How do I figure the measurements to cut an angle?" and "construction." The information we needed was right there. Needless to say, we found that we need the Pythagorean theorem. This is a real world application of geometric skills. You could also type in "real-world geometry" (or any other skill) and get plenty of information to help you when planning lessons.

3) Do the following before planning lessons.

√ Practice the math skill to be taught

√ Read the chapter or selection you plan to use in class

√ Practice the experiment

By doing these things BEFORE you plan out your lesson, you'll find that this helps you prepare for potential questions, glitches in procedures, problems, and misunderstandings that might occur during the lesson. It will also help you know what to expect when you actually present the lesson with students.

Veteran teachers have the benefit of having taught the skill or experiment in previous years and as such know what they are doing. As a new teacher, much of your planning time should be spent in gaining that knowledge and experience with the concept.

2.) Understanding People

Why do teachers need to know about human psychology? Well, the more you know about human behavior, the more you will be able to motivate students to want to behave and learn in your class. Take some time to review the concepts you learned in your psychology course and brainstorm ways you can adapt your own behavior to create positive relationships with your students.

Each student in your class is a unique individual who has specific needs. It is easy to forget that fact when dealing with a classroom full of faces. We can get caught up in curriculum, deadlines, grades, accountability, and forget that we hold in our hands the fragile psyches of adolescents who often need more than just good grades to help them bloom into successful adults.

> *"A well-prepared teacher reads content and practices skills when planning lessons."*

Hint:

When do you have time to read all of this? Try one or more of the following:

- -in the bathroom

- -while taking a bath

- -while walking on a treadmill

> *"An effective teacher takes time to get to know students as individuals."*

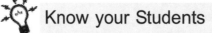 ## Know your Students

1) Get to know your students as individuals.

2) Be flexible and know that you can't react exactly the same to every situation and every student.

3) Be understanding.
   Look further into what may be causing the problem rather than immediately assuming the student is a troublemaker or is "out to get you."

4) Take the time to talk with students.
   Don't make assumptions, but rather talk out the problem, assist with mediation between students, or just take time to talk with the student about life in general.

Boys in today's classrooms

In talking about human psychology and meeting individual needs, I want to bring up a topic that may cause some controversy - Boys. Most classroom teachers, being female, do not understand boys and how they operate. They find themselves at a loss in trying to help these boys find a place within the classroom.

For the longest time girls have been a major focus in teacher training because they were often being left out of class discussions. The goal was to help our girls become more assertive in the classroom and receive the attention they deserve. This has been an issue of concern in the past and is currently being addressed. The following information is not in any way intended to propose that we stop encouraging our girls to be successful in the classroom, only that we need to understand our boys so that they can also see success.

Psychologists and social scientists are warning our society that we are in the middle of a major crisis among boys. We can see this ourselves when we look at the number of boys commiting horrifying types of violence in our schools. So why are we addressing this issue here? We feel that the more you know about the types of behavior you are likely to see from boys, the better prepared you will be and the more effective you will be as a teacher.

Dr. James Dobson, in his book Bringing Up Boys, states that understanding how boys are "hard-wired" is the first step. Let's take a look at the information he provides.

1) **Higher levels of Testosterone** (T) in boys cause traits of high risk including physical, criminal and personal risks. The more (T) in a person, the more risky behavior is exhibited.

2) **Boys have lower levels of Serotonin**, the hormone which calms the emotions. This hormone also facilitates good judgment.

3) **Boys have a large amygdala** which is the fight/ flight part of our brain. It does not think or reason, but puts out a chemical that causes a "knee-jerk" reaction which can lead to violence in some instances.

All of these elements are the backbone for why boys generally engage in risky behaviors including acting out in class, wrestling with other boys, and a seeming lack of common sense.

Does this mean that your boys are a hopeless case? Absolutely not! What it does mean is that we must understand the need of most boys to be physically active. We also need to have an understanding behind the cause of often irrational reactions by boys to events and people in the school. For example, boys are much quicker to "shut down" when in a controversial situation with a teacher.

What can I do?

1) We strongly recommend that you read Bringing Up Boys by Dr. James Dobson, The Wonder of Boys by Dr. Michael Gurian, or Raising Cain co-authored by Dr. Michael Thompson. All are excellent books on understanding and helping boys.

2) Keep in mind the strategies for knowing your students that we discussed earlier in this chapter.

3) Provide opportunities for your active boys to move around or wiggle. You would want to seat them in the back of the room where they cannot distract others. **ex:** *let them stand, wiggle a leg, bounce up and down, use squeezy balls while working, etc.*

4) Provide a place where students can calm down until they are ready to join the class. I used my reading corner as "Australia" for them to get away.

Teacher Testimony:

"One of the boys in my room was very active and had difficulties with prior teachers in the school. He was brilliant, but often caused disruptions because of his need for movement. I moved his desk to a place where he would not distract others, and let him stand or wiggle while working. This gave him the outlet he needed.

The year before he had been in and out of the Principal's office all year long. The year I had him, he went to the Principal's office maybe two times all year. His parents were pleased with the progress and he was able to be a positive member of my class."

How do I deal with angry or difficult students in my class?

There are different reasons for angry or difficult students.
- picked on by other students
- assumes he/she will always get in trouble (from past experiences with teachers)
- issues at home
- feels no one likes/appreciates them
- feels the need to "prove" they are tough
- feels stupid
- doesn't trust the teacher because of past experiences

Steps to Determining Root of Problem

1.) Identify the specific behaviors exhibited by the student.

2.) Is this happening in just your class or in other classes as well?

3.) Is this behavior recent (past few days or months) or has it been going on for several years?

If behavior has changed recently:
  -you've seen a change in behavior/attitude
  -student was not behaving this way last year

Then ask:
Has something happened recently to the student either at school or home?
  -bullied   -family issues   -changes in family life
  -a recent move   -a friend moved   -death in family

These types of events can affect a student's attitude and behavior resulting in a shut-down in the classroom.

4.) Once you've identified the cause of the change in behavior, work towards a solution

√ Offer a place for students to go to calm down. They may rejoin the class when they are ready.

√ Talk one-on-one with the student to determine the cause of the anger or problem. Talking out issues is oftentimes enough to help the student build a sense of trust in you.

√ Allow students to talk to the counselor.

"The more we get to know each of our students, the better we can help them to be successful."

"Sometimes all it takes is a kind word or "I believe in you" to turn an angry or difficult student around."

If the student's behavior is long-term, begin to work with parents and the counselor to resolve the problem.

- Be flexible rather than overly rigid.

- Offer a place for the student to calm down every time he/she is angry or frustrated and allow them to rejoin the class when they feel ready.

- Encourage positives shown by the student.

- Utilize leadership qualities within the student and use in a constructive way to help you. *"I could really use your help as a leader in my classroom."*

- Talk with the student instead of making assumptions.

- Slow down and take your time when working with the student. This shows you care.

The more time spent=building trust=building respect

- Many angry/difficult kids are ignored, yelled at, and/or demeaned at home. They need something better from you if you want their cooperation.

- Implement a non-threatening environment in your classroom.

3.) Understanding How the Brain Learns

Studies done by researchers show us that there are certain elements which increase students' chance of learning. We're going to use a very simplified explanation and application to the classroom, but in order to fully understand how the brain learns best, we strongly suggest that you read authors including Eric Jensen, Howard Gardner, Leslie Hart, and Susan Kovalik. We have listed several different books in the back of this chapter as additional resources for your review.

The first element of a brain-based classroom is a non-threatening environment. What is a non-threatening environment and why is it so important that our classrooms be this way? An environment is non-threatening when students feel comfortable sharing their thoughts, ideas, and dreams with the teacher and also with other students. We want to strive to have an atmosphere in the classroom where no one is judged by anyone else. Every idea is welcomed, no one is ridiculed, no one is fearful of overly harsh punishments, and no one is put down. Our classroom should be a place where students can make mistakes and still be cherished.

Teacher Testimony

One year I had a student who came to class angry every day. He was in a complete shut-down. The merest hint of another kid touching him would result in a total melt-down. I looked in his Cumulative folder and saw that he had been a problem for most of his school career. He was in Special Education, but for Speech reasons only. However, he kept telling me, "I can't do that. I'm stupid." After talking to the mom, who threw up her arms in exasperation, I decided that extra care was needed with this one. Whenever I saw him get angry, I would let him go to the reading area to calm down. When possible, I would go and talk with him about whatever had happened. After a while he began going to the corner less and less. One day, I saw him doing some of the more complicated class work with ease. I said to him, "Boy, you sure are smart. Look at what you can do!" He simply beamed. I told him this over and over. By the Winter Holidays it was like I had a totally different student in my class.

As teachers we can create a non-threatening environment by:

- Insisting upon positive life skills.
    kindness, cooperation, team-work, flexibility,
    friendship, integrity, honesty, dedication, loyalty, etc.

- Character education is an additional way to create a positive classroom climate.

- Do not stand for bullying, teasing, gossiping, and other negative behaviors in your classroom.

- Implement your consequences and defend those students being hurt by others. Show that you will not tolerate it.

Of course, all of this is well and good, but if you do not practice what you preach, you will never have a non-threatening classroom environment.

Why is this so important? Remember that amygdala we mentioned earlier in the chapter? When our classrooms are full of negativity and hurtful behaviors from either the teacher or students, the amygdala kicks in and student learning shuts down. Let's take a look now at how the brain operates.

The Triune Brain

Simply put, the brain is made of three parts. This is called the "Triune Brain." There are technical terms for each part, but I use more simplified terms to explain this concept to my students. The terms in parenthesis come from Leslie Hart in his book Human Brain and Human Learning.

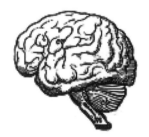

1. The "Thinking" Brain - (Neomammalian)
    This is where we learn, store, and retrieve knowledge. Our memories are housed here as well as our creativity.

2. The "Regulating" Brain - (Paleomammalian)
    This part of our brain is much smaller and somewhat below the thinking area. This part of our brain takes care of all our bodily needs such as eye blinking, swallowing, digesting, heart beating, eating, etc.

3. The "Reflex" Brain - (Reptilian)
    This is the smallest part of our brain (the amygdala) which resides just below the regulating brain and just above our spinal cord. This is the control of our emotions, as we discussed earlier. The "fight vs. flight" reflex is exhibited through this part of our brain.

I like to explain this to my students so that they will better understand how they learn and why sometimes it seems so hard for them to learn.

There are several things that can keep us from using our "Thinking" brain. For example, if we are starving because we haven't eaten anything all morning, our brain downshifts into the "Regulating" part and all we can think about is our hunger. No learning can take place because every thought we have revolves around food.

Are students only thinking of food?

Another strong example is anger. If someone makes us angry, our brain downshifts to the "Reflex" part, and all we are able to do is be angry. All of our thoughts revolve around our anger. No learning can take place while we are still emotional. This goes for all emotions including joy and fear.

Take a moment to think about a time someone made you really angry. Were you able to think straight? Often this is how people describe a haze of anger. How can our students learn if their thoughts are consumed by hunger, bodily needs, anger, or other emotions? Also, how can we teach well if we are consumed by those same things?

Anger inhibits learning

Let's apply this theory to the classroom. What would happen if our students walked into a classroom where they were constantly picked on by other students, ridiculed or belittled by the teacher, and punished for every little mistake they might make. Can learning occur in this classroom? Definitely not! Students will enter the room and immediately downshift to their "Reflex" brain so that they are better able to protect themselves from possible harm, be it physical, emotional, or mental.

Now, what about a classroom where chaos rules? Before long, the teacher is the one who becomes fearful. The entire class is spent with the teacher operating in survival mode. No quality teaching can take place when the teacher is spending every minute using his/her "Reflex" brain.

One last application of this theory is in the school itself. It is important for administrators to create the same type of non-threatening environment for his or her teachers. When teachers are fearful for their job, ridiculed or talked about by other staff members, or not allowed an open exchange of thoughts and ideas, they are not able to be effective teachers. Every thought and concern is focused on their situation within the school and therefore is not focused on teaching, where it should be.

Does chaos rule?

> *"A well-prepared teacher plans how to implement brain-based strategies in their classroom and determines expectations for student use of freedoms."*

Teach Students about the Triune Brain

At the beginning of the year, explain to your students the concept of the Triune Brain. Give specific examples from your own life of when you have "downshifted".

> *For example: "When I was taking the GRE exam, I arrived very early and brought a book to read while I waited. Although the test had not yet been passed out, a test-monitor came by my seat, snatched the book out of my hands and threw it on the floor near the opposite wall. "No outside materials aloud," she harshly told me. Well, let me tell you, I was so angry that I couldn't think of anything else except for that woman for a full fifteen minutes or more into the test. I couldn't concentrate on the test until I had calmed myself down."*

This is a perfect time to explain to students the implementation of the other ideas presented in this section. I discuss at length my expectations for student use of these privileges and freedoms along with the consequences if they are abused.

Keep Healthy Snacks Available.

To help students stay in their "Thinking" brain, I keep a huge jar of pretzles, goldfish crackers, or some other healthy type of snack available for everyone. If a student comes to me and is hungry for whatever reason, I let them grab a handful of crackers to help ease that hunger.

Clear Transition from Play Time to Work Time

When the class is having a lot of fun and everyone is joking, it is necessary to make a deliberate stop and point out to students when "play time" has stopped and "work time" has begun again. This can be done by saying something like, "That was fun." (pause) "Now it's time to get back to work. Everyone focus on..." Most students have trouble moving from play to work without this transition help from the teacher. Too much excitement can inhibit learning as well.

Hint:

One way to transition students and re-focus their attention is to say,

"Look at the ceiling. Look at the floor. Look at me."

Thank you to Kim Arthur, Frisco ISD, for sharing this idea with us!

Allow Students some Freedoms

When students need to use the restroom, I allow them. All they have to do is let me know they are going (not during my instruction of course) and sign out. When they return, they sign themselves back in. This allows me to keep track of where and when everyone has gone. I feel that this shows students more respect than demanding that they ask permission to leave when "nature calls." However, if students abuse this freedom, there are consequences. *(See "My Time")*

CONCLUSION

A brain-based classroom is one where collaboration between students and teacher occurs on a daily basis. It is a place where everyone feels comfortable working and sharing ideas with one another. Can it really occur in the real world of teaching? You bet! We've been there and have experienced it ourselves. However, it is up to the teacher to create this type of an environment through their knowledge and actions. By being life-long learners ourselves, we foster a love for learning in our students. How? By reading and researching all we can about the concepts we teach, our students see our own desire to learn more. Additionally, when we take the time to get to know each of our students as individuals, they begin to trust and respect us as their guide. Lastly, when we understand how the brain works, we can better meet student needs. When these needs are met, learning takes place every single day, which, after all, is our ultimate goal.

Additional Resources

Multiple Intelligences: Theory into Practice
by Howard Gardner

The Unschooled Mind
by Howard Gardner

Brain Based Learning
by Eric Jensen

Human Brain and Human Learning
by Leslie Hart

Bringing Up Boys
by James Dobson

The Wonder of Boys
by Michael Gurian

Raising Cain: Protecting the Emotional Life of Boys
by Dan Kindlon and Michael Thompson

Questions for Reflection

1) Why is it important for you to be knowledgable in your content area?

2) Why should you get to know your students? How will it help you as a teacher? How will it help your students?

3) How does knowing about the Triune Brain affect your teaching style and your classroom?

4) What can you do to encourage a non-threatening environment in your classroom?

Activities

1) Take one concept you will teach this year *(see your State Standards or the district/school curriculum)* and learn as much as you can about it through research. How can you relate this concept to students' lives? Develop an introduction that will "hook" students and one activity that will make this concept come alive for students.

2) Develop a plan for how you will make your classroom a brain-based learning environment.

3) Do some further research on boys in the classroom or students with anger issues. Develop a list of strategies you can use to help these students be successful in the classroom.

Notes/ Reflection on Chapter

Brain-Based Teaching Strategies

Another aspect of the brain-based classroom is engaging students in their learning. We want students to be active, not passive participants in the learning process. What exactly does it mean to be active versus passive?

Take a look at the learning pyramid below to see the average retention rate for different styles of teaching. Which of these encourage passive learning through listening or watching and which encourage active learning through doing?

I want to keep my students actively engaged in class!

How do I begin?

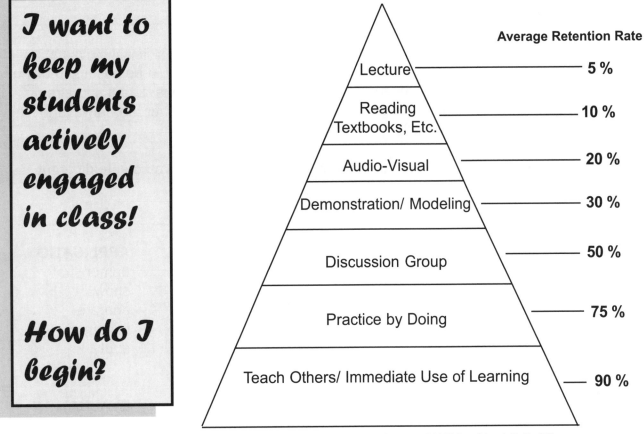

Average Retention Rate

Lecture	5 %
Reading Textbooks, Etc.	10 %
Audio-Visual	20 %
Demonstration/ Modeling	30 %
Discussion Group	50 %
Practice by Doing	75 %
Teach Others/ Immediate Use of Learning	90 %

NTL Institute for Applied Behavioral Science, 300 N. Lee Street, Suite 300, Alexandria, VA 22314. 1-800-777-5227.

Students need to be actively manipulating information through a variety of activities in a brain-based classroom. Being actively involved is motivating and you'll find that students won't want to leave your class because they are having so much "fun." Can you imagine a classroom where students are being challenged to think at higher levels, create products that demonstrate and apply their learning, and teach others what they have learned? This is what a brain-based classroom looks like. Let's start by taking a look at higher level thinking skills.

Bloom's Taxonomy

Bloom's taxonomy of cognitive skills includes:

KNOWLEDGE

COMPREHENSION

APPLICATION

ANALYSIS

SYNTHESIS

EVALUATION

"Increase critical thinking skills by utilizing higher levels of Bloom's Taxonomy"

Knowledge is the lowest and most basic skill while evaluation is the highest cognitive skill. Our students should be assessed using each of these cognitive levels. This helps our students to stretch and challenge their critical thinking skills rather than always testing basic facts.

Below are some terms you can use to help you create different types of activities:

KNOWLEDGE	**COMPREHENSION**	**APPLICATION**
define	explain	demonstrate
list	summarize	show
identify	interpret	operate
describe	rewrite	construct
match	convert	apply
locate	give example	
ANALYSIS	**SYNTHESIS**	**EVALUATION**
compare	create	judge
contrast	suppose	appraise
distinguish	design	debate
deduct	compose	criticize
infer	combine	support
categorize	rearrange	

Here are some sample activities for each level in Bloom's:

KNOWLEDGE

- Define the following vocabulary
- Identify the main characters
- List the properties of a gas
- Locate England on the atlas
- Describe the scientific method

COMPREHENSION

- Retell the story in your own words
- Give an example of how the main character is a hero
- Explain how a gas is different from a solid
- Explain how an island is born
- Give 5 examples of mammals

APPLICATION

- Predict what will happen in the sequel to this book
- Demonstrate how a liquid becomes a solid or gas
- Demonstrate how a volcano can create an island in the ocean
- Show how erosion changes land features

SYNTHESIS

- Imagine that the villain and hero are friends. What might happen in the story because of this?
- Suppose we breathed liquid rather than a gas (air), how would our lives be different?
- Design your own island using three different land features
- Design the front page of a newspaper that might have appeared in Great Britain in the year 1100

EVALUATION

- Choose an issue from the story to debate
- Which is better to breathe, solid, liquid or gas? Support your opinion
- Using what you know about landforms and tectonic plates, criticize or support the notion that California will one day "fall into the ocean"

"Use Bloom's taxonomy to help you assess different levels of student learning."

Team/Group Activities

Another aspect of the brain-based classroom is cooperative learning. Working together as a team is an important skill students will need throughout their lives. Also, when students work together as a group they learn from one another.

Although we may not see some of the benefits immediately, our students are learning important social skills. They are also learning different ways to think and respond to situations by observing the others in their group. If handled properly, group activities not only motivate students, but also enhance student learning.

Team Roles

It is important to discuss team roles with your students so that they each know what is expected of them. In the beginning you will need to model what you expect each "role" to look like and sound like. Just telling students, "Okay, you are the leader" does not teach them how to be a leader. Instead model what the leader of a group might say and do.

> **Example:** (leader) "We are supposed to read this chapter and respond using the questions on this sheet. Why don't we break up the chapter and each read a section aloud. Who would like the first two pages? (etc.)" ... when getting off task leader might say, "I think maybe we are getting off topic. Who is supposed to read next?"

A good book to read besides Johnson's *Cooperative Learning* is *Learning Thru Discussion* by WM. Fawcett Hill. It will give you additional ideas on how to model a good team for your students.

Additionally, *Choice Theory* by William Glasser also discusses the concept of teaming within the classroom.

"The workplace is becoming less isolated with workers behind partitions and more a dynamic system of people working together in teams."

Hint:

Are you looking to get students actively involved in a lesson? Try putting them together in a group to become "experts" of a section in the chapter or to create a product using the skill/concept you just taught.

Before every group activity, have students review the roles and rules of working as a team.

Leader - The person guiding the group. This person begins discussion and leads the team in the activity. They also redirect when the group gets off task.

Recorder - The person who writes down the specifics of the activity, takes notes, etc.

Reporter - The person who presents information to the class.

Materials - The person who gather necessary materials.

TimeKeeper - The person who watches the clock and makes sure the group meets their deadline.

(These roles are taken from different Learning Group Models)

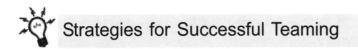 Strategies for Successful Teaming

- **Have guiding questions and activities** to help students know what to do. Remember, you are the overall guide and facilitator of this activity.

- **Constantly monitor students.** We use the Clipboard Monitoring method mentioned in the Classroom Management chapter. A simple spreadsheet on a clipboard will help you keep track of student behaviors and academic progress.

- **Using bonding type activities** at the beginning of the year, or anytime you change groups, to help students work better as a team. We have several activities listed in the First Day of School chapter that you could use for this purpose. Additionally, you might look up information on ROPES activities which are designed to build trust between groups of people and emphasizes problem solving skills.

Hint:

Use Bloom's Keywords to help structure group discussions or group activities.

We sometimes use a concept called "Cube It" shared with us at a G/T training.

The idea is to take a box, cover it with colorful paper, and put the keywords for each level on each side of the box.

Give one cube to each group of students and have them create their own questions or activities based on one or more of the keywords listed on each side.

You could tell students to "Cube It" and have them do one question/ activity for each level.

Or, you could assign a level to the student groups depending on what you wanted them to do.

Teaming Strategies Continued...

- **Remember, your students will not do this perfectly the first time.** It will take constant practice before they become adept at working together as a group.

- **Remind students before group activities what your expectations are.** Take some time to model what you want to see and hear, not just one time, but throughout the year.

    Example: *"We had some problems during group work today. Let's remind ourselves of what group work looks like and sounds like."*

"Working together in a group situation requires skills that students will use throughout their lifetime."

Please don't think that you can say to your students, "Okay everybody. Get into groups of four and discuss the implications of war on a new country," and they'll do it. Oh no, not by a long shot. You probably won't even be able to get them to do a simple activity such as illustrating a concept just taught.

You have to show them how to work together, or how to guide and participate in a discussion. It is a lot of work on your part, but you'll find it is so worth the effort in the long run! Just stick with it and keep reminding your students what is expected of them. Before you know it you'll have students actively engaged in their learning rather than bored to tears.

 Grouping Strategies and Ideas

Think-Pair-Share
With this strategy, have students take a minute to think about the topic or question you have posed. Then have them share with a partner or neighbor. After a few minutes of sharing, have the pairs choose another pair and share again as a larger group. This activity gives students a chance to think both independently and gain new ideas from others.

Jig-Saw

This strategy calls for small groups of two-four students. Each small group becomes an "expert" either with reading a selection, with research, or with a partiuclar skill or concept. Every group is responsible for a different passage or concept.

The second step is to have one "expert" from each group get together in new larger groups and share their information with each other. This activity helps make an otherwise boring assignment exciting and different. It also allows students to see how others work and it keeps them moving.

Group to Individual

Anytime you are presenting a new skill or concept for students to manipulate, work through an example as a whole class. Next, have students do the activity as a group. Then, have students do a similar activity with the skill in pairs. Lastly, have students show application of the skill/concept as individuals.

This strategy allows students the opportunity to practice the skill or concept several times and gather input from other students before having to show comprehension and application on their own.

Any Activity to Enhance Learning

Pretty much any activity that engages students actively in their learning can be done as a group. Below are a few ideas to jumpstart your thinking:

Games - Playing board and other types of games such as Scatergories, Mastermind, and Monopoly encourage thinking skills and require students to take turns

Scavenger Hunt - Students read through a chapter or part of a chapter and work together to create scavenger hunt questions for the class to answer.

Scripts - Students work together to turn a historical event or a story into a play. Students could work together to explain a concept or skill through a skit or play. I always require a written out script to show the different reading parts.

> *"A well-prepared teacher uses a variety of teaming strategies so that group work does not become as dull as lectures."*

Discovery and Experiential Learning

Another aspect of the brain-based classroom is discovery, or learning through experiences. Students learn best when they experience something and add that experience to their knowledge base, or schema. Science and Social Studies provide excellent opportunities for this type of learning. Instead of telling students about the Civil War, take them to see a reenactment of a battle. If a student asks a question about whales, have them research the answer for themselves and share it with the class.

Allow your students to find and experience the knowledge for themselves. If that seems the easy way out to you, you are wrong! From an outsider's point of view it may seem as though the teacher is doing nothing. However, students need guidance and encouragement to find the right answers. Some students need that extra push to do more than just what is expected of them. Your job, contrary to popular belief, is not always the purveyor of knowledge. It is also to guide your students and teach them how to gain that knowledge for themselves.

Here are some ways of allowing students to discover knowledge for themselves:

 Expert Advice

This is a slight twist on the Jigsaw teaming activity we mentioned on the previous page. Break your students into groups of four or five. Assign each group a subsection of the unit and/or chapter from the textbook. Instruct your students that they have _____ (minutes/hours/days) to become an expert on their section/ concept. They need to read the section, discuss it, and be prepared to teach it to the rest of the class.

Encourage them to ask questions of each other and you. Also, their presentation should be creative. Then hold EVERY student accountable for the information presented through a test or other assessment. You will be surprised at how motivated students are to read when THEY are the ones who have to teach everyone else.

"An effective teacher teaches students HOW to learn so that they can become life-long learners."

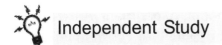

Independent Study

Have each student choose one concept/ person/ idea related to your unit to research. Create a checklist for them to follow. Have them write a research paper, create a visual, and present the information to the class. Hold students accountable through an assessment over the information presented.

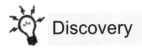

Discovery

Pose a question to your class and discuss it. Help them to discover the information through questions and discussion. For example, you might ask your students, "I wonder why George Washington was elected the first president?" Then guide them through a discussion to help them discover the answer. This is a wonderful way to encourage questioning skills that will help in student research.

Use objects to jumpstart "I wonder" questions. Pass around an object and ask, "I wonder what this is used for?" Encourage students to come up with their own "I wonder" questions about the object.

When students ask a question about a particular topic, or ask a "why" question, help them use the internet to discover the answer for themselves. Then they can share their newfound information with the rest of the class.

"I wonder" questions are a wonderful way to integrate different subject area topics and skills. You might pose a question regarding the use of triangles and other shapes used in building bridges and other structures in a math or science class.

Use "I wonder" questions to encourage research as part of the learning experience. We discuss research projects later in this chapter.

"The gift of knowledge is often not appreciated unless it has been earned!"

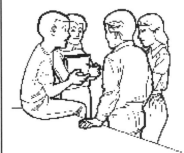

"Field trips are a great form of discovery learning."

Experiments

Don't just discuss a question or concept, experiment. Are you discussing Egypt and the Nile? Try an experiment showing how the Egyptians were able to use the floods to their advantage in farming.

Discussing space exploration? Experiment with balloons to show how a rocket works. Discussing plant life? Have students design and plant their own garden.

AIMS has some wonderful experiments that are easy and can be connected to all subject areas.

Scholastic and Teacher Created Materials also have some fantastic books available of kitchen table experiments that could be done in any classroom.

Get your students doing, not just reading!

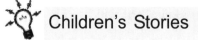

Children's Stories

Have students read a chapter from the textbook and rewrite it as a children's story. It must be from one person's point of view (ex: Caesar's story about the fall of ancient Rome) and should include all of the important information from the chapter. Have students share their stories. You could even have them share their stories with younger grade levels.

Children's stories are also a great way to introduce a unit and make connections between literature and the subject area. Getting ready to learn about onomatopoeia for a poetry unit? Why not read the book Mr. Brown Can Moo? Although a simple Dr. Suess book, Mr. Brown Can Moo is full of onomatopoeias and provides excellent examples.

There are such a plethora of children's books that reach across all subject areas. Not sure what you are looking for? Do a search through Amazon or another online bookstore with the concept as your keyword. With Amazon you can go to the Children's Books section and then browse only in that area. You're sure to find what you need!

Hint:

The internet is an excellent source to look for experiments you can do with your students. When doing a search be sure to type in "student experiments" and the keywords of your topic.

You might also try Yahooligans when searching.
www.yahooligans.com

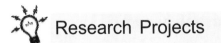

Research Projects

In this "information age" research skills are some of the most important and useful tools we can give our students. These skills should be taught and practiced from first grade all the way up through high school. Children are naturally curious about the world around them, and what better way to learn than to discover the answers to questions through research?

"Oh, no," you may say to yourself, "my kids aren't ready for research." Perhaps you are the one who is not ready. For those of us who remember 20 page writing assignments, the word research can have a very negative connotation. However, research can be as simple as looking up the answer to a question.

Here are some tips to help you along:

√   **Start out simple and easy.**

Have students use primary and secondary sources to find the answer to a question relating to your topic of study.

Be sure to teach note-taking skills before requiring any formal research.

Set a limit of 3-5 double-spaced typed pages for each paper. Every 9th grader should be able to write a 3 page paper and every 12th grader should be able to write a 5 page paper.

In our opinion, students should be required to complete at least 3 research projects each year. As students get into upper grades, the requirements should become more stringent. This will better prepare them from college and vocational school where research is a common learning tool.

√   **Take it step by step.**

When you do your first research project, take the students through the process step by step. Model each step for them as a class and then allow students to complete that step for their own project.

One way to help students get comfortable with research projects is to do the first one as a group project, the second one as a partner project, and the last one, or next ones, individually.

√   **Allow student choice.**

Choose a timely and global topic, but then allow your students to choose the specific area within that larger topic.

Teach students appropriate library skills as part of the research process.

Hint:

The library and librarian are excellent resources. Be sure to talk with the librarian before you begin planning a research project for your students. Know what is available and how you can use the library.

"No matter what time of year, projects are a great tool to use in the classroom.

Students are excited to learn and enjoy the collaboration."

√   **Determine ahead of time what you expect.**

What elements do you expect in the project? Do you want a written part, visual, and an oral presentation? Within each of these, what do you expect? Is this to be a group or individual project? Can the written part be creative like a story or skit, or do you expect a formal essay of some sort?

√   **Create a checklist for students to follow.**

Make sure you include every aspect that will be assessed. Include directions for the project at the top of the page. You can make the checklist as specific and detailed as you feel your students need.

I use mine to show students the steps to follow when completing their project as well as tasks and products to be done for each section. Some students need a lot more structure than others. You might even consider including due dates for completion of each section.

√   **Teach students how to write the formal paper, if required.**

When it is time for students to write their essay, it is important to go through the process with them step by step, especially the first couple of times.

> ***Example:*** *I teach students how to write an introduction in class. Then, that night they are required to write an introduction for their paper. The next day I read and help students revise their introductions. We follow the same process for the body and conclusion of the paper. It really helps students to go through the process one step at a time, especially if this is their first formal paper.*

√   **Monitor students constantly.**

This is not the time to sit behind your desk. Monitoring is not difficult as long as you are prepared. Use the Clipboard Monitoring form found in the Classroom Management chapter to help you keep track of who is on/off task and who is having trouble with the process.

In our opinion, students should be required to complete at least three research projects each year. As students get into upper grades, the requirements should become more stringent. This will better prepare them for college and vocational school where research is a common learning tool.

Teaching Note-taking Skills

Not only do students need to know how to take notes from a class lecture, but they also should be able to take notes from a reading source as well. This skill is of extreme importance to students going on to college. The first step you should take is teaching your students how to take notes from a book, magazine, or internet site. Don't just leave this up to the English instructor. Students should be required to take notes for research or class instruction in EVERY academic subject!

√   **Introduce**

One of the easiest ways to train students is to use one of the following:

- A Big Book (the type used by primary teachers)
- A Magazine article
- A News article

Choose a book or article that is easy to read (never use an encyclopedia to start) and either make transparencies or enough copies so that each student can easily read the information.

Follow the steps below several times with your students as a class, then have them work in small groups, then as pairs, and finally individually. This process helps give students confidence to take good notes.

Hint:

Continually practice note-taking skills as a whole class with the teacher writing information in outline format on a transparency. This simply helps reinforce the idea of what you expect students to do when they read non-fiction.

√   **Steps**

- Write the title/general topic of the book as your main heading or topic

- Read each page (including the picture captions) carefully.

- Ask students to tell you what that page was mostly about (main idea).

- Write the main idea as your subheading on a transparency or butcher paper.

- Ask students for details from the page that support the main idea.

- Write these as one or two word details under the subheading.

- Make sure you show the student the pictures and discuss the information in each caption. Is it necessary or extraneous?

THE SOLAR SYSTEM

THE SUN
- a medium sized star
- nine planets orbit
  -Mercury, Venus, Earth, Mars, Jupiter, Saturn, Uranus, Neptune, Pluto
- provides light and heat

INNER PLANETS
- Mercury, Venus, Earth, Mars
- Solid
  -mostly rock
- closest to the sun
- short orbits

"Research projects should be utilized as a learning tool in all subject areas."

"Practice taking notes with your students before sending them off to research!"

Have students apply this knowledge of note-taking skills when researching and taking notes from a source, including the internet. Instruct them to take notes exactly as they have practiced in class. When students begin taking notes in this manner, using only one or two keywords for each detail, you'll find that they are not able to plagarize from the source. You may even want to practice taking notes from an encyclopedia or other non-fiction book to help students make the transition from simple paragraphs to more complex source material. Don't forget to have them write down the title of each source at the top of their notes.

Here is a set of instructions you can give to older students to help them during the research/ note-taking process.

Instructions for Taking Notes

1. Read each paragraph - does it contain information you need?
    -if yes, go on to #2
    -if no, read the next paragraph

2. What was that paragraph mostly about?
    - Write the main idea on your paper

3. What are the details in this paragraph?
    -Write the supporting details in one or two words as bullets under the main idea
    -Limit 3 words for each bullet

4. Read the next paragraph

**Remember, you do not need to copy EVERYTHING down. Taking notes is the art of pulling out only the information you need.

Making Connections between Subject Areas

Another effective teaching strategy is integrated study. This section will offer some of our thoughts on why you should integrate as well as some suggestions for your classroom. Most of these ideas come from Susan Kovalik's ITI for the Classroom. Another excellent resource for integrating is a book entitled *The Way We Were, The Way We Want to Be* by Ann Ross, written for secondary teachers. Both of these are excellent resources to have in your library!

WHY?

With everything we are supposed to teach each day it often seems as though we can never fit it all in. However, by integrating subject matter, concepts, and skills, not only can we cover everything we need to, but we can also help our students make important connections in their learning.

Integration is the connection of several subjects under a topic or theme of some sort. Brain research shows us that students learn best when ideas are connected across subject areas. As adults, we know that science cannot be separated from math, and that social studies concepts are closely linked to both language and science.

How then can we ask our students to learn in isolated compartments for each subject? In doing so, we push students farther back rather than leading them forward in their studies. One way we can work towards making connections is through thematic units. Susan Kovalik, in her book ITI for the Classroom, states that themes should be motivating to students and relate to the real world.

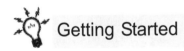 Getting Started

1.) Start with a topic of study required for your grade level and/or subject area
      -Science and Social Studies are the easiest to use as a starting place

2.) Brainstorm skills/ objectives usually taught for that topic

3.) Brainstorm connections with other subject areas
      -find the common links in skills/concepts (ie - graphing is a skill used in math, science, and social studies)

> *"An effective teacher helps students see connections across their learning."*

> *"Making connections in learning encourages higher level thinking and is supported by brain-based research."*

Example:

Let's say that you have an upcoming unit on Volcanoes. You would first want to list skills and concepts to be taught for the topic. Next, as a team, you would brainstorm Social Studies, Math and Language Arts connections with volcanoes. Some of your ideas might include:

☞ Have students locate volcanoes along the *Ring of Fire* using latitude and longitude (Social Studies). This could even include a video about the *Ring of Fire*.

☞ Students can read about or research famous historical events surrounding volcanoes such as Mount St. Helens or Vesuvius (Language Arts and Social Studies).

☞ A study of landforms could also arise since many mountains began as volcanoes. In addition, students can learn how new islands are created (which goes well with the *Ring of Fire* study). With the study of islands, students can also apply mapping skills. Those skills can be applied by creating their own "island" and using graph paper to create a map of cities, rivers, etc. on this island (Social Studies).

☞ Additionally, there is a very definite sequence to what happens when a volcano erupts and how it creates an island over time. This works well for including the reading concept of sequencing (Reading).

☞ Students can also study the geometry of volcanoes by discussing cones and triangles. Students can also study how seismic instruments work to measure pressure, etc. (Math).

"Can you think of any ways to incorporate art or music into this unit?"

💡 Use a Graphic Organizer when Planning

MATH
  Triangles
  Angles
  Cones
  Volume
  Measurements

SCIENCE
  Tectonic Plates
  Layers of the Earth
  Creation of new land
  Effects of pressure
  Environmental changes

VOLCANOES

LANG. ARTS
  Sequencing of events
  Research - note taking
  Descriptive Mode
  Non-fiction reading

SOCIAL STUDIES
  Latitude & Longitude
  Landforms
  Mapping/using a grid
  Ancient Romans - Italy
  Mt. Vesuvius
  Current Events

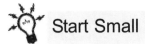 **Start Small**

If you jump in with both feet, you will more than likely meet with disppointment. Not only does it take a while to get used to a new idea, but it also takes some time to implement a new type of strategy in the classroom. Just like our students, we all have different ways of learning. Some of us need to go for the gusto, but others need more of a trial period before being ready to undertake a project like this. Integrating takes experience and it takes logical thinking. It works best when you have two or more teachers working together to brainstorm the connections and make them work in a lesson or unit.

For those of you who read the above tips and examples and thought immediately, "That is way too much work for me right now," please understand that you do not need to start out so big. You are probably already integrating without even realizing it. Every time you use a teachable moment to help students reach an understanding, whether it relates to your subject matter or not, you are integrating.

Here are a few ways to start out with small steps:

 When reading a story or novel, incorporate history from the time period used in the setting.

 Provide students with a timeline of interesting events that occurred during the time the author either wrote the novel or during their lifetime. A neat way to do this might be to create a "In the Year Of" poster that shows prices of everyday items, popular music, famous people, etc.

Point out cities and countries on the map for authors, story settings, famous scientists or mathematicians.

Point out ways the environment affects a story, historical event, or world culture. This includes landforms, temperature or seasons, climates, and/or animal and insect life.

 Use timelines to show other events happening at the time of a scientific discovery.

Use research projects in Science and Social Studies to study a topic in further detail.

 When teaching a concept/skill in Math or Science that has a practical application, try to either show or discuss these with students.

How can I integrate if I don't know what I'm supposed to teach?

Every State has a Department of Education website where they post important information including the State Standards. These standards are what the State expects students to learn in each grade and subject area.

1) Print out the State Curriculum Standards (may be called something different) for the grade level and subject areas you will be teaching.

2) Scan each subject area for skills that are duplicated. For example, the skill of graphing shows up in Math, Science, Social Studies, and Reading.

3) Look for a Science or Social Studies topic that can connect skills/ concepts from the different subject areas.

4) Use the advice in this chapter to begin developing an integrated unit.

Remember - you don't have to start out with a full-blown integrated unit. Try starting with small steps so that you will not be overwhelmed.

Interdisciplinary Study

Integration is not an impossibility in the secondary classroom. If you are truly interested in integrating subject matter, there are several ways to go about it.

"Students learn best when they are able to see the connections between different subject areas."

- You and your team members need to agree that integration is the best thing for your students.

- Share the different skills and topics that will be taught throughout the year.

- Work together to determine a yearlong theme and subsequent six weeks themes.

- Planning together will make integration much easier for everyone.

- Each class will cover a part of the lesson for the day.

For example:
If you were doing a mini-unit on volcanoes, each class would build on the others.

- Science would discuss how volcanoes are formed and would experiment with volcanoes.

"The real world does not consist of separate compartments."

- Social Studies might plot various known volcanoes on a map of the world and study latitude and longitude.

- Language Arts might read about some historical volcanic eruptions such as Vesuvius or Mt. St. Helen's and may write a How To essay on making a model volcano.

- The art teacher could be a part of this unit by actually allowing students to make a volcano (or it could be done in another class).

- Lastly, Math might be able to study cones, ratios, percentages, and probability.

Learning Centers

Another way of enhancing your instruction is through learning centers. As high school teachers, we often do not utilize the learning center for the following reasons:

- Takes up too much room

- Takes too long to create and organize

- Takes too much effort to monitor

- Takes too long to evaluate students

In our classrooms, we finally found a way to utilize learning centers so that they were not a burden, but instead were a helpful tool.

Enrichment Centers

Students use the enrichment center when they are finished with a class assignment and have nothing else to do. We also used it as a reward. Here is how you set it up:

1) Create a "thinking folder" for each student with a manila folder
2) Place these folders in an easily accessible place
3) Copy logic puzzles, think-a-grams, and other word puzzles, glue them on colorful construction paper and laminate them
4) Separate puzzles by type & place them in clearly labeled manila folders
5) Write the directions for the center on the manila folder
6) Place vis-a-vis pens in a can on a table
7) Students choose a puzzle, complete it and write the answer on their own sheet of paper.
8) Then they put their paper into their "thinking folder."
9) Lastly, have students wipe the original puzzle clean and put it away.

- Students can work these puzzles at their own seat which means that you don't have to have a whole "center area" prepared. All you need is a spot to keep the puzzles.

- Every three weeks check the folders & grade the puzzles.

- Give students extra credit for correct answers and feedback for wrong answers to help them do better the next time.

"A Thinking folder is an easy way to monitor student work from the learning center."

Field Trips

Field trips are important discovery learning tools. They provide hands-on learning for students and serve as a great way to get children to experience the community around them.

Students love field trips! Think about it...you all get to go somewhere exciting and it gives you a break from your daily routine. Field trips also provide wonderful educational opportunities for students and teachers alike. However, without planning and organization, field trips can be a nightmare for teachers.

A large part of this planning process is soliciting parental support in the form of chaperones. Most museums, theaters, and other cultural places require a small student to teacher ratio of 5 to 1 or 10 to 1. When you have a class of 30 or more students, this means that you'll need several adult volunteers to help.

"A well-prepared teacher plans ahead and in detail for all field trips."

"Remember to get your lunch count in early. The cafeteria staff must make sack lunches for your students AND lunch for the rest of the school. They have a lot to do!"

Helpful Tips

The number of chaperones you will need depends on -

- your class size
- the type of field trip (inside vs. outside)
- the number of students requiring special attention

The more chaperones you have, the lower the student to adult ratio. Smaller groups give parents/ volunteers greater control over their charges.

Whenever you go on an inside field trip, you want lots of structure and control to maintain a quiet and non-disruptive environment.

Sign up parent volunteers well in advance of your trip.

Notify other teachers in the school of the dates and times for your field trip.

Notify the cafeteria if you will be out during lunch time. This helps them better prepare for lunch that day. Also, you may have several students who need a sack lunch from school. A lunch count needs to be done at least 2 weeks before your trip.

Put in a request for a field trip to your principal as soon as you begin your initial planning. All field trips must be approved by the principal.

 Have a clear educational objective for your field trip. Why are you going? If it is just for a free day or to give students a break, the trip probably won't be approved.

 Be ready with some sort of a scavenger hunt or focus questions for adult volunteers to use with their groups to help make the most out of this great educational experience.

 When signing up parent volunteers, write down their names on your calendar so that you can remember to call them with reminders.

 Organize and write down your expectations of both students and adult volunteers during the field trip. Give each adult leader a clipboard with the following information attached:

- Their assigned bus
- A list of students in their group
- Teaching tips for the trip

  ⇨ questions volunteers should ask students during the trip
  ⇨ topics that need to be discussed during the visit
  ⇨ special exhibits for students to focus their attention
  ⇨ back up procedures for supervising difficult students

Hint:

Give each adult a clipboard with important information for the field trip.

Have each student bring a clipboard or pocket-folder to hold focus questions, scavenger hunt, or some other type of activity.

Teacher Testimony

"I remember the first field trip we ever took. My Mentor planned like a crazy person and I thought she was going a little overboard. The entire grade level was going to the city art museum as part of a unit we had planned. What struck me, about half-way through the day, was how loud and out-of-control the other classes were. The teachers looked harried and ran from group to group. Meanwhile, my class and my Mentor's class were looking at the art, filling out their scavenger hunt on their clipboards, and staying pretty much engaged (with the usual exceptions). Parent chaperones were using their own clipboards, helping students when needed and I was able to stick with my group of students. It was nice not feeling as though I needed to run from group to group to help the chaperones know what to do or where to go. I guess my Mentor wasn't so crazy after all."

Hint:

If you are taking a large group of students, assign each small student group to a specific bus. Determine how many groups will fit on each bus. Create signs (Bus #1, etc.) to place in the front passenger window of each bus. This will help keep confusion to a minimum.

All of this takes prior preparation and planning on your part. Visit your destination ahead of time so that you can prepare this information for the field trip.

Have name tags ready for everyone. This helps the volunteers know the students in their group AND the other adults in the group.

Thank the volunteers for joining you even BEFORE the field trip begins.

Ask volunteers to arrive 15 minutes before the departure time to receive instructions.

Have signs made up for the buses (especially when taking a large group) so that students can easily identify their assigned bus.

Get several large plastic tubs on wheels to hold lunches. I like to have one for each group, but some people simply have one for each class.

"Ask volunteers to arrive early so that you can go over field trip information."

If you or the school can't afford to get these types of tubs, gather several large empty boxes to use. They aren't as easy to get from the bus to the eating area, but they do work to keep lunches together.

Hint: Visiting a field trip destination ahead of time does not have to be drudgery. Take a date, a friend, or a member of your grade level and enjoy the outing. Just be sure to take a little notebook and jot down questions/ideas for a field trip activity.

Field Trip Permission Form

Dear Parents,

    We are taking a field trip to _____. For the students' safety and well-being, it is important for you to know where we will be going and the purpose of this trip. Please note the following important information about our upcoming event.

Place: _____

Date: _____

Time: _____

Purpose: _____

_____

_____

Please fill out and sign the form below. Detach the bottom portion and return it to me in the next couple of days. If you have any questions or concerns, please feel free to contact me at school during my planning period, or leave a message with the school secretary for me to return.

Sincerely,

- -

I, _____ give my permission for _____

to attend the field trip to _____ .

I will _____ send a lunch for _____ purchase a school lunch

My teen has the following special needs to take into consideration _____

_____

Parent Signature: _____ Date: _____

Field Trip Instructions

DATE:_____

TIME:_____

PLACE:_____

GROUP:_____ VOLUNTEER NAME:_____

LIST OF STUDENTS	SCHEDULE FOR THE DAY: (including rotation schedule of exhibits if necessary.)

Please be sure to ask your group to think about or discuss the following:	Be sure to visit the following places/ exhibits:

CONCLUSION

A brain-based classroom is also one in which students are actively engaged in the learning process. Human beings naturally have a sense of curiosity about the unknown. Unfortunately, the isolated nature of traditional lectures and textbook reading has a tendancy to squelch that curiosity. Students become bored and refuse to learn. We hope that this chapter has inspired you instead to use cooperative learning tools such as discovery learning, integrated content, and learning through experiences to foster life-long learning within your students.

Additional Resources

Learning Thru Discussion
by W. M. Fawcett Hill

Teaching with the Brain in Mind
by Eric Jensen

Integrated Thematic Instruction
by Susan Kovalik

The Way We Were, The Way We Can Be
by Ann Ross

Synergy
by Karen Olsen

Questions for Reflection

1) Why is it important to keep students actively engaged in the classroom rather than passively listening?

2) What are some different ways you can keep your students actively engaged?

3) How might you implement discovery or experiential learning in your classroom?

4) Why should you consider using research projects throughout the year rather than just once a year?

5) What is your opinion of integrating subject areas? Is this something you might implement in your classroom? Why or why not?

Activities

1) Take a chapter from a textbook you currently use in the classroom. Develop 5 different activities that will keep students actively engaged

2) Create an activity/project for an upcoming unit or lesson using the Bloom's Keywords listed in this chapter.

3) Develop a one-day integrated lesson based on either a children's story or a required science or social studies topic for your grade level.

4) Create 2 or 3 different "portable" enrichment centers to use in your classroom. Take time to make these ready to implement in the classroom.

Notes/ Reflection on Chapter

Assessment

Not sure of what to do to assess, or evaluate, your students' abilities and progress?

How do I assess my students so that their abilities and progress are accurately reflected?

Don't worry. This chapter will give you a clearer understanding of assessment and will provide ideas that you can use right away. Not only is it important to have a philosophy of assessment before you begin the year, but you also need some practical know-how. Throughout this chapter, we will provide you with various assessment strategies, grading techniques, and practical ideas for your gradebook to help you prepare for assessing your students.

First, you need to realize a few things about assessment.

- Even experienced teachers have to continually check their assessment techniques. By doing this, effective teachers make sure that their assessment is a reliable and valid tool to show student achievement.

- Proper assessment can be a challenge.

- It is important to vary and adapt assessment tools to fit different learning styles and instructional needs.

"An effective teacher continually re-evaluates his or her assessment techniques."

Philosophy of Assessment

Here are some tips to help shape your philosophy on student assessment:

- **Assessment is so much more than just assigning a letter grade. It should provide teachers with detailed information to share with parents.**

  - Proper assessment throughout the school year will:

    - Measure the progress a student has made
    - Show students' strengths and weaknesses
    - Allow a teacher to check for understanding

- **By varying the ways we measure student achievement, we can tap into different kinds of learners and accurately represent student progress and achievement.**

"An effective teacher uses a variety of assessment methods to get an accurate measure of their abilities."

For example

   If a student has difficulty with writing and every single method of assessment in a Social Studies class is an essay test, what kind of grades do you think this student will get in social studies? If, however, you vary your assessment tools and give an oral interview or observe the student discussing concepts with other peers, then that student has a chance to really show you what has been learned! This student may be able to tell you the entire history of the Civil War if you asked him, but when he has to write it down, he fails and receives a poor history grade. Is that a fair assessment of his historical knowledge? This is an important issue for teachers!

> **Teacher Testimony**
>
> *My second year of teaching I had one student in particular who was a concern. It seemed that he could not pass any test that I gave him. However, I knew that he understood the content because of discussions we'd had in class. After a while, I gave him some oral examinations to see how well he would do. He passed every time. This student had a hard time getting the information from his head onto paper. Had I not ever thought of varying my assessment for him, he would not have passed my class.*

- **Know what you want to do for assessment before you present your lesson.**

  - Are you going to have students create a timeline of important dates during the American Revolution? Then you need to teach your lesson or give students notes in a timeline format.

  - Essay questions require a classroom discussion where students can express their thoughts and opinions.

"Your lesson should reflect the type of assessment tool you use."

- **If a student does not understand what the teacher's expectations are, it will be difficult to get a true picture of what that student has really learned.**

  Do you expect your students to be able to compare and contrast fractions with decimals? Make sure that students know this. Students cannot meet your expectations if you do not tell them what they are.

- **Directions for any evaluation should be clear and precise. When students are confused, they cannot show their knowledge of the skill or concept being assessed.**

  Use simple language and sentences. Too many compound or complex sentences will cause your students to bog themselves down in your instructions.

Strategy:

Give the students a problem at the end of the class session that they will turn in. They do not need to write their names on these papers. When reviewing the answers, you can get an idea of what students learned and what still needs to be discussed in further lessons.

"Give clear and specific directions."

"Let students know what you expect ahead of time."

Thank you to Sheri Langendorf, High School Teacher, Illinois for sharing this strategy.

Alternative Assessment Tools

There are a variety of ways to assess student work and learning. A common dilemma among first year teachers is how to find different ways to assess students other than paper and pencil examinations. Here we have provided for you different ways you can evaluate your students' learning. You may not use every method, and you may vary your assessment tools with each class and/or each student. You will make these decisions once you get comfortable in your teaching. Whatever methods of appraisal you choose, just be sure to use a diversity.

Observation

- **Teachers can observe students in various situations and can keep records for grading purposes.**

    Most teachers think that grading has to be done on paper. This is not true! In your grade book, you can give many different grades, such as participation and discussion. These kinds of grades often help students who do not normally perform well on written assignments.

- **You are the teacher and should be evaluating your students constantly. How can you do this?**

- **Walk around the room -**

    If you walk around the room, you can more accurately observe students without them necessarily knowing that you are grading them. Students often freely share their knowledge when they are not intimidated by the pressure of getting graded!

- **Observe students in cooperative group discussions -**

    Are they participating? Are they showing knowledge of a concept or comprehension of a reading passage by the comments they make in a discussion? Are the students correctly using a skill that was taught?

"Your lesson should reflect the type of assessment tool you use."

- **Keep records of behavior & participation -**

If you are grading based on observations, YOU MUST KEEP ANECDOTAL RECORDS! Written records of observations, behavior, and social skills provide tangible evidence and explanation of grades for the teacher, parents, principal, and other teachers.

Clipboard Cruising **is one way of keeping records on observations of each student. Have one clipboard for every subject (Math, Language Arts, Social Studies…)**

Make up a large index card for each student, and tape the top of the cards vertically along a clipboard in alphabetical order, so that you can easily flip through them. For each observation, date the entry and make a short, but detailed statement of what you observed. You do not have to make a record of each student every time! Just record noticeable observations on that day. You'll want to replace the index cards each grading period, and put the old card in the student files.

We have another example in the Classroom Management chapter with a spreadsheet that is also effective in the classroom.

Example:

Suzy Smarts – Social Studies	
9/20/98	Great discussion and reasoning of why the Southern Confederacy was fighting to preserve their way of life. Logical thinking and specific examples used!
10/05/98	Provided few specifics – conference with Suzy about reading requirements.
10/15/98	Excellent work on timeline project, showing knowledge and comprehension of material – good improvement since conference!
11/01/98	Showed excellent discussion and critical thinking skills today, as she worked with her group to finish the presentation assignment on the 13th Amendment. Great participation!

> *"A well-prepared teacher keeps records of observations to help assess academic learning and as documentation for parent conferences."*

"A Mind Map is an excellent assessment tool for students who like to draw."

Student Reflection

When students are asked to reflect on their own growth and knowledge of a concept or theme, it forces them to take reponsibility for their own learning. Students create their own meaning instead of memorizing and regurgitating information, which provides the teacher with a clear picture of what the student actually learned and internalized. You might use this assessemnt tool after students read a book or passage, after students have studied a unit, or with student projects.

Clear and Unclear Windows

This is another variation of student reflection. In this format, students fold their paper into two or more sections. They label half of the paper as clear windows, and the other half as unclear windows. In the clear window boxes, the students write what they have learned and understand about a topic, reading, or concept. In the unclear window boxes the students write about the concepts that they do not understand or where they need clarification. This is a great resource for teachers as they can shape future lessons to accommodate for unclear windows.

Semantic Web or Mind Map

This is a fabulous method of assessment as well as a great way to teach students how to organize information. Students need to learn how to make connections and find relationships among varying facts and concepts. The students place a main topic in the middle of the paper, and then branch off with related details. Each branch then might have another branch off of it and/or connecting that fact or statement with another detail. This can be written or drawn. Using this as an assessment really shows the teacher how a student's knowledge is organized in their brain, or if they don't understand a concept at all.

As with all of these different types of assessment, it is important that you model for students what you expect to see when they turn in their work. Model how they would create a mind-map around a specific concept or skill.

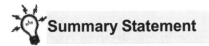

"I learned..." Statement

This assessment can be used after a short activity, such as a lesson or film, in order to measure whether or not the teacher's objectives were met. It could also be used as a culmination to a large thematic unit in place of the dreaded unit test! In the "I learned..." statement, the students simply express what they have learned either orally or by writing the sentences. It is best to narrow this assignment to five or less statements so that students are forced to prioritize the information instead of throwing out trivial little facts. This is another assessment where Bloom's Keywords can come in handy.

"An effective teacher periodically checks for student understanding throughout a lesson or a reading."

Summary Statement

This is longer and takes more depth than the "I learned" statements. The students are asked to summarize what they have learned in a coherent paragraph. This may also be an oral or written assignment. A summary should require the students to make connections among the various facts they learned instead of simply stating isolated data. This type of activity requires higher-level thinking skills on the part of students.

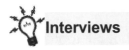

Interviews

Oral interviews can be held with individual students on any topic to see how much a student learned, or to check for understanding. The interview should be short and last no longer than five minutes. The questions should include a range of lower level to higher level thinking. The lower level questions will provide opportunities for success and build student self-esteem. The higher level questions will allow you to assess student reasoning ability. Teachers should take notes during the interviews for grading and record-keeping purposes.

"Inteviews in the classroom are great practice for high school students.

They are Real World Assessments."

Visual/Pictoral Assignments

Visual learners can often express their knowledge beautifully through many different types of artistic and creative assignments. Here are some great examples of visual assessment tools: Illustrations to go with writing and to show comprehension of material, pictures with captions, cartoon drawings, murals, mobiles, dioramas (shoe box scenes), students creating their own maps, charts, graphs, posters, travel brochures, and mind maps. There are several different activities of this nature in the Motivating Students chapter which can be used to assess student learning.

K-W-L Chart

Prior to a lesson or unit have the students create their own KWL chart. Students fold their paper into three sections. Label each section K, W, or L. The students complete the K section (what they already know about the topic), and the W section (what they want to know about the topic) prior to the lesson or unit. At the end for an assessment, the students finish the L section (what they learned about the topic).

Checklist of Objectives

When students have a lengthy assignment, a helpful tool for teachers to evaluate student progress is to have the students fill out a checklist. When students are given time to work on the project in class and you don't want to grade in depth until the final project, you can ask to see the student's checklist along with corresponding work. That way a brief glance shows you whether or not a student is on track. An easy grade can be given at this point for effort and progress, or completeness of that particular section. Earlier we discussed how Bloom's keywords can be used to create a checklist so that students are required to use all levels of thinking. See our example on the next page.

"Use writing assignments such as journals, travel brochures, poetry, and research assignments as meaningful assessment tools."

Native American Project

_____ 1. Identify, locate, and illustrate on a map the area(s)
            where your tribe lived. (Knowledge)

_____ 2. Explain the culture and daily life of your tribe.
            (Comprehension)

_____ 3. Construct a visual teaching tool to demonstrate the
            lifestyle of your tribe. (ex: diarama, model, poster, video)
            (Application)

_____ 4. Compare and Contrast your tribe with another tribe
            when looking at food, dwellings, religious ceremonies,
            and geographic location. This will require you to
            communicate with one other group. (Analysis)

_____ 5. Organize a presentation that incorporates all of the
            information you have gathered about your tribe in order
            to teach others. (Synthesis)

_____ 6. Determine how well your tribe would be able to survive
            in America's modern environment. (Evaluation)

"Using Bloom's Keywords will help you develop projects that require students to use higher level thinking skills."

Student Evaluations:

Evaluate your group on the following:

____ Cooperation within the team
____ Individual participation
____ Information gathered
        ___ amount   ___ correctness
        ___ elaboration

____ Visual teaching aid
        ___ creativity   ___ best quality
        ___ accurate   ___ use in presentation

____ Presentation
        ___ individual participation
        ___ clearly spoken
        ___ loud voices
        ___ creativity

See pages 234-235 for an explanation of Bloom's Taxonomy.

Portfolio Assessment

Many teachers do not rely on portfolios when assessing students because they are confused about what a portfolio is and what it should be used for. Do we only use the best student pieces or do we put both "good" and "bad" work in to show improvement? Also, how do we grade the portfolio? If the work is already graded, do we grade it again? The following is a brief "How To" on portfolios.

Goals

- Decide what your goal is. What is the purpose of the portfolio? What is unique about you and your students? Your goal should reflect your classroom and your students. Some possible goals might include the following:

  - Student Improvement
  - Mastery of Certain Skills
  - Amount of learning occurred
  - Collection of student work

*Remember that your goal should reflect you, your classroom and your students.

> *"A well-prepared teacher has a goal in mind before using the portfolio as assessment."*

Assessment

- Before using portfolios, you need to decide how you will grade them. Once again, what is the pupose of this portfolio? Assessment of the portfolio is closely tied to your goal.

  - Quality of work in the portfolio
  - Amount of work in the portfolio
  - Improvement
  - Knowledge of skills

Student Portfolio

The easiest way to assess a portfolio is on a rating scale. The rating scale must also reflect your goal. You must decide for yourself what you are looking for in each portfolio entry, or in the portfolio as a whole, and then create a rating scale to reflect that. For example, let's say your goal is to show the amount and quality of learning that has occurred over the semester. You might evaluate each entry as Correct (mechanics), Complete (information), and Comprehensive (thought provoking) with the student receiving a score of 1-4 in each area:

1 = not at all   2 = somewhat   3 = mostly   4 = entirely

The scores then would be added up to give a grade for the entire portfolio.

Ask another teacher to help you assess the portfolios in order for them to be a reliable form of evaluation. Why? Well, we often grade according to the student. If the work in the portfolio is absolutely terrible and not up to standards, but we know that this is the best the student can do, then we might be more lenient on our rating scale than another teacher who doesn't know the student. Thus, the impartial evaluator helps to make the portfolio a much more reliable and accurate form of assessment. The two grades can be averaged and used as the grade for the portfolio.

"Before you use portfolios, you need to decide three things:

What are your goals?

How are you going to assess it?

How will you involve your students?"

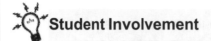 **Student Involvement**

Student involvement is a very important part of the portfolio process. After all, it is the students we are evaluating. There are three main components to student involvement.

- **Understanding** -

It is very important that students understand what the portfolio is, your goals, your rating scale, the pieces you want included, and how it will be used. This needs to be explained at the beginning of the year. If you wait until the end of the semester, your students will not be as involved with the portfolio and you will not get a true reflection of their thoughts and feelings about their work. If your students understand what is required of them, they will be much more likely to create what you want in a portfolio.

- **Choice** -

Choice is an extremely important aspect of the portfolio. There are some pieces that you will want them to include so that you can accomplish your goal, but there should be some entries that express and reflect the student's personality and preferences. You may be able to give students some choice even in the work you require, but it is absolutely vital that your students be allowed to choose work that is a reflection of them or their progress whether it is bad or good.

- **Reflection** -

Students should write a reflection of their thoughts and ideas about each portfolio entry. You may want to ask students to write why they chose to include certain pieces, or how they felt about an assignment. These reflections will give you an even clearer picture of the student's work, learning, and progress throughout the year.

Another important aspect to reflection is a discussion between teacher and student of each piece and reflection in the portfolio. Some sort of dialogue needs to occur between student and teacher so that a clear understanding of the portfolio occurs. The student and the teacher should be able to explain each entry.

Sample Portfolio Outline

An outline of details regarding how you plan to use the portfolio will make things much easier for you in the long run. It will also help you to remember what you decided at the beginning of the year. Below is a sample portfolio outline for a Language Arts class. It is not absolutely necessary that you produce an outline with the same detail, but it does help.

PORTFOLIO ASSESSMENT

GOAL: To show the amount of learning that has occurred over the semester.

FOCUS: The focus will be on the reflection statements for each entry since most of the work has already been graded.

ITEMS TO BE EVALUATED: Students must include one narrative, two expository (how to; compare/contrast, etc.), journal entries, and three poetry pieces. In addition, students must choose 5 other assignments from class to put in the portfolio.

STUDENT INVOLVEMENT: Student choice of 5 assignments should show what they have learned over the semester. These entries can be both good and poor work samples. Students must write a reflection over each entry. The reflection should express the purpose of the entry in the portfolio, the skill(s) it shows accomplished (or working on), any thoughts or feelings about the entry and why they put it in the portfolio. Before the portfolio is evaluated, the student and teacher will have a conference to discuss the entries included and the portfolio as a whole.

CRITERION: Each reflection/entry will be evaluated as being Correct (mechanics), Complete (information), and Comprehensive (thought provoking) with the student receiving a score of 1-4 in each area where 1 = not at all; 2 = somewhat; 3 = mostly; and 4 = entirely.

RELIABILITY: Two teachers will score the portfolio. One teacher will be myself, the main instructor, and the other teacher will be one who is not as familiar with the students. These two scores will be averaged and used as a final grade for the semester.

VALIDITY: This portfolio will have content validity because it measures the student's awareness of what was taught in class. Students reflect on what they learned through each experience or project done in class.

In the back of this chapter is a conference sheet and grading sheet you can use for your portfolios.

Grading

Once you have an assessment tool, how do you grade it?

So far in this chapter we've discussed different methods for assessing students, but we haven't talked much about grading. Here are some tips that should help you when actually grading students.

> **Organize your grade book.**

There are several ways you can do this.

1) Set aside six pages for each class period (one for each grading period). Group all of the subject pages together.

Set aside six pages for attendance.

> *Attendance - pages 1-6*
> *Remedial Reading -   pages 7-12*
> *English - pages 13-18*

2) Set aside pages for attendance and each class you teach. Then, create six "groups" of these pages (one for each grading period).

1st Six Weeks: Attendance, Reading 1, Reading 2, American Lit., American Lit. 2, Speech & Debate - pages 1-6.

2nd Six Weeks: Attendance, Reading 1, Reading 2, American Lit., American Lit. 2, Speech & Debate -   7-12

> Note: These examples are assuming that your school has 6 six weeks grading periods. If not, adjust accordingly.

- Use stick-on tabs (these can be found at any office supply store) to mark different sections in your grade book. This makes finding a particular subject or class period easier.

"Use stick-on tabs to mark different sections in your gradebook. It makes life so much easier!"

What grading scale are you going to use?

Percentages

You can grade using a 100 percent scale. Out of 100 percent, how many did the student get correct? For assignments/tests that do not meet 100 points, use a grading tool that can be bought at any teacher store. It will automatically determine the grade by the number of items on the assignment/test.

	1	2	3	4	5	6	Avg.
Julie	80	75	99	78	88	100	520/ 6 = 87
Robert	77	99	86	87	100	98	547/ 6 = 91
Grace	85	87	88	96	98	100	554/ 6 = 92

Points

You can grade by a point scale. Out of 25 points, how many did the student get correct? Write this as a fraction (20/25). Divide the top number by the bottom and get a decimal. This is the student's grade. For example: 20/25 = .8 which would be an 80. In the grade book you can simply record the number of points the student got correct and do the division at the end of the grading period.

"A well-prepared teacher thinks through how he/she plans to record student grades before school starts."

	1	2	3	4	5	6	T.pts./Out of	Avg.
Julie	18	25	18	30	28	16	135 / 160	84
Robert	19	20	20	25	18	20	122/ 160	76
Grace	20	19	20	27	28	25	139/ 160	87

Grade subjective assignments according to a rubric.

- Decide what skill(s)/objective(s) you want the student to show

- Write these down in a checklist format

- Grade each skill/objective on a scale of 1 to 4 where
  1 = poor, 2 = fair, 3= good, and 4 = excellent

- Average the numbers to get a total score for the assignment.

- Final scores should look like this:
1- = 60	1 = 65	1+ / 2- = 70	2 = 75
2+ / 3- = 80	3 = 85	3+ / 4- = 90	4 = 95
4+ = 100			

"A rubric makes subjective grading easier!"

"A well-prepared teacher provides a copy of the rubric to students at the beginning of a project or assignment so they know what to expect."

Diorama of American Revolution

3	**Scene from American Revolution**	1	2	3	4
3	**Correct Information**	1	2	3	4
4	**Complete sentences used on** index card	1	2	3	4
3	**Colorful**	1	2	3	4
2	**Creative**	1	2	3	4
3	**Neat**	1	2	3	4
18	**Total Points = 18/ 6 = 3 = Grade 85**				

Comments:

It is important to use a rubric when grading subjective assignments so that you don't end up comparing students which is completely unfair to everybody.

Grading Writing Assignments

Technically writing assignments are subjective, and as those of you who use writing projects will see, it is one of the hardest areas of grading. Writing assessments are used in many classes, such as History, Science, Economics, Political Science, English, Literature, and more.

Here are a few tips to help you with this challenge:

- Use a rubric like the one above. Grade only the skills you have already covered in class.

- Use an overall rubric. With this students will receive one grade for their entire paper. A sample overall rubric is provided in the back of this chapter. Also, your district, school, or perhaps the state, may have developed a writing rubric that they expect you to use. Ask other teachers or the Language Arts department chair for this information.

- Give students two separate grades for their paper. One for content and one for mechanics.

When giving two separate grades on writing assignments –

The content grade can be a 1-4 on the ideas expressed and how well they followed the writing mode. The mechanics grade can be on a scale of 1-100 with one point or 1/2 point taken for each grammar error in the paper. You can then average the two grades, OR keep them separate for your grade book. If you teach Economics, History, or any subject other than English, you might not choose to weigh the grammar as heavily as the content, depending on your goal.

"Giving students two grades on writing assignments allows them to see specific feedback on their grammar skills versus the content."

Teacher Testimony

It really concerned me as I was grading student work that they were receiving a grade that reflected their effort as well as the grammar skills demonstrated. During my student teaching, my cooperating teacher told me to grade one and then judge the others according to that first paper. They would be either better or worse. In my mind that is not acceptable. It does not take into account the individual differences of my students. In the end I decided to give students two grades, one for grammar and one for content. This way they are able to see some success and get the constructive feedback they need to improve. With an overall grade, students do not receive the specific feedback in either grammar or content to become better writers.

Modifying Grades

Once you get into the classroom, you will see that not all students are equal and that some of your students can not be graded on the same scale as everyone else. These students usually have an I.E.P., or Individualized Education Plan. How do you grade students like this? Well, most states have laws that require you to modify for your special education students in one way or another. The one thing you must remember is that the student's I.E.P. will outline exactly how you must modify for that student. These modifications must be followed exactly as they are written on the I.E.P. It is the Law! However, some I.E.P.'s will be written to provide the teacher some flexibility. In this case, some teachers modify the lessons and tests while others will modify the grading scale.

"You MUST modify for your Special Education students. It is the Law!"

For example:

Let's say that one of your students has an I.E.P. that states they should have only fill in the blank and multiple choice items on any tests they take. Also, they must get 75% of the items correct. You, however, have a test that includes an essay question. What do you do? You need to cross out the essay question and then grade the student's test. Once the student has a grade, refer to your modified grading scale (in the back of this chapter) to determine the grade for your gradebook. If the student scored a 76 on the test, then they would receive an 81.

Testing and Test Anxiety

Whether or not you agree with standardized tests as a valid assessment tool for student performance, they are here and it doesn't look like they will be going anywhere for a while. In fact, it seems that the public is leaning more towards these types of tests than they ever have before. What does this mean for us and our students? Well, basically it means more stress.

We are stressed out because, for many of us, our jobs are directly affected by how well our students perform on these tests. Some of us feel the need to "teach to the test" while others take a "back to the basics" approach with students.

One factor that is not often discussed, though, is student test anxiety. I believe that low student scores are often a result of fear and frustration rather than lack of knowledge. This is especially true of our border-line students, or the students who are on the verge of a passing score.

Just imagine yourself in their place. *You know how to work algebraic word problems. You've done it a hundred times in class and most of the time you pass with an average grade. Then a test is placed in front of you. You are told that this is a very important test, and that how well you score will determine what you have and have not learned. You might even be told that this will effect whether or not you go up to the next grade level. Now you are getting nervous and your palms are sweating. You have butterflies in your stomach. You think that you can do this, but you aren't quite sure. The more you think about it, the more nervous you get. Suddenly all you can think about is how nervous and/or scared you are. The teacher announces that it is time to open the test booklet. You see the first question and your mind goes blank.*

Have you ever experienced that same sensation? I know I have, both as a student and as an adult. This is test anxiety. It is a fear that, as we mentioned in the previous chapter, causes your brain to downshift to a lower "gear." When going through test anxiety, it is virtually impossible to concentrate on working through individual test questions.

On the next pages are some tips you can use to help your students deal with their test anxiety.

"Many students cannot think clearly under the pressure of a high-stakes test."

Understanding How the Brain Works

It doesn't take long to teach your students how their brain works. No matter how old or young, your students should be able to understand the basics. In a previous chapter we discussed the theory of the Triune Brain. Here is just another way you can use this research to help your students.

- Explain the basic theory to your class. Be sure to put it into terms they can understand.

- Discuss/Brainstorm different events that can cause them to shift from their "thinking" brain to one of the smaller sections of their brain. These might include being hungry, having to use the bathroom, fighting with someone, being angry, being frustrated, being tired, being afraid, etc.

- Work out with students ways to overcome these stumbling blocks during a test. Prepare, with your students, a classroom environment that will help them stay in "thinking" mode throughout the test.

"Understanding how the brain works is the first step to helping students understand what happens to them in testing situations."

Create Favorable Testing Conditions

- Have healthy easy snacks, high in carbohydrates if possible, available for students in the classroom. Always approach this as both a necessity and a privilege for students. Be sure that you explain your expectations regarding food in the classroom in detail. When students understand why food is available and your expectations, they will be less likely to take advantage of the situation. Goldfish crackers, triskets, apple slices, trail-mix, and popcorn are good snacks for testing days. Be sure that you have disposable bowls and napkins as well.

- If you have a morning testing class, provide a small breakfast. You might offer muffins and juice or a ready-to-eat fruit.

- Be sure the lighting in your classroom is adequate. If not, bring a few lamps from home to add more soft light. Also, check the temperature of the room. If the conditions are too cold or hot, students will be more concerned about the temperature than the test. Lastly, are students moderately comfortable? You don't want things too cozy, but if a large student is crammed into a small desk, his/her brain will not be on the test.

- Explain restroom procedures to students. Make sure they understand that they are not required to "hold it," but that they need to give you a signal. Some teachers like to give each student a small piece of colored construction paper folded in half. The student places this card on their desk to signal the teacher when they are in need of assistance, a snack, or a restroom break. You might want to laminate these cards and use them all year long.

- Encourage students to eat a good meal and get at least eight hours of sleep the night before a big test. This will help students arrive to school rested. Also, you want to encourage students to arrive a little bit early so that they do not feel rushed before taking the test.

 **Teach Students Calming Exercises**

What do you do with a student who has severe test anxiety or who clams up suddenly during a test? Here are the steps you can teach your students when they are feeling nervous or tired during a test.

1. Close your test booklet and place your answer sheet in the middle of the booklet (or turn the test over).

2. Close your eyes.

3. Imagine yourself in your favorite place - somewhere quiet where you feel calm and relaxed.

4. Slowly count to ten or take several slow deep breaths.

5. Don't think about the test, but try to keep your mind empty/ calm (in other words, don't start thinking about what you are going to do later in the day).

6. When you feel ready, open your test booklet and begin again.

Hint:

How can students know when they need to take a breather?

- I'm feeling sick to my stomach/ butterflies/ anxious.

- I'm thinking about everything except the test.

- I'm feeling frustrated.

- I'm feeling angry at someone or something.

- I'm blanking out on each question.

- I'm tired.

- I'm hungry.

- I'm thirsty.

- I have to use the restroom.

Brainstorm additional "clues" with your class. You'll be surprised at how many they come up with during your session.

A Writing Rubric

Score	Characteristics

Score   **Characteristics**

4   Correct purpose, mode, and audience
Elaboration for each point and in each paragraph
Consistent organization
Clear sense of order/completeness
Smooth flow - almost no grammatical errors

3   Correct purpose, mode, and audience
Moderately well elaborated (a few points/paragraphs)
Somewhat organized
Clear language - few grammatical errors

2   Correct purpose, mode, and audience
A little elaboration (one point/paragraph)
A few specific details
Lists items rather than describing them
Gaps in organization
A lot of grammar and spelling errors

1   Attempts to address the audience
Brief/ vague
No elaboration at all
Off topic/ thoughts wander
No organization
Wrong purpose/mode
Grammatical errors make it difficult to understand

0   Off topic
Blank paper
Foreign language
Can't read the paper
Copied the prompt (nothing else)
Profane language
One paragraph written, but no more

For Texas teachers, an updated thorough writing rubric for TAKS can be found at
http://www.tea.state.tx.us/student.assessment/taks/rubrics/writing.pdf
We suggest that you use that particular rubric when grading writing to help students better understand the process. In fact, we highly recommend the TAKS writing rubric to all teachers.

Portfolio Conference Sheet

Student Name _____   Date_____

Teacher Name _____

Directions: Make comments about the discussion under each entry of the portfolio.

Title of Entry

1. _____

2. _____

3. _____

4. _____

5. _____

6. _____

© 2003 Survival Kit for New Secondary Teachers

Name _____   Grade _____

Class _____   Teacher _____

Description of Entry	Complete (1-4)	Correct (1-4)	Comprehensive (1-4)
1.			
2.			
3.			
4.			
5.			
6.			
7.			
8.			
9.			

The grade is marked in the smaller box with comments in the larger box.
Each student should have a reflection of about 5 to 10 sentences for each entry (upper elementary).

Teacher _____

Modified Grading System Grading Scales

	50%-75%		55%-75%		60%-75%		65%-75%		70%-75%
A	75 = 100	A	80 = 100	A	85 = 100	A	90 = 100	A	95 = 100
	74 = 99		79 = 99		84 = 99		89 = 99		94 = 99
	73 = 98		78 = 98		83 = 98		88 = 98		93 = 98
	72 = 97		77 = 97		82 = 97		87 = 97		92 = 97
	71 = 96		76 = 96		81 = 96		86 = 96		91 = 96
	70 = 95		75 = 95		80 = 95		85 = 95		90 = 95
	69 = 94		74 = 94		79 = 94		84 = 94		89 = 94
	68 = 93		73 = 93		78 = 93		83 = 93		88 = 93
	67 = 92		72 = 92		77 = 92		82 = 92		87 = 92
	66 = 91		71 = 91		76 = 91		81 = 91		86 = 91
	65 = 90		70 = 90		75 = 90		80 = 90		85 = 90
B	64 = 89	B	69 = 89	B	74 = 89	B	79 = 89	B	84 = 89
	63 = 88		68 = 88		73 = 88		78 = 88		83 = 88
	62 = 87		67 = 87		72 = 87		77 = 87		82 = 87
	61 = 86		66 = 86		71 = 86		76 = 86		81 = 86
	60 = 85		65 = 85		70 = 85		75 = 85		80 = 85
	59 = 84		64 = 84		69 = 84		74 = 84		79 = 84
	58 = 83		63 = 83		68 = 83		73 = 83		78 = 83
	57 = 82		62 = 82		67 = 82		72 = 82		77 = 82
	56 = 81		61 = 81		66 = 81		71 = 81		76 = 81
	55 = 80		60 = 80		65 = 80		70 = 80		75 = 80
C	54 = 79	C	59 = 79	C	64 = 79	C	69 = 79	C	74 = 79
	53 = 78		58 = 78		63 = 78		68 = 78		73 = 78
	52 = 77		57 = 77		62 = 77		67 = 77		72 = 77
	51 = 76		56 = 76		61 = 76		66 = 76		71 = 76
	50 = 75		55 = 75		60 = 75		65 = 75		70 = 75
D	49 = 74	D	54 = 74	D	59 = 74	D	64 = 74	D	69 = 74
	48 = 73		53 = 73		58 = 73		63 = 73		68 = 73
	47 = 72		52 = 72		57 = 72		62 = 72		67 = 72
	46 = 71		51 = 71		56 = 71		61 = 71		66 = 71
	45 = 70		50 = 70		55 = 70		60 = 70		65 = 70
F	44 = 69	F	49 = 69	F	54 = 69	F	59 = 69	F	64 = 69

Source Unknown

This page may be reproduced for classroom use only.   © 2003 Survival Kit for New Secondary Teachers

Mid-Term Progress Report

The grades below reflect your child's grade mid-way through the current grading period.

Student's Name _____

Reading _____   **Language Arts** _____   **Art** _____

Math _____   **Science** _____   **P.E.** _____

Social Studies _____   **Foreign Language** _____   **Behavior** _____

═══ CONCERNS ═══

_____ **Low grades on homework**

_____ **Does not complete assigned work**

_____ **Poor homework/ study habits**

_____ **Does not pay attention in class**

_____ **Does not make up missed work**

═══ COMMENTS: ═══

- -

I have seen my child's mid-term grades.

Student _____

Parent _____

Detailed Progress Report

Student Name _____   Date _____

WORK HABITS	E.E.	M.E.	N.I.	COMMENTS
Completes assignments on time				
Follows directions readily				
Uses time wisely				
Contributes to activities/ discussion				
Works neatly and carefully				
Works Independently				
BEHAVIOR				
Follows school/ class rules				
Respects authority				
Considerate of peers				
Cares for school property				
Is self-disciplined				
ACADEMICS				
Reading				
Writing				
Social Studies				
Math				
Science				
Extra-curricular				

EE = Exceeds Expectations   ME = Meets Expectations   NI = Needs Improvement   *(Developed by Spring Branch ISD Summer Program)*

MISSING ASSIGNMENTS:

Parent Signature _____   Date _____

If you have any questions, feel free to call me at _____ .

This page may be reproduced for classroom use only.   © 2003 Survival Kit for New Secondary Teachers

Missing Assignments

Name: _____

Assignments:

_____

_____

_____

_____

_____

_____

_____

_____

_____

_____

_____

_____

_____

_____

_____

_____

_____

_____

Parent Signature: _____

CONCLUSION

In order to be effective, we must think about how we will assess students in the early stages of lesson planning. The fact that many of our classroom activities can be used as a way to assess student learning is a time saver. However, if we do not take this into consideration, we could find ourselves trying to evaluate students in a manner that is neither valid nor reliable. Always be sure that your assessment matches what you have taught and that it addresses different learner needs. This can be done by varying the type of activities you use. Also, take into account your special needs students, and determine ahead of time how you plan to modify assessments so they are valid. In short, student assessment should not be an after-thought to lessons, but rather a pre-planned effort in order to effectively evaluate learning.

Additional Resources

Classroom Assessment: What Teachers Need to Know
by W. James Popham

Great Performances: Creating Classroom Based Assessment Tasks
by Larry Lewin and Betty Jean Shoemaker

Classroom Assessment for Students with Special Needs in Inclusive Settings
by Cathleen Spinelli

Questions for Reflection

1) Why do you think it is important to develop a philosophy of assessment?

2) How can you be sure that your assessment accurately represents student achievement and progress?

3) In what ways can a portfolio be used in the classroom? How would you use a student portfolio as an assessment?

4) Why should teachers be concerned with the issue of test anxiety?

5) What are some strategies you might implement to help overcome test anxiety?

Activities

1) Develop your own philosophy of assessment within one or two paragraphs.

2) Develop your own grading policy to use with your students.

3) Describe how you plan to set up your gradebook and the type of grading scale you plan to use.

4) Choose four different assessment strategies from this chapter and explain how you plan to use them in the classroom. (**Example:** *I plan to use the mind map to assess student learning of the concepts discussed within a history textbook chapter.*)

5) Write a letter to your administrator supporting your decision to implement different strategies that will help students overcome test anxiety. Use additional sources of information and research to back up your position.

Notes/ Reflection of Chapter

Motivating Students

> Some of my students are not excited about learning!
>
> What can I do?

One of the most difficult aspects of teaching is motivating students. In fact, William Glasser, in his book entitled Choice Theory in the Classroom, states that trying to teach students who do not want to learn is impossible. In our own experience, the middle and high school student is especially challenging in this area. Add to it the fact that you will most likely have students from a lower socio-economic background, where survival is more important than learning, as well as students with learning or language difficulties, and you have a challenge.

Remember, the more engaged your students are, the more they will be motivated to learn. Engaging activities are ones where students must manipulate the information, skill, or concept in a variety of ways. This can include working in teams, discussion, projects, research, or creating a product of some sort as we discussed earlier.

Take a few minutes to think about classes that you've attended throughout your lifetime. Which ones do you remember as positive and motivating experiences? Which ones were so boring that you spent every minute counting the seconds until it was time to leave? Generally classes where the teacher or professor lectured at students or required students to do meaningless work, busy-work, or repetitive tasks are the most boring. Classes which get students actively involved in discovering their own learning, interacting with each other, and encourage respect between the teacher and students are the most motivating. Look back at the Brain-Based Classroom and Strategy chapters for more detail about these motivating attributes.

Additionally, it is important to be prepared with a variety of activities that will engage students in their own learning. If a lesson seems to be faltering or you notice a glazed-over look in the eyes of your students, smile a big smile, do a little dance, and pull out something different to capture their attention. Have you been doing all of the talking and action for the lesson? Think quickly how you can get students involved instead.

In this chapter we will share additional easy-to-use strategies to help you engage and motivate students. These can be referenced when planning lessons, or in many instances, used at the spur-of-the moment when you see that glazed-over look.

Atlas Activities

- When reading a story or novel, have students find the city/town/country of the setting on a map. Discuss where it is located in relation to where the school is located. Older students can determine the latitude and longitude to practice Geography skills.

- Discuss the culture, environment, and weather of the area. How does this affect the story, if at all? Is the setting a true representation of this actual city/town/country?

- If the story has a make-believe setting, where is the author from? Does the story reflect the culture and weather of the author's hometown?

- Identify historical events on the map.

- Identify place of birth/residence of different Scientists, Mathematicians, Artists, Musicians, Sports Figures, Famous People, etc.
    - How did the culture, history, geography, weather of where they live(d) affect them?

- Have students create their own city/town/country. Students exhibit Geography skills by drawing a map. Be sure they include important elements such as the Legend/Key, landforms, a grid system, etc.

Books and Brainstorming Activities

- Children's books are an excellent way to introduce units and lessons. Everyone loves to be read to, even if older students won't admit it! If you're not sure how you can introduce a particular concept or skill, see if you can find a children's book that can be used as a jumping off point for your lesson. Amazon.com and other online bookstores are a great way to search for books. With their search engines, all you need to do is type in the keywords in the children's books section and many titles should pop up for you to browse.

- Brainstorming provides students an opportunity for input in class decisions and class discussions. It also offers a way for students to voice out loud what they already know (or think they know) and generates ideas for everyone to think about. Brainstorming is an excellent pre-writing strategy as well as a way to stimulate thinking when beginning a new concept. Jot lists can be done independently and then shared with the group. Be sure that each and every idea is valued and none ridiculed. It does not matter how impossible an idea might be, during brainstorming everything is to be included. We want to encourage our students to think "out of the box" rather than all conform to one way of thinking. You can use brainstorming to:

    - Generate writing topics
    - Generate questions for guest speakers
    - Generate questions for interviews or research projects

Concept Board Activities

Students love to share and displaying their work is vital. A fun way to encourage this is by allowing them to create tri-fold concept boards. They are great when you are working on experiments in science or doing book reports. Concept boards also come in handy when reviewing previous skills, and parents love seeing them displayed for curriculum fairs and parent nights.

Concept Boards do not have to be huge. Students can create mini tri-fold boards out of 1/2 or even 1/3 of poster board. Once they've cut the posterboard in half or one-third, students need to fold the remaining portion into three sections. Now you have a ready-to-use mini concept-board!

Dioramas and Drawing Activities

After reading or learning about a new concept, have students show what they've learned by making a diorama, or shoe-box scene. Using a shoe box, have students create a 3-D scene using construction paper and other materials such as grass, twigs, plastic figures, fishing wire, etc.. On the outside, students should write a short paragraph telling about the scene or explaining the concept.

Have students draw about a topic before reading or writing about it. This helps focus students on what they are about to learn. It is also a great way to encourage students who do not feel successful when reading or writing.

Utilize the mind-map strategy. The mind-map is very similar to webbing except that students draw pictures instead of only using words. Each thought or idea branches off of the main topic. This can be used in all subject areas to show relationships between ideas, events, people, etc.

Everybody Activites

Get everybody involved by using pass-along stories, or round-robin stories. Each student will write one beginning sentence on their paper. They then pass their paper on to the next student who adds another sentence or two continuing the same thought. This is an excellent way to teach the importance of staying on a topic and learning about fluent story lines.

The round robin concept can also be used when solving equations or sequencing events.

Fun and Freedom of Expression

Don't be afraid to have fun and laugh with your students. Fun is an important need of all human beings. Once you have established work time vs. play time, enjoy humor in your classroom. Share a joke or funny story with your students and encourage them to share some with you.

Provide your students with lots of options. Every person is better at one medium than another. Let them try their hand at writing music lyrics, poems, raps, and plays. They will love the chance to explore their creative side.

Games and Getting to Know Students

Using games is a great way to teach teamwork. There are many new and old games that involve skills we teach in school. Monopoly and Backgammon involve the problem-solving skills we like to encourage, while Scrabble promotes vocabulary and spelling. Other fun games that also stimulate the brain are Scatergories and Mastermind.

You can become a game creator as well. Our students love to review for tests by playing bingo, overhead football, and jeopardy.

FunBrain.com is a great way to introduce online games to your students that challenge their thinking. It has a great resource for teachers as well.

Students also love to create their own game. This type of activity really forces them to use higher level thinking, although they never realize it! Have students make up a game using information they've learned. How will they teach others the skill and/or knowledge they've learned through their game? Is this a review type game or a teaching type game. Stress the importance of clear and precise instructions.

The more you know your students as people, the better you will be able to relate to them. Each student in your class is a unique individual with their own personality, their own wants, needs, likes, and dislikes. Do you really know them as a person or are they just another face to you? Our students are often motivated to work harder for the teachers who take time to get to know them on a personal level and show that they care. This is often done in primary grades, but as students get older, it happens less frequently.

Helping

Helping others can be motivating to students. It provides them with a chance to show what they know and to be appreciated. Provide opportunities for your students to help you as a teacher assistant.

Students can help one another when partnered together in class for activities and projects. Have students create study groups within the class. This also helps with developing important skills of networking with others.

Integrating

The more students can see the connections between what they are learning and real life, the more they will be motivated. Even subjects or reading material that can be viewed as dry and dull takes on new meaning when presented in a way that connects it to the real world or to student's lives. How can you present your subject material so that it comes alive for students?

Journaling

Writing out information often helps students conceptualize information and place it in their long term memory. For example, think about how you would write out an explanation of "3 x 5." Journals can be utilized in all classrooms. In fact, a famous gymnast, when teaching his students, has them keep a journal of their work-out to solidify in their minds what has been done and what needs to be done.

Journaling, continued

Students can create a learning log by writing down what they have learned for the day. It can also be used on a weekly basis. The only rule is that students must use complete sentences. Journaling provides the transfer necessary to make a concept real. It also allows the teacher to check periodically on a student's individual progress. Journals are a great way to demonstrate knowledge of a concept, show understanding, and give directions on how to complete a task or solve an equation. A journal entry also works great as a closure activity.

We discuss additional ideas for using Journals in all subject areas in the Reading and Writing Across the Curriculum chapter.

K-W-L

KWL stands for Know-, Want to Know-, Learned-, and is written across the top of a chart, chalkboard, or paper. Students fill in the first two sections as a class before a new unit or concept is learned. The last section is completed at the end of the unit or lesson. With primary students this can be done orally or as a class using large sheets of butcher paper.

Life Size and Letter Writing

Students love anything different from paper and pencil activities, so give them a large piece of butcher paper and markers and let them make life sized timelines in History, graphs in Science and Math, solve problems, create storyboards, or brainstorm ideas.

Writing letters to the President, Governor, local Congressman or Senator, or to other famous figures, is extremely motivating to students. Many addresses for government officials and businesses can be found in the almanac and on the internet. This is an excellent way for reviewing both friendly and business letter formats with students. Not only do they have a real audience, but also have a variety of topics to write about. This can also be used as a tool for assessment since students have to know the subject in order to make a coherent letter. Everyone will be excited when they receive a reply letter in the mail.

There is an excellent book called "Letters from a Nut" (will have to edit some of the material for appropriateness), that uses letters written in a serious format to poke fun at the world. The author has written letters to actual businesses with either a compliment or a complaint and has published the return letter. This book is a fun way to introduce writing letters to businesses to either compliment or complain about a particular product or service.

Mobiles

Mobiles are a fun way to display information. Students can make mobiles of atoms, story settings, and timelines. Require written explanations of the mobile. This is great for visual learners and can be used as an assessment tool. We've used everything from coat hangers to dowel rods to make mobiles. Students can be creative in what they decide to hang when representing a concept.

Note Writing

We are forever picking up notes in class, so it is time to use this time worthy tradition by encouraging students to write informal letters for information, send birthday notes to a classmate, or even write notes to their best friend about their day.

With computers and specialty paper, it is easy to create personalized note cards to give to students. At the beginning of the year you could use Microsoft Publisher or any Card Maker program to create a variety of cards with different messages on them. Then, throughout the year, pick a card and personalize it for the student.

Everyone likes to get a card that shows someone is thinking of them. If a student seems sad all day, give them a "Cheer Up" or "Hang in There" card. Don't just make cards to show appreciation for hard work and improvement, but think of other situations where a personal card would make a difference to a student. If you make up a wide variety of cards with different messages, then you can just write in, "Dear_____," jot a quick note, and sign your name. If you have a few minutes, then write more.

Don't get so caught up in the day to day business of teaching that you forget your students are people with feelings and needs.

Odd Shapes and Open Sharing

Octagon, squares, stars, and other shapes make learning fun. Use various shapes to help students see similarities and differences, categorize items, or order concepts. For example, a triangle is an excellent way for students to visualize hierarchies.

A variation on this activity is to make these objects 3-D and place instructions or questions on each surface.

Allowing students to share in class helps create a positive learning environment and makes students feel important. Have them share what they have written or learned. Encourage students to relate their learning to their life. Have they ever been in a particular situation described in the story or event? Have them share relevant experiences.

Paper Bag Activities

Students can use paper bags as an alternative to routine paper/pencil tasks. Fill the bags with flash cards, sequence strips, or character traits. Decorate the outside of the bag and put in exciting events from history, a script for a skit, events of a novel, etc. Students can complete the activity found within the bag.

This is a great way to jump start an activity with student groups. Have them predict what the activity will be based on the outside of the bag. Encourage student cooperation with paper bags. If each group has one or more items another group needs to complete their task, they will need to cooperate with one another in sharing and exchaging needed information.

Students can also put their work inside a paper bag and illustrate the outside. The possibilities are endless! When using paper bags as part of a project, be sure to use a checklist so that students know exactly what is expected of them.

Poems, Paper Bags, and Pop-up Books

Poems can be written about seasons, historical events, and even math. The more they write, the better writers they will become. A Bio-Poem is a fun way to show knowledge about a historical figure or concept.

The pattern is:

Line 1: Person's name/ Concept
Line 2: 2 adjectives to describe
Line 3: An action phrase with an -ing word
Line 4: An action phrase with an -ing word
Line 5: An action phrase with an -ing word
Line 6: Wrap up word or phrase that is a
            synonym for line one

Examples:

Abraham Lincoln
Honest and just,
Fighting a bitter war,
Leading a broken nation,
Living on through time,
A Man for the Ages.

Volcanoes
Hot and Fierce,
Spitting out ash and rocks,
Spilling out lava,
Covering everything in sight,
New land is formed.

Pop-Up Books

Pop-up books are such a fun way to publish student writing. Just for something different, have students publish their information in an illustrated pop-up book. Students simply fold one or more pieces of construction paper in half for their book. The title should be written on the front and an "About the Author" on the back along with illustrations. Inside, have students write their paragraph(s) on the bottom half of each side and illustrate the top. Glue or staple the pages together on the crease.

A pop-up image can be created by folding a small piece of cardstock or construction paper in an "L" shape and pasting it on the page. You might also ask your art teacher to help you with other ideas for creating pop-up images.

Quotes

As students make profound, or humorous statements, have them write these down and display them on a bulletin board or walls of your classroom. What a great way to let students know that what they say is important!

A variation to this activity is to have a quote of the day or a quote of the week from different famous figures. Use the quote as a springboard for your discussion that day or week.

For example, a music teacher might use, "We are the music makers and we are the dreamers of the dream," by William Shakespeare. Students can interpret what they think this quote means.

Another variation for quotes is to have students finish the quote. Provide students with the beginning of a famous quote or saying and have them finish it in their own words. You'll enjoy reading the results as will the parents! Afterwards, discuss each quote and its meaning with students.

The internet is an excellent source to find books of quotes or even websites full of quotes ready to be used.

Remembering Names and Researching

Students are motivated to work for people who care about them. Remembering their name after the first day of school is one way to show that you care. Play the Name Game or another type of game that will help you remember each student's face and name together. You'll see their face light up, no matter what age, when on the second day you say hello to each along with their name.

Have students research more often and less formally to establish a love of searching out answers. Research does not have to be massive, but can be an easy quest for knowledge. Assign mini-research topics using a variety of resources. Let students research information to answer questions they may have on a particular topic. Make it as non-threatening as possible so that students will enjoy seeking information and reveling in the success of finding it.

Have students research fun, interesting, and unusual topics. For example, when studying a culture, have someone investigate hair-styles, clothing trends, or favorite desserts! In Chemistry, how many elements are used in health and beauty products, to make jewelry, or in cooking?

Sentence Strips

You can use this same concept in just about any class. Use strips of paper to organize or categorize information into a T-chart, timeline, Venn Diagram, or any other graphic organizer. Type out statements, words, ideas, etc. and cut them into strips. Have an envelope or baggie with the strips ready for each student group. Students then work together to put information in correct order or correct category. They can paste their final product onto construction paper or a large sheet of colored butcher paper. This activity helps students mainpulate information in a variety of ways.

Transparencies and True/False

To add enthusiasm to your class, divide students into teams and let them solve problems or answer questions on an overhead transparency. Students can then share or explain this information to the class.

During a class discussion, allow students to come to the overhead and write their answer or idea using colored Vis á Vis pens.

Reviewing facts in class can be fun using the game True or False. Have student groups work together to create three to five statements regarding a recent lesson that are either true or false. Have the groups go to the front of the room to share their statements. The other students in the room then decide whether each statement is true or false. Students really enjoy this game because they have a chance to "trick" other students with their statements. It works great as a review because you can stop after each statement and discuss why it was or was not true.

Unwrapping and Underlining

Students describe a famous person, place, or concept on a sheet of paper. Encourage creativity with illustrations and/or objects that help represent the information. Have students put their information in a box, wrap it up, and exchange their "gift" of knowledge with another student.

Give students special colored pens, pencils, or highlighters when they have to underline a reading passage. Another fun way to use underlining is in teaching the parts of speech. Have students use a different colored pen or pencil to underline each part of speech in a sentence. This is a great group activity where each team member has a different colored pen. They must work together to identify the parts of speech in a sentence.

Vacation Brochure

A brochure is a great way for students to show their creativity. They can use it to market a "time travel" vacation. Students design the brochure to convince people to travel back to a specific time period in history. Who will they see? Where will they go? What will they experience?

Have students plan a trip to anywhere in the United States or the world. What will they see? What route will they drive? How many miles is it? Will they need to fly? What is the cost? Where will they stay? Math concepts are integrated by figuring the cost of gas/travel, and setting a budget for food, lodging and attractions. How much will the total trip cost? For older students, how long will each leg of the trip take when traveling x miles an hour? Also, if they were able to save x dollars each month, how long would it take them to save up for the trip?

When students are studying a new math concept, have them make a travel brochure to with tips on how to solve this type of math problem.

When studying world cultures, have students make travel brochures to convince people to travel to different countries.

When studying any concept, have students create a travel brochure to visit the "Land of ..." (atoms, volcanoes, baseball, etc.) in which they explain information about that particular concept.

W is for Walkabout

The Walkabout is a type of research adapted from a traditional practice of Aboriginal Australian tribes in which adolescents are sent alone into the outback for several months to prove their readiness for adulthood. Dr. Maurice Gibbons, in his book, The Walkabout, Searching for the Rite of Passage from Childhood and School, adapted this practice into a form of real-life teaching to help students want to learn.

The Walkabout is a year-long project in which students explore one topic of interest to them. Students must go on an adventure, create something unique, research one aspect of the topic, do a community service, and show professional skills attained. Pictures, journals, and information gathered for each section are organized into a 3-ring binder and presented to a panel of teachers, peers, and parents at the end of the year.

X-tra Small or Large

Have students do their assignments on extra large or extra small pieces of paper. This makes boring, repetitive type tasks more fun. Another way to spruce up their work is by providing them with brightly colored paper or index cards.

"Xcellent"

Praising students is an excellent way to motivate them. When they share an answer with the class, thank them. Say, "Excellent answer!" or "Excellent effort!" You will be surprised at how many more hands will begin to go up when you do this.

Yard

We're talking about the school-yard here! Take students out and about on beautiful days. Walk around and pick up different kinds of leaves, look at trees and roots, pick up rocks to identify, or notice different cloud shapes. There is so much for us to learn from our world that we should take advantage of it and spend some time outdoors. Who says that all learning must occur inside buildings?

Take some time to play team-building games outside or use chalk to do math. Have students make butter, bricks, or other objects that reinforce your topic of discussion. Measure the distance from the sun to each planet with chalk, or have student groups use their bodies create "live" mini solar systems with "planets" rotating around the "sun."

Go outside to write poetry or stories and let the great outdoors inspire your writers and artists. There are so many different ways that you and your students can enjoy the outside world and learn at the same time!

Zooming In and Zest

Have students take a broad topic and "zoom in" on one tiny detail to explore fully. For example, when studying a culture, focus on hairstyles or clothing. It is also easy to "zoom in" in science by using microscopes and magnifying glasses to write about what students see.

Add zest to your classroom by participating in the activities you require of your students. They will love to see your product and will be more motivated to put time and effort into it when they see how much effort you put into yours. This is an excellent way to model your expectations as well as a way for you to enjoy being with your students.

Working with Special Needs Students

This section is in the Motivating Students chapter because oftentimes these are the hardest students to motivate. Mainstreamed students include Special Education and ESL (English as a Second Language) students. As teachers we know that our job is to teach ALL students regardless of their inherent ability. However, we also know that there are some students who are harder to reach for whatever reason. This section contains tips that will help you find a way to cope with the varying abilities of your students.

 **Special Education Students**

The Special Education teacher comes into your room a few days before school begins and tells you that you have a few students with special needs. What can you do to accommodate them?

- Do not treat these students any differently than the others.

- Pair them with someone in your class who is patient and willing to help.

- Read each I.E.P. (Individualized Education Plan). If you don't understand it, ask your Special Education teacher to explain what that particular student needs. **It never hurts to ask for help!**

- Remember, you are required by law to follow each I.E.P. exactly when modifying for the student.

- If you do not feel comfortable modifying tests or assignments, ask your Special Education teacher to help you.

- Get textbooks that you can highlight. Some I.E.P.'s request this. Your Special Education teacher will know where to get them or may have some you can use.

- Modify tests BEFORE you hand them out. It only takes a few minutes to cross out or highlight sections for the student to complete. Don't embarrass the student by making them wait while you modify the test or assignment right at their desk.

"Do not hesitate in asking the Special Education teachers for help!"

"Take the time to find out what interests each student and use that to help motivate them."

- Find out if your school has a walk-in room, resource room, pull-out room, or other place where you can send Special Education students for help.

- Get to know your Special Education teacher. He/she can really help you out of tricky situations!

- Find out if your school has an adaptive behavior classroom or some other place for emotionally disabled students.

- Do not tolerate jibes or funny remarks about Special Education students by others – even other teachers!

- Answer the questions on the referral paperwork the best that you can.

- Read to and with these students every day, even if it is only for a few minutes. That extra time reinforces that they are worth your attention.

- Do not make a big deal about Special Education students leaving your class if they go to a resource classroom.

- Be prepared for pages and pages of referral forms! Ask for help with these forms if you need it. Be aware! Referrals can be anywhere from five to fifteen pages long.

- Be aware that the referral process can take a VERY LONG TIME with lots of paperwork and meetings in between.

- Try not to lose your temper and if you do, apologize. Kids understand that everyone has bad days.

- Be Patient!

- Find out what that student is interested in and use it!

- Be prepared to explain the concept or lesson in a different way for them.

- Be sure to attend all ARD (Admission, Referral, Dismissal) meetings prepared with your gradebook, samples of student work, and possible recommendations from what you observe in the classroom.

- Some students need to move to learn. Allow an active student to sit in the back and move around a little, as long as he/she doesn't disturb anybody.

- Find out how that student works and be flexible! If a student needs to draw to listen, then let him/her draw.

- If you don't feel comfortable with modifying tests and assignments, you also have the option of modifying grades for Special Education students. (See the back of the Assessment chapter)

- Trust your gut instinct!

- Don't get discouraged! It is hard when you know a student needs help, but they don't qualify according to the state requirements. Do what you can.

- Keep your eyes open for students who need help and are not getting it. Not everyone needs Special Education resources. Check it out first to make sure that the student is not just goofing off.

- Don't try to fill out a referral form alone for the first time! Find a veteran teacher or the Special Education teacher.

- Ask about other programs, such as tutoring and Big Brother/ Big Sister, that might help your student.

- Have documentation of any behavior and/or academic problems the student has exhibited in your classroom.

- If your student does not qualify for special education services, but you still feel they need extra help, discuss a 504 plan or speech referral with your special education teacher.

- Remember that parents are not always happy about their child being referred for Special Education services. Many times parents feel that you are simply trying to label their student as "dumb". Reassure them that you are trying to find a way for them to be successful in the classroom.

"Keep your eyes open for students who need special help.

Do you see a discrepancy between their intelligence and their abilities?"

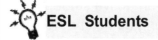 **ESL Students**

It is frustrating to have someone in our class who can't understand anything we're saying. How do we know that they are learning anything or that they are being successful? This is often the case with our ESL students. Many times students arrive in our class having just entered the country. Others, however, have been here for some time, but do not have a good grasp on the English language. Whatever the case, we need to be prepared to offer these students a good education. Here are a few tips used by effective ESL teachers that you can use with ESL students in the classroom.

Students with no English language skills

- Provide ample listening opportunities

- Use mixed ability groups

- Create high context for shared reading

- Use physical movement

- Use art, mime, and music

- Put yourself in their shoes to gain perspective and understanding

- Demonstrate

- Restate/ paraphrase

- Use Gestures

- Explain or define any and all terms used in class.

- Use illustrations and photographs; label items in the room

- Remember, these students are scared and confused and do not understand anything that is going on in the classroom.

- Do not force them to talk until they are ready. Respect their silence.

- Pair with a student who can fluently speak their language and can help translate.

"Respect an ESL student's need for silence when faced with a new language."

Students with extremely limited language skills

- Ask *yes/no* and *who? what? where?* questions.

- Continue to provide listening opportunities.

- Have students label pictures and objects.

- Have students complete sentences with 1 or 2 word phrases.

- Use pattern books and picture dictionaries.

- Try to help them understand what is going on in your classroom.

- Pair them with a student who is fluent in English as well as in their home language, if you can.

- Build vocabulary in the content areas using visuals and meaningful experiences.

Students with less limited language skills

- Ask open-ended questions.

- Model, expand, restate, and enrich student language.

- Have students describe personal experiences.

- Use predictable and patterned books for shared and guided reading.

- Use role-play and retelling of content area text.

- Have students create books.

- Do not assume that the students have the appropriate academic skills.

- Teach students academic language – what is a noun, subtraction, etc.

- Help students by modeling thinking aloud. Encourage students to only use English then at school.

Hint:

Have students create understanding thermometers to help them show you their level of comfort and understanding.

Use heavy cardstock paper for the thermometer. Cut the page into three sections approximately 4" by 7". Label the top "Understanding Thermometer" and draw a line down the middle. On the right side of the line write "No Clue," then "Confused," then "Questions," then "I get it." On the left side of the line draw faces to represent these statements. Cut a hole at the top and bottom of the line. Thread a piece of yarn with a bead. Next, thread the yarn through the holes so that the bead is on the front of the card. Tie the yarn in back. Students can move the bead up and down the thermometer to show you how they are doing.

"Keep your ESL students involved in all class activities.

ESL students, just like all of our students, work best in groups."

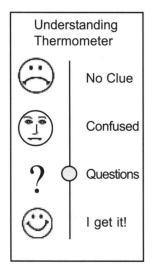

Understanding Thermometer

No Clue

Confused

Questions

I get it!

Thank you to Connie Skipper, ESL teacher, Garland ISD for sharing this idea with us!

Students with fluent language skills

- Pair them with another student who needs help.

- Use group discussions to help them continue practicing their language skills.

- Guide them in the use of reference materials such as dictionaries, almanacs, atlases, and encyclopedias

- Provide higher level reading materials.

- Have students write their own stories.

- Provide realistic writing opportunities.

- Provide visuals to help with comprehension.

- Publish student writings.

- Encourage them to use both of their languages as a translator.

All ESL students

- Do not let them use their lack of language skills as a crutch!

- Be understanding and flexible with the ESL teachers. Ask for strategies and ideas to help you in the classroom.

- If you see that a student needs help and you do not feel that you do an adequate job, send them to their ESL teacher for extra help.

- Begin with shortened assignments and gradually increase them as they gain fluency.

- Do not make a big deal of students leaving your classroom for their ESL classes.

- Keep them as involved as you can in your classroom. They need to do everything the other students are doing!

- Have students do the regular assignment and then modify their grade if necessary.

CONCLUSION

Remember, the more motivated your students are, the more learning will take place. When students are energized and engaged, their minds are like sponges absorbing new information and storing it. This happens so easily when they have a fun activity to connect with concepts learned. Additionally, many of these activities help our Special Needs and ESL students to feel success and enjoy the learning process. Thus, planning motivating lessons is not such a difficult task when you use simple activities like the ones in this chapter to add zest!

Additional Resources

Reading, Writing, and Learning in ESL (2nd Edition) by Suzanne Peregoy and Owen Boyle

Exceptional Lives: Special Education in Today's Schools (3rd Edition)
by Ann Turnbull, et. al.

Motivating Your Students: Before You Can Teach Them, You Have to Reach Them
by Hanoch McCarty and Frank Siccone

Choice Theory in the Classroom
by William Glasser

Questions for Reflection

1) If you could use one word to sum up how to motivate students to want to learn, what word would you use? Why?

2) Why is it helpful to have quick and easy ways to make learning fun?

3) What are three things we need to keep in mind when working with Special Education students?

4) What are some ways you plan to help ESL students at different levels in your classroom?

Activities

1) Incorporate two or three of the strategies mentioned in this chapter into one or more lessons you are currently planning, or describe how you would incorporate different strategies into lessons for particular concepts/skills (ie - Colonization, Oceans, Novel study, etc.)

2) Brainstorm how you would set up a "creative center" in your classroom. What materials will you include? How will you set it up? Draw a sketch of what your area ideally would look like. Remember, most classrooms are small, so don't go overboard.

4) Develop a series of notecards on the computer to use with students for praise or encouragement. Print them out and save them to use in your classroom.

© 2003 Survival Kit for New Secondary Teachers

Notes/ Reflection of Chapter

Technology in the Classroom

To be effective, teachers need to be prepared to use a variety of technological hardware and software when teaching students. While the computer is becoming a major tool within the classroom, technology comes in all shapes and sizes. Not every school is fully equipped with computers and other types of high-tech hardware. This can be frustrating to tech savvy teachers. Even more frustrating is the fact that many teachers across the United States are equipped with computer presentation stations and other hardware/software options that they rarely or never use.

There are lots of different, helpful, and motivating ways you can use technology in your classroom to enhance student learning. However, we must stress the importance of attending training provided by your school or district in how to use these tools. A well-prepared teacher strives to stay on top of the latest technology available to them. If we are not familiar with using certain types of hardware or software, we will not use them in the classroom. This hurts our students who need that exposure to help prepare them for life in the new millennium.

> *My school has really embraced technology in the classroom.*
>
> *Where do I start?*

Computers

Computers have so many different uses in the classroom. Whether you have a presentation station, one computer for the whole class, or several workstations, computers can be used in a variety of ways to enhance your learning environment. We are going to discuss both teacher use and student use of equipment and software programs for the computer in this section.

Teacher Use of the Computer

Presentation Station

A presentation station includes a Television Set, a computer, and sometimes a VCR and internet connection. All of these items are hooked up together so that the teacher can present information from the computer/internet for students to view on the TV. Schools across the country are moving towards this type of setup for teachers to make technology more accessible as a teaching tool.

Computer/TV Hookup Cables

These days computers can easily hook up to the TV through a series of cables which your librarian may have available. If not, Radio Shack and other Computer stores will be able to help you find the correct cables to use.

LCD Panel

These panels will also project information from the computer to a screen, usually the overhead screen. Some schools may have an LCD panel available for check-out through the library. However, the LCD panel does not provide as crisp of a picture and can be hard to see clearly.

Projector Unit

Some schools have projector units that connect to a computer and project the information directly to a screen. These are clear projections, unlike the LCD panel, and can often be used to project other images as well.

Of course, the ideal is that every teacher would have their own presentation station to be able to present lessons using a variety of technology and media.

Okay, now I have the equipment, but what do I do with it?

There are a plethora of fantastic software programs that will help you with lesson presentations, creating forms, developing web pages, contacting students and parents, and more! On the next couple of pages we are going to review some of the different programs you might find useful.

Power Point

Power Point is a program that is used to present information. The pages can be changed manually with the click of a mouse, or automatically through the slide show mode. You choose how many seconds or minutes you want to pause in-between each slide.

Power Point can replace the overhead transparency when presenting notes, pictures, or information. Simply type your notes, information, or insert pictures onto each page (called a slide). When teaching, either time the slides to automatically switch or use the mouse to click over to the next slide of information. This is a great way to integrate pictures along with information. You can use digital camera images or clipart. The program includes a nice little collection of clipart that is easy to insert.

Other Uses include:

- Post class objectives, the date, homework assignments, or your focus assignment (warm-up, sponge, bell-ringer, etc.). This helps keep your whiteboard or chalkboard open for other teaching needs.

- Post Vocabulary or Spelling words for students to copy or look up in the dictionary.

- Post your Word(s) of the Day or Quote of the Day

- Print the outline version of the slides to use as notes when presenting the lesson. You could also give these to students who were absent or special needs students who cannot copy as quickly.

- Review for a test. Create one slide for each review question. Set the time between each slide to give ample opportunity for answering the question before it switches to the next slide. This keeps you free to monitor students while they work and to help answer questions. This method saves on copies and is a great alternative when the copier is broken or the school is out of paper.

- Post directions for assignments, lab rotations, or group work.

- Have you run out of room on the overhead or whiteboard? Think about posting some of the information using Power Point.

"Power Point can take the place of the chalkboard and multiple handouts for students."

Word Perfect or Microsoft Word

You can use Word for the same reasons as Power Point. The difference is that multiple pages will not change automatically. Also, you must remember that students can only see what is visible on the screen. With Power Point, once you start the slide show, each slide will adjust itself to fit perfectly to the screen.

Use Word to:

- Create and save letters to parents
- Create note cards or post cards to give to students
- Create tests
- Create welcoming letters for parents and/or students
- Create forms to use in the classroom
- Create checklists for assignments
- Create assignment handouts
- Create lesson plans
- Create lesson handouts
- Teach editing skills -- Have students point out mistakes in a typed paragraph. You can correct the mistakes on the computer while students are watching. You might use a different color to fix the problems in order for the changes to stand out.

"Creating letters and forms using Word or other word processing programs allows you to save on disk an edit as needed."

EXCEL

Excel is a spreadsheet program and has many different uses. We highly recommend that you take a course in using Excel to learn all of the different ways it can be used in the classroom. Here are a few examples:

- Graph data or information to encourage higher level thinking with students.

- Keep and average grades if your school/district does not have an electronic gradebook. The spreadsheet will actually calculate the averages for you if you set up the equations correctly.

- Make a spreadsheet to keep track of student work, absences, etc., or to use for the Clipboard Management techniques we discussed earlier in the book.

- Create databases to use for mailing labels

Also, you can use your presentation station to teach students how to use any program through demonstration.

Microsoft Publisher

With this program you can create multiple text boxes to hold typed information and place them anywhere on the page. You can also insert and place graphics much easier than with Word. Publisher is a much more versatile program. You can use it to create note-cards, postcards, newsletters, flyers, labels, coupons, brochures, websites, and more with their ready-to-use templates.

Additionally, any document you create can be saved as HTML to upload as a webpage. Publisher is a WYSIWYG (What you see is What you Get) type of HTML editor. Your web pages will look exactly as you create them on the page. You can make text and graphics into hyperlinks to make your site as interactive as you wish. There is even an option for creating response forms and adding your own HTML code, if you know it.

Here are a few ideas:

- Post class information/ newsletters as a website for parents and students to view
- Post tests and assignments for students to complete online
- Post student work for parents to view
- Post your professional portfolio

Can you think of any other ways you could use a classroom website?

Student Use of the Computer

- Use the computer(s) you have in the classroom as a Learning Center for student enrichment.

- Computer games are a fun way to teach valuable skills, and they won't even know they are learning!

- Teach word processing skills for writing pieces and projects.

- Students can practice or learn to type on the computer.

- Use the internet to research information (closely monitored by the teacher).

- Email famous figures, experts, and government officials to ask questions related to units of study.

Hint:

Students can use software programs such as Publisher, Word, and Power Point to create presentations for the class, write research reports or essays, create brochures, flyers, class newsletters, or websites exhibiting information they've learned. Excel can be used to create their own charts and graphs as a way of organizing and intepreting data.

Give students meaningful uses of computer programs as part of their learning and watch them blow you away with their abilities!

•CD Programs can extend lessons and units, and can be used creatively for all kinds of research projects.

Educational CD programs are now widely available through Office Supply stores, Computer stores, Teacher Supply stores, Bookstores, and places like Wal-Mart and Target. Most programs cost between three and thirty dollars although some are considerably more costly.

A few good programs for classroom use are:
> The Animals – San Diego Zoo
> Atlas Pack
> Grolier's Encyclopedia
> Guinness Records
> Compton's Encyclopedia
> Magazine Article Summaries
> Time Almanac
> Magic School Bus
> News Lines
> American Journey – Exploring American History
> Where in the World/US is Carmen Sandiego

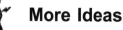 **More Ideas**

Math

- Create spreadsheets using mathematical equations
- Study and draw geometric figures using Draw or Paint programs
- Create graphs, charts, tables and diagrams to represent information
- Practice math skills using the variety of math programs available
- Create a website to help other students practice or learn more

Science

- Use CD Roms, Software, Internet and Email for research
- Create data bases of information
- Write research reports and science projects
- Use pictures/images from CD Rom and Software programs to enhance science projects, especially for the Science Fair!
- Create spreadsheets, graphs, tables, and diagrams for representing data
- Create a website to teach others

"Don't forget the importance of allowing students to locate information using the computer."

Social Studies

- Use CD Roms, Software, Internet and Email for research
  Example: *Take a "Tour of the White House" over the Internet!*

- Write research reports and complete projects
  *The computer has different fonts and images that can make historical reports look authentic!

- Create graphs and charts showing information

- Create Maps and Travel Brochures for geography

- Create slide show presentations for lessons and/or student projects

- Create a website to help other students practice or learn more

Language Arts

- Write compositions

- Create 'About the Author' Pages using the digital camera to place a picture of the student on the page with their biographical sketch

- Use the computer for Final Drafts or to Publish students' works
  *Poetry can look beautiful when using the variety of fonts and illustrations from the computer!

- Use *Print Shop*, Draw and Paint programs to illustrate stories and projects

- Create cards for classmates and family

- Students can practice grammar and reading skills using programs in your school.

- Create a website to share information or publish written works

Hint:

Check with your librarian and/or computer technician on your campus for help with locating software programs and CD Roms already in your school. Don't run out and buy any programs yet!

See our list of web sites at the end of this chapter for ideas.

Scheduling Computer Time

It is important that each of your students has a chance to work and practice on the computer. Sometimes teachers tend to only allow their top students to use the computer, because they are usually finished with their work first and already know how to use computer technology. Your goal should be for every student in your class, no matter what learning level, to have a certain amount of time on the computer each week or month…whatever you decide.

Organizing Computer Time in your Classroom…

If you only have one or two computers in your classroom, you will probably utilize your computer(s) daily as learning and practice centers, and often as research centers for projects. For daily use, teachers might let students take turns on the computer instead of their silent reading time or other daily events. You will want to create a schedule or a method of keeping track, so you ensure each student has their fair share of time on a computer.

"Computers are an excellent learning tool!

Every student can benefit from time spent on the computer."

Notebook method

Each student's name is written along the side of the paper with days or weeks in a month written at the top. The students must record their time on the computer in the appropriate section. The teacher checks the notebook weekly to verify that all students are taking their turn. Once a student has used their time, they may not work on the computer unless it is approved by the teacher.

Posting a schedule

Each week or each month the teacher posts a large schedule above the computer table, which displays each student's time slot.

Tips of the Trade: How to effectively utilize school computers!

➔ When working on special projects that need computers for research, be sure to consult with your librarian. Libraries often have extra computers and printers that can be rolled down to your classroom, or the librarian may allow students to come to the library and work. Your librarian is an excellent resource!

➔ Many school districts issue laptop computers to teachers. When planning special projects, coordinate and reserve the use of teacher laptops to add to the number of computers in your classroom. Give other teachers plenty of advance notice and explanation for what you are doing. Most teachers would be happy to cooperate!

➔ Don't hesitate to use the computer lab if your campus has one. Teach word processing/editing skills, how to create databases, spreadsheets, graphs… Sign up in advance if you want to use the lab for special projects, as this will often require more time than the standard 30 minutes.

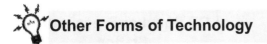 **Other Forms of Technology**

TV/VCR/DVD

Do not hesitate to show meaningful videos, clips and images from videos, commercials, recorded TV productions, DVD presentations and other visual tools in your classroom. You know the old saying: "A picture is worth a thousand words!" A visual picture can often capture a student's interest or help students to understand what you are teaching.

Tips:
- Always preview videos, video clips and computer programs before showing them to your class! It is negligent if you don't!
- Almost any production will allow you to show their piece for educational purposes, although you may be prohibited from using the video for entertainment purposes for your students.
- Always have an educational reason for showing any videos.
- Always get permission from your principal before showing videos in your class, and be ready to explain the educational value!

Ways to use this technology:
- Good Videos for Classroom use:
  - National Geographic videos on Nature, Geology, Animals, and History
  - Videos of IMAX films
  - Relevant appropriate movies that tie into your unit

- The Nature, Discovery, History, and Learning Channels provide great resources! Watch your TV Guide and plan to record programs that coincide with upcoming themes!

Cameras/Digital Camera

- Take or bring pictures to class to enhance your lessons. Often your life experiences with travel can bring learning to life for students! Many students have never traveled out of their own city, and have never been to an art museum, arboretum, or any historical monument!
- Have students take pictures for special projects.
- Pictures can easily be integrated into documents on the computer with the digital camera or scanner.
  - *Example: About the Author Pages – Pictures of the students can accompany an autobiographical paragraph for their writing projects. It gives students the feeling of "being published!"*
- Integrate pictures into parent newsletters, student projects, etc.

" A short video or music clip is an excellent way to introduce a lesson.

Always preview videos, computer programs, and internet sites before showing them to your class."

Hint:

Places like Wolf or Ritz Camera can now put pictures directly onto a CD as well as prints. This makes life much easier and negates the need for a scanner or digital camera.

"For most teacher observations and appraisals, using technology in your lesson is part of the evaluation."

Hint:

If you have high-tech equipment in your classroom, your principal will expect to see it used when observing to give you higher marks for the technology domain of the professional assessment tool.

Calculators

When doing special projects that require complicated math computations, think about using calculators and adding machines. If your goal is not to assess math skills, but to integrate subject areas where math is involved, why spend the extra time having students do lengthy calculations?

Example: During our space unit, I had my students calculate their ages and weights on each different planet in our solar system. This was a fun project, but would have taken up days of class time had we not used calculators!

LCD Panel or Presentation Station

Depending on the level of technology available at your school, use one of these to show images from the computer screen on the overhead screen or television, so the whole class gets a good view.

- Notes for lecture
- Teach editing/word processing skills
- Show students how to use a particular computer program
- Give class presentations

Video Camera

Video cameras are a great tool to motivate students to do their very best. When you video tape them giving presentations of any kind, they are immediately more concerned about their appearance and preparation time. When you show the videos back to the entire class, it is a terrific learning experience!

Overhead Projector

Yes, this is technology! The use of an overhead can make giving notes, showing statistics, reading aloud, and working math problems so much easier and more efficient than using the chalkboard. You can save notes for absent students, instead of erasing from the chalkboard! Give it a try, even if you love writing on the chalkboard! It didn't take me long to make the switch!

Tape recorders/Cassette players

Use this for students to record and give presentations, oral exams, practice speeches, reading aloud, and even for some homework assignments. Almost every student has a tape recorder at home, so it is a great tool the students can use.

- This works great for shy students who find it hard to make speeches or presentations to the whole class.
- Having your students tape record their work can be fun and motivating!

Internet Web Sites

There are many interactive internet sites which offer free services for students. These can include review of facts/concepts, games, and other online type programs that are educational. Be sure you personally review any website before allowing students to view them. In the last few years we have seen an increase in unacceptable adult websites buying expired education domain names. This practice is horrific and can cause major problems. For example, we had a link to a site for lesson plans which at one time hosted fantastic teacher lesson plans. Just recently we checked our links and found that this domain name now leads to an adult-only website. Needless to say, we took that link off immediately. This story is just to caution you to preview all sites before letting students view them.

In the next few pages we have listed some internet sites that you might find helpful in the classroom. We have checked all of these links and updated them. However, as with everything on the internet, there is no telling when site names will change or disappear. Your best bet is to spend some time previewing and investigating these and other sites to be sure of what you will find.

Teacher Resources:

Beginning Teacher's Tool Box http://www.inspiringteachers.com
TeacherNet http://www.teachers.net/
Teachers Helping Teachers http://www.pacificnet.net/~mandel/
Tenet Halls of Academia   http://www.tenet.edu
Education World   http://www.education-world.com/
Classroom Connect   http://www.classroom.net/
Busy Teacher's Web Site   http://www.ceismc.gatech.edu/BusyT/

Content Resources:

Color Landform Atlas of the United States
http://fermi.jhuapl.edu/states/states.html

National Geographic
http://www.nationalgeographic.com/main.html

Presidents of the United States
http://ipl.sils/umich.edu/ref/POTUS/

"Remember, always preview web sites before students look at them.

It is important to closely monitor internet use by students."

**My Own Favorite
Web Sites:**

Content Resources Continued:

This Day in History
http://www.historychannel.com/thisday/

The History Channel
http://www.historychannel.com

Yahoo! Countries
http://www.yahooligans.com/

World Cultures
http://www.kent.wednet.edu/curriculum/soc_studies/text gr7.html#top

U.S. Government
http://www.vote-smart.org/index.html

White House for Kids
http://www.whitehouse.gov/kids/l

The Exploratorium
http://www.exploratorium.edu/

National Park Service
http://www.nps.gov/parks.html

American Museum of Natural History
http://www.amnh.org

Ask Dr. Math
http://forum.swarthmore.edu/dr.math/dr-math.html

Math Forum
http://forum.swarthmore.edu/

Mrs. Glosser's Math Goodes
http://www.mathgoodies.com/

Mathematics Archives
http://archives.math.utk.edu/k12.html

Eisenhower National Clearinghouse for Mathematics
http://www.enc.org/about/nf_index.html

Content Resources Continued:

Bill Nye - The Science Guy
http://billnye.com

The Nine Planets
http://seds.lpl.arizona.edu/nineplanets/nineplanets/nineplanets.html

Science Hobbyist
http://www.eskimo.com/~billb/

How Things Work
http://howthingswork.virginia.edu

NASA
http://www.nasa.gov/

Magic School Bus
http://scholastic.com/MagicSchoolBus/

Weather Channel
http://www.weather.com/twc/homepage.twc

Cells Alive
http://www.cellsalive.com

San Diego Zoo
http://www.sandiegozoo.org/

VolcanoWorld
http://volcanoworld.org

My Own Favorite Web Sites:

Books

Looking for a particular book or books on a particular topic? Try Amazon.com or any other large online bookstore. They have a great database that is easy to search. Once you've found the book you are looking for, you can buy it or try to find it at the local libarary.

Amazon.com   http://www.amazon.com

Searches

Do searches for information, interactive sites for students, or websites for teachers using keywords for your topic. String several keywords together for results that will meet your needs. We recommend the following Search Engines:

Google   http://www.google.com
Ask Jeeves   http://www.askjeeves.com

CONCLUSION

Technology is an integral part of our society, and therefore should be an integral part of our classrooms. There are so many different ways to incorporate technology into our daily lessons that we really have no excuse not to. It is vital to our students that they have exposure to computers in order to prepare them for the outside world.

Additional Resources

Best Lesson Plan Websites
by Karla Spencer

The Busy Educator's Guide to the World Wide Web
by Marjan Glavac

Teaching with Technology: Creating Student Centered Classrooms
by Judith Haymore Sandholtz, Cathy Ringstaff, David C. Dwyer

Questions for Reflection

1) Why is it important to attend training for different hardware and software programs and then use those programs frequently?

2) What are some different ways you can incorporate technology in the classroom if computers and other high-tech hardware tools are not available?

3) What are some different uses of the internet as a teaching tool?

4) Why is it so important that we preview websites before using them with our students?

Activities

1) Develop one or more class activities or assessments which utilize Power Point, Excel, or Publisher. Create directions and a checklist for students for each activity you design. The purpose of this activity is to develop activities which can be implemented in any unit or lesson.

2) Create a website using Publisher or another type of editor. This can simply be information about you and your portfolio (to share with administrators), information about your class for parents and students to view, interactive activities for students to complete online, or sharing your ideas with other teachers.

3) Think through how you would use one computer station in the classroom. Write out a plan that can be implemented in the classroom.

4) Think about and list the different ways you plan to use a computer presentation station daily in your classroom.

Career Bound

It isn't easy knowing what to do when you first get out of college and are looking for a job teaching. For the most part your college should have a career center to help you with your resume and interviewing skills. Your student teaching professor should get you started on a portfolio and dossier to use when applying for jobs. At many universities, and in many cities, teaching job fairs are held during Spring Semester where you can meet with different districts.

However, if your college doesn't have a big education department you may be left with a feeling of frustration due to a lack of information. Also, most university career centers are geared for students going into the world of business which doesn't help you much at all.

Additionally, you may be someone looking to change careers and become a teacher. Although you do not have your certification, most states now have an Alternative Certification Program to help you make the transition. You will still be required to attend teacher training courses and get your state certification, but you are allowed to teach while you work towards that goal. Contact your State Department of Education to locate different programs available in your state. The US Department of Education website - http://www.ed.gov - lists all of the state departments for your reference.

This chapter is designed to help you understand what public school districts are looking for and how they hire new teachers. Whether you are a recent graduate or trying to change careers, you will need to find a teaching job somewhere. We hope you will find these tips to be helpful. Please remember that every state is different, so not every tip will be useful to you. Still, it can't hurt to have some information on your side.

I'm ready to start teaching in the classroom and need a job.

What do I do?

The Application

First of all, most school districts have an application that has to be filled out. The best course of action is to decide which school districts you are interested in, call them and ask for an application. It will arrive in the mail between 1 and 5 days within your phone call.

If you don't know the districts in your area, the college or public library will have Patterson's American Education which lists every school district for every state. It is organized by state, city and then districts in that area. Each district has a little blurb about it along with the address and phone number. Don't forget about private and charter schools as well when putting in applications.

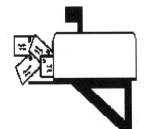

It is your responsibility to mail the form, along with an addressed stamped envelope, to each reference.

When filling out the application, be sure you have:

- **Basic biography information** - name, address, etc.

- **Schools where you have previously taught**
(your student teaching experience will work fine for this area) — name of school, name of district, address, phone number, how long you worked there, and possibly a supervisor's name.

- **Other work experience**

Be ready to provide References.

- Cooperating teacher
- Principal of your student teaching school
        (if he/she observed you teaching)
- A professor in your major subject area
- Your student teaching professor/supervisor.

Be sure you know their address and phone number. Also, make sure you tell them that you are using them as references.

Remember: Most districts do not like personal references!

Many districts will want your references to fill out a form. **YOU** have to get the form to your references **AND** give them an addressed/ stamped envelope to send the form back to the district. Sometimes the form is a rating chart and other times there are general questions about your performance. Make sure you choose people who will take the time to fill it out.

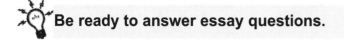
Be ready to answer essay questions.

Some typical questions include:
- Why did you choose to become a teacher?
- What do you feel are your strengths as a teacher?
- What do you feel are your weaknesses as a teacher?
- What is your philosophy of teaching?
- What do you believe is the most important part of teaching?
- How do you incorporate special needs students into your classroom?
- How do you build a positive climate in your classroom?
- How do you incorporate technology into your lessons?

Some questions are more specific in relation to the goals of the district. Answer all of these questions truthfully and as fully as you can. Some districts will only ask one or two questions whereas other districts may ask up to ten questions.

When answering questions about how your classroom works, answer with what you've done during your student teaching as well as what you plan to do when you are hired.

"Think about your first, second, and third choice of teaching assignments."

Think about the type of Teaching Assignment you want.

- Think about your first, second and third choice of teaching assignments.

- **DO NOT** put down something that you are not comfortable teaching. You may be interviewed for that position.

- Be aware that districts are often in need of teachers for 6th - 9th grades. Also, many districts are in need of Math, Science, ESL, and Special Education teachers.

Also, think about activities you would like to sponsor such as student council, yearbook, student clubs, or coaching.

 **Getting Noticed**

You have filled out the application and everything is in order. Now all you need to do is let the principals know you exist and are ready to teach. Getting yourself noticed is one of the first things you need to do. Here are some tips for getting your foot in the door.

- **Be a substitute teacher in the district where you applied.**

If you are in between college and a job, or if you just graduated at an awkward time, subbing is one of the best ways to get your foot in the door.

"Subbing is a great way to get noticed and gain classroom experience!"

Call one or more local districts and ask for the Personnel or Human Resources Department. Let them know that you would like to be a substitute. They will give you directions on what you need to do.

When subbing in a building, be sure to introduce yourself to all of the teachers you meet as a new teacher who is subbing for experience. Let them know you are looking for a teaching job.

It is not enough to just sub, you also need to be excellent in the classroom. Show what you can do. Everyone will be watching how you handle the students, how well you handle the curriculum and/or teacher plans (or lack of plans).

Offer to help during the planning period and ask if you can sit in on planning sessions. Once again, let them know that you are a new teacher and that you want the experience. The other teachers will give you whatever help they can.

- **Meet the principal**

If you are subbing in a school, do everything you can to meet the principal in a positive situation. Introduce yourself with confidence and offer some positive feedback about the students and the school. Be sure to use phrases you know will catch the principal's attention and will show you are knowledgeable.

The Cover Letter

A good cover letter that stands out from the rest can also help get you an interview. Here are some tips for a good cover letter:

 **Use paper that draws attention, but isn't too flamboyant.**

Florescent green or yellow certainly stands out, but it isn't professional and it turns decision makers off! A page with school buses all around is cute, but too distracting from the message you want to convey.

Choose one logo to represent you and place it at the top of all letters, resumes, thank-you notes, etc.

Businesses use a logo to gain visual recognition. It will work for you as well. If the principal sees your logo often, he/she will begin to associate that image with you.

Use a colorful folder or envelope when sending your cover letter and resume.

Once again, use good judgment when choosing a color. You want it to be noticed, but not be offensive. Create mailing labels that use the same logo as your cover letter and resume so that it creates a solid image of you. This portrays confidence and organization, both of which are important qualities in a teacher.

Use active voice in your writing.

Active voice portrays confidence which is exactly what you want to communicate to your potential employers.

Keep it brief.

Principals do not have time to read through lengthy cover letters and resumes. You do not need to fill the page to be effective. Think, "Less is More."

"Your cover letter should briefly introduce you to potential employers."

Example:

"When mailing a resume, it is vital to have a cover letter!"

Sara B. Teacher
4000 Teachaway Rd. • Schooltown, USA 89999 • HM (999) 444-8888

June 18, 20___

Mrs. Principal
Verifine School
200 Peachy Street
Friendship, TX 78994

Dear Mrs. Principal,

I want to applaud you and the other teachers at Verifine High School for your commitment to student learning. I visited your web site and noticed that every teacher in your school has a web page with pictures of students learning as well as a bulletin board for parents to view assignments and upcoming events. I also saw many pictures of you and your teachers actively working with students in the classrooms and hallways of the school.

I would very much like to be a part of the Verifine team. As a newly graduated teacher from United University, I believe in team work within a school staff. I firmly believe that teachers and students learn best when actively involved tin a positive and caring classroom environment where trust and respect are highly valued. I can see these same values and beliefs within your school, and feel that I would be a positive addition to your team.

I would like to meet with you to discuss the wonderful work you are doing at Verifine High School and how I might fit one of the teaching positions you currently have available. I look forward to hearing from you soon.

Sincerely,

Sara B. Teacher

Cover Letter Elements:

- Introduction with positive comments about school
- 2nd paragraph has university information and teaching philosophy
- 3rd paragraph requests a meeting

How do you get personalized information about the school?

Research!

Log on to the internet and locate the district and school web page. Use the information you find there to write a personalized introduction. If you know the name of the school/district where you are applying, you should be able to do a search using Google or some other search engine to find the web page. Otherwise, you might try locating the school through the State Department of Education website. These can be found at http://www.ed.gov/.

Follow up:

You want to follow up the cover letter and resume with a phone call if you don't hear back within several days after mailing it out.

When you call, simply confirm that the letter was received by the principal. You don't want to sound too pushy or desperate.

If you still don't hear anything in a couple of weeks, it is okay to send a follow up note. Be sure to use the same logo and color scheme as your cover letter and resume. If you have a web site, use this second letter as an opportunity to mention it to the principal. This keeps your name in circulation without badgering.

Hint:

Create a website for yourself that includes a picture, biographical information, your teaching philosophy, and other important items for principals to review.

You might even want to post your teaching portfolio on a website rather than having to leave your original with an administrator.

The Resume

Your resume does not need to be extensive, but it should definitely be clear and concise. Principals do not have a lot of time to read a wordy resume. Only put down the most important information. A sample resume is printed below to give you an idea.

"Your resume should be clear and concise!"

Sara B. Teacher

4000 Teachaway Rd.	HM (999) 444-8888
Schooltown, USA 89999	WK (999) 665-8888

EDUCATION:

- TEACHER UNIVERSITY, Houston, TX - BA, English, May 20__; GPA 3.0
  - Honors/Offices — Served as House Manager, Kappa Kappa Gamma Sorority. Appointed Sophomore Advisor, Served as fundraising chair, Residence Life Association.

CERTIFICATION:

- Texas Provisional Certificate— Secondary English, 7-12
  Secondary Reading, 7-12

EMPLOYMENT:

- STUDENT TEACHER - ROSEWOOD MIDDLE SCHOOL -
  Rosewood I.S.D., Rosewood, Texas 200_-200_
    - Taught four classes of English and Reading
    - Created a six weeks unit on poetry for 8th grade students
    - Participated in staff development on 4-MAT lesson planning
- AFTER-SCHOOL COORDINATOR -
  LIVSEY ELEMENTARY /YWCA, Rosewood, Texas   200_-200_
    - Established, developed and organized after-school program for Livsey Elementary School.
    - Held supervisory position over two counselors.
    - Conducted monthly staff development meetings.
    - Successfully completed all regulatory state records.
    - Responsible for and implemented overall program budget.
    - Established interpersonal relations with parents and school.

SKILLS

Proficient with IBM and MacIntosh computers. Proficient with various software programs including Power Point, Publisher, Word, and Excel. Proficient with the Internet and emailing systems. Experienced with Scanners and Networked systems.

HOBBIES

Enjoy writing stories, reading, swimming, cross-stitching and playing the flute.

The Portfolio

A portfolio should be a well-organized presentation of yourself. Although a portfolio is not necessarily a requirement in an interview, having one definitely can set you apart from other applicants. Below are some tips for creating your portfolio and using it to help you get a job.

Presentation:

- 3 ring-binder
    - should be new
    - zippered binder keeps loose papers inside and neat
    - vinyl binder is okay
    - leather binder/ portfolio is not necessary

- Use nice paper
    - linen paper
    - designer paper (don't use too much of this or else your portfolio will look crowded and more like a scrapbook)
    - a heavier weight typing paper will work fine

- Professional
    - don't tape pictures to construction paper
    - use photo sheets or picture corners to keep pictures on a page
    - use binder folders to hold loose papers

Artifacts to include:

- Resume
- Teaching certificate(s)
- Recent observation reports (for you)
- Copy of degree(s) earned
- Sample lesson plans
- Photos
- Letters of accommodation or thanks
- Professional Development certificates, if you have any

"Your portfolio should reflect both who you are as a person and as a teacher."

Organization of Portfolio:

There are a variety of ways to organize your portfolio. Here are a few that you can consider using:

"An organized portfolio presents and organized teacher."

- **By artifacts**

  Use tabbed dividers and label each section according to the artifacts found within. Some sections might include:

  -Teacher qualifications
  -Lessons/ units
  -Photos
  -Letters
  -Observations
  -Professional development

- **By teaching standards**

  You might want to organize your artifacts according to different teaching standards and/or responsibilities. Your sections might include:

  -Professional qualifications
  -Curriculum and Instruction
  -Classroom Climate
  -Technology
  -Parental Involvement
  -Meeting needs of ALL students (ESL, Special Education, Gifted/Talented)

  Many states have specific teaching standards listed on their education department web page. You might also consider using those standards when organizing your portfolio.

Other Portfolio Tips:

- Use copies of your certificates and degrees so that you won't accidentally lose the original.

- Put your portfolio on CD using browser/ web technology. This will help set you apart from other applicants. Also, you can make several copies of the CD portfolio and leave them with each principal as you interview.

- Create a portfolio on a web site. Use a brightly colored manila folder to hold your resume and web site address. This is another way to stand out from the crowd.

The Interview

Your first interview most likely will be with someone in the Personnel Department of the district. This is a screening interview and it is usually with only one person. During this interview you will be asked very general questions similar to the ones on the application. Some districts use a video interview process while others conduct more of a casual conversation.

In certain places, you may be asked to present a demonstration lesson. If you have a chance during student teaching, you might want to video a couple of different lessons to show during an interview. Having a video tape like this will also help set you apart from other applicants when talking to individual schools. Make several copies so that a principal can keep one for a couple of days, if necessary.

Some interview questions will include:

- What is your philosophy of teaching?
- How did you reach this point in teaching (or in your career)?
- What makes a good teacher?
- What are two of your greatest strengths?
- What is your biggest area of weakness?
- How do you feel about student retention?
- How do you feel about mainstreaming and/or inclusion?
- Describe for me a typical day in your classroom.
- Describe for me how you would deal with an upset or angry parent.
- Describe for me how you would deal with a student discipline problem.
- How do you incorporate technology in the classroom?
- How you do you communicate/ involve parents in the classroom?
- If we were to walk into your class at any given moment, what would it look like?
- ·What are some lessons/units you have planned?

"The District Screening Interview comes first, then you'll be contacted by interested administrators."

"Dress professionally for your interviews!"

Don't worry about having a smooth, off-the-cuff answer for each question.

The interviewer expects you to be nervous and knows that you might stumble over your answers.

Do You Know About These Issues?

It is important that you give the impression that you have thought about and are still thinking seriously about the issue. This impression will only come from actually thinking about these types of questions.

Philosophy of Teaching

The interviewer is looking for your beliefs about teaching. There are two ways to go about your philosophy of teaching. One way is to create an educational philosophy. This should be no longer than 2 or 3 sentences at the most.

Example:

> Teachers and students learn best when actively involved through hands-on learning, discovery learning, and real experiences in a positive and caring classroom environment where trust and respect are highly valued.

"A well-prepared teacher has given thought to their educational platform."

When developing your philosophy, remember that school administrators are looking for people who emphasize working as a team with colleagues and students, and working to meet the needs of ALL students.

Principals also like to know that life-long learning, parent communication, and working toward school goals are important issues to teachers.

A second way to communicate your philosophy of teaching is through an **Educational Platform**. An educational platform is a sheet that begins with the statement I Believe and then lists your beliefs.

Below is a sample Educational Platform:

I BELIEVE...

- Teachers should guide their students in learning, not just give information.
- The classroom should be student centered, not teacher centered.
- Learning should be hands-on. Students learn best through discovery learning and experiences.
- A faculty should work together to be better teachers for their students.
- A principal should support his/her teachers.
- Learning concepts should be integrated so that students can see connections.
- Students should have lots of experiences with critical thinking skills.

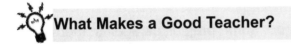 ## What Makes a Good Teacher?

This is part of your beliefs. Do you believe that a good teacher guides students rather than spouting out information? Does a good teacher have strong communication skills with parents, students and faculty? Include statements about a good teacher in your platform.

Strengths and Weaknesses

Be honest, but also be aware of what the school is looking for. You want to find weaknesses that actually are strengths. For example, you might say, "One of my biggest weaknesses is that I tend to put everything I have into my work. I often arrive early and stay late. Since I know new teachers often burn out quickly, I need try to take a little time for myself every now and then. This will be hard for me, but I know it will be better for my students in the long run."

Another area that many principals understand as an area of weakness is integrating technology into the classroom.

Areas that will not be acceptable as your weakness:
- Math
- Reading
- Parent Communication

Hint:

What would your strengths be as a teacher? Below are some examples:

Strong rapport with students

Utilize proactive classroom management strategies

Have a natural flair for delivering interesting lessons

Use higher-level thinking skills and questioning techniques to expand lessons.

Retention

This is the process of holding a student back a grade instead of passing them. There are two basic beliefs.

One belief is that a student should not be held back unless it is absolutely one hundred percent necessary. This school of thought believes that retention is ultimately harmful to a student for the following reasons:

- They will be older than the other students

- They may lose their self esteem

- They will be bored because they've already experienced the curriculum

- The teachers may harbor some prejudices against them from the previous year.

- Tutoring and summer school are held as the best alternatives to retention.

"Before your interview, research the district's policy on student retention."

The other school of thought holds that students who cannot do the work required by that particular grade need to be held back another year for the following reasons:

- They have already experienced the curriculum and may better understand it a second time.

- They will gain better self-esteem because they experience success rather than failure.

- They are often held up to the younger members of the class as leaders because of their age.

Educators of this school of thought may feel that retention is not a stigma on a student, but rather offers them a "do over".

 **Mainstreaming**

This is the process of placing special education students in a regular classroom. This process is also known as inclusion. Schools experience a wide range of mainstreaming from totally self-contained classrooms to totally mainstreamed classrooms. Regular teachers may have students with learning disabilities, emotional disabilities, or even physical disabilities along with their other students.

Some educators feel very strongly against the issue of mainstreaming, while others would rather have all students in their classroom. It is important that you think very carefully about how you would feel to have children of such widely ranging abilities together in your classroom. The best solution is to be open-minded and accepting of whatever students you may receive. Remember, no matter how much you pretend, children can always sense how you feel about them.

 **Typical Class/ Typical Day**

This is an especially hard question for new teachers who have never been in a classroom. Take some time to imagine how you **would** run your classroom in the most practical sense.

- **Think about your subject area.** How would you begin the class to get students engaged? Would you use sponge activities? Would your lessons be hands-on or textbook oriented? How would you close your lessons?

- **Observe your cooperating teacher** and ask yourself, what do they do that I like? dislike? Then, imagine how you would do it if it were your classroom. Earlier in this book we discussed some different ways to manage and plan for a successful classroom that you can use as a reference.

"Students can always tell how you feel about them, even if you don't verbalize it."

*Remember, a sponge activity is an assignment ready for students to complete as soon as they enter the classroom.

Typical Class...continued

With this question Administrators are looking for the following:

How will students be engaged from the moment they walk in the door?

Example:

> When students first enter the classroom they get their class materials and pull out their journal. Before the bell rings students are already in their seats writing about the journal topic.

How will you handle administrative tasks?

Example:

> While students are writing in their journal, I use my seating chart to take attendance. After I have put it out to be picked up, we answer the warm-up science review questions.

Example of typical day answer:

> If you were to walk into my classroom during class, you would see students actively engaged in learning. We would be engaged in discussion of various topics, or students would be working in cooperative lab/group situations with activities that apply and enrich the topic of study. I teach through mini-lessons rather than lectures as I feel that lectures tend to make students passive learners rather than active learners. I prefer to have students actively engaged in activities that help them discover and apply the information themselves.

"A well-prepared teacher constantly thinks about how their classroom will operate."

 **Technology**

If you could have the ideal classroom, what kind of technology would you include? Here is a list of some very useful tools for the classroom

- Computers
- Internet access
- CD-Rom
- Video camera

- Presentation Station
- TV
- VCR
- Digital Camera

Some of you who are more technologically advanced may even know of some other hardware items that would be useful. Discuss how you feel about using these tools in your classroom. How would you use them?

Also, remember that most schools will not have these things and you may have to do without. However, principals these days are looking for teachers with that extra technological edge even if their school does not have the necessary equipment.

 **Student Discipline**

What would you do if a student spoke back to you in a disrespectful tone of voice? Would you immediately send them to the office, punish them verbally in class, put a check on the board, or discuss their behavior with them privately? Principals are looking for generalities. In general, do you talk with students and work through the problem, or do you rely on immediate punishment strategies? It is important to think about what we know about human behavior when thinking about this issue. Look over our Classroom Management and Teaching Strategies chapters to help you in answering this question.

Parent Communication

The biggest thing principals want to hear is that you are willing to discuss issues with parents. The best method is to use a calm voice and to encourage the parent to voice their concerns. After all, you are both interested in what is best for the student. This is not a competition, but a cooperative effort in creating a successful environment for that student. See our chapter on parent communication for more ideas on answering this question.

"Remember, a classroom built on trust and respect generally does not have discipline problems."

Be genuine in the way you answer each question.

Districts are looking for enthusiastic, energetic teachers, not automatons. You may do yourself more harm than good if you write out an essay answer for each of these questions, memorize it and then try to recall it in the interview. Do some serious thinking about each issue and you will find that at the interview it will not be hard to answer the question.

Remember to send a Thank You note to your interviewer.

Usually you will be given a business card by the interviewer with their address and phone number. Reiterate in a thank-you note your interest in working for their district and how excited you were to meet and talk with them.

Once the intial screening interview is over, the next step is to wait.

"Most districts follow similar hiring procedures."

Unfortunately there is no set time of waiting. Some people who have applied and interviewed early have had to wait several months while others have gotten a job right away. Other people have applied and interviewed closer to the start of school only to find that there are no more jobs left, while still others do the same and get a job that day.

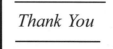

Thank You

Remember to write a thank-you note!

The Hiring Process

Most districts follow similar policies for hiring procedures.

If you have applied early, say in February or March, you can pretty much depend on waiting until at least May or June before you are called again.

Teachers who are already under contract with the district must be placed in a school before any new hires can take place.

That means that principals are looking at people already in the district for their openings first. Many principals would often rather have new teachers, but they must still follow the same process. Then, around early summer, the transfers have been taken care of and schools begin interviewing possible new teachers.

If you do not receive a call by June, do not panic.

Some principals don't get around to hiring new teachers until the end of July and some even hire up to the day school starts. This does not make the situation easier for you since you need a job, but at least you will go into the whole process with a little prior knowledge about the system.

Keep in mind that most school administrators take off two to three weeks in June or July. You may not receive a call simply because everyone is on vacation.

"If you do not receive a call by June, do not panic!"

"Districts are required to handle their in-district transfers before they can hire anyone new."

Be Patient! Although time seems to crawl while you are waiting - your turn will come!

School Interviews

Once you are called back for an interview at a specific school, you may see a variety of interviewing techniques.

- You may be interviewed by the principal alone.
- Some schools have both administrators interviewing.
- Other schools interview in a group setting.

- By group setting, we mean that several people may be interviewing you including the principal, a couple of teachers and maybe a parent or two. For many people this is the most nerve-wracking, but it can turn out to be better for you.

- With a one person interview, you are counting on one person liking you instantly. With a group interview, there are several people who have input, and if one person does not think that you will work out, there may be two or three who think you are perfect for the job. Usually the majority rules.

"Don't feel pressured to accept the first job you are offered!"

Before the interview:

- Research information about the school. Most districts and schools now have a web page which will tell you their vision and mission as well as show you the various activities going on at the school. By looking through their site, you should be able to determine the issues they feel are important. Address these issues in your answers and in the questions you ask them during the interview.

- Put your resume or vita in a bright colored manila folder. Print out a label with your name and phone number to put on the tab for easy reference. If you have a CD with your portfolio or a video of you in the classroom, place them in a bright colored envelope with a label. Be sure that your folder and envelope match so that the principal will know which items are yours. Don't use florescent colors.

The questions at the school interview are a little more specific to the school.

- Be prepared to discuss why you would be qualified to teach specific grade levels and/or courses. Do not hesitate to specify grade levels/courses you would feel most comfortable teaching. If you leave it up to the principal, you may end up teaching just about anything.

- During this time, the interviewer will tell you what makes their particular school special or different.

- They may ask you how you can contribute to their vision of the school.

- Also be ready to explain how you teach certain subjects such as math, language arts, science and social studies. Think about your ideal classroom.

  - **Describe classroom setup** (groups, learning centers, tables, desks, display student work, motivating and colorful environment?)

  - **Classroom management philosophy** (how would you handle discipline problems, unruly students, exceptionally gifted students, rewards, and consequences?)

  - **Hands-on versus textbook/ worksheet?**

  - **Typical Lesson** (Opening, Meat of Lesson, Closing)

    - Do you use manipulatives or experiences to introduce a new concept?

    - Do you lecture or use questioning techniques to teach the concept?

    - Do you use student groups and guide them to learning and/or applying the information?

    - Do you have them reflect in journals or review concepts in their own words as closing?

"A well-prepared teacher knows the issues that are important to each school when interviewing."

Prepare a list of your own questions for the principal.

These questions should include some of the following:

- What is your vision for the school? (long term goals)
- What is your philosophy of teaching and learning?
- Describe the climate of your school for both staff and students.
- In what ways are the parents included and how do they show support for the school?
- Please describe the demographics of your school.
- How do your grade levels/ departments support each other ? Do you do vertical planning?
- How is grade level/ departmental planning implemented in this school?
- In what ways does the district provide support for the staff and students in this school.

If you have done some previous research about the district, you might ask something like:
When looking at your website, I noticed that your district emphasizes _____. How does your school work towards that goal?

- Carefully evaluate the answers the interviewers provide for you and the discussions during the interview session.

- Be sure this is an environment you would be comfortable working in. Your philosophies should closely match those of the principal and staff. You may be offered a position right after the interview. Do not hesitate to ask for time to think about it. However, if you feel this is the perfect place for you, take the job right away.

If you leave the interview feeling excited and confident, this would be the right job for you. If you leave with questions or concerns, consider going on other interviews before accepting a position. Be sure to write a thank you note to the principal who interviewed you. You never know what may happen later in your career.

Every school is different! There should be a good fit between the school's expectations and your teaching philosophies.
This is of *key* importance!

CONCLUSION

The hiring process can really be a time of stress and uncertainty. However, you can help yourself in getting a teaching job by standing out from the crowd. Take the time to prepare a good presentation of yourself through your cover letter, resume, and portfolio. Keep in mind the hot issues of concern to principals today and research information about the schools and districts where you interview. Although the teacher shortage in some areas pretty much guarantees almost anyone a job, there are places across the country and world where you must present yourself as a "must have." Remember the following when interviewing:

- Be confident, but not cocky.

- If you don't know the answer to a question right away, ask to have it rephrased. Take a moment to think about it before answering.

- Be assertive, but not aggressive. Use your "teacher" voice and mannerisms.

- Show enthusiasm for working with students. This will show in your eyes, voice, and body language during the interview.

In short, be a professional in every way from attire to conversation and demeanor, and you will find yourself a bonafide classroom teacher!

"Use as many different resources as you can to help you get started!"

Additional Resources

How to Develop a Professional Portfolio: A Manual for Teachers
by Pamela Cignetti

The Teaching Portfolio: A Practical Guide to Improved Performance and Promotion/ Tenure Decisions
by Peter Seldin

Inside Secrets of Finding a Teaching Job
by Jack Warner, Clyde Bryan, and Diane Warner (Contributor)

How to Get the Teaching Job You Want: The Complete Guide for College Graduates, Returning Teachers, and Career Changers
by Robert Fiersen and Seth Wietzman

Questions for Reflection

1) When applying for a teaching job, what are some ways you can get noticed or stand out in the crowd?

2) Think about your strengths and weaknesses in the classroom. How do you plan to communicate these to a principal when interviewing?

3) How would you improve your weaknesses?

4) Although a group or team interview seems overwhelming at first, why might it work to your advantage?

5) Why would it be a good idea to research a district's website and philosophies before the interview?

Activities

1) Summarize your philosophy of teaching or create your Educational Platform.

2) Compose your cover letter.
   a) Choose a school district with which you intend to apply
   b) Research and become familiar with this district's vision and unique traits, demographics, etc...
   c) Apply this information for use in your cover letter.

3) Brainstorm additional "hot topics" for education and support your position on each. Think of this as preparation for those unexpected questions you might be asked during an interview.

Notes/ Reflection on Chapter

REFERENCES

N. Atwell, *In the Middle: Writing, Reading, and Learning with Adolescents*, (Upper Montclair: Boynton/Cook, 1987).

P. Cunningham and R.L. Allington, *Classrooms That Work: They can ALL Read and Write*, (New York: HarperCollins, 1994).

J. Dobson, *Bringing Up Boys*, (Wheaton: Tyndale House Publishers, Inc., 2001).

H. Gardner, *Multiple Intelligences: Theory Into Practice*. (Basic Books, 1993).

H. Gardner, *The Unschooled Mind*, (Basic Books, 1993).

W. Glasser, *Choice Theory in the Classroom*, (New York: HarperCollins, 1988).

D. Hershman and E. McDonald, *ABC's of Effective Parent Communication*, (Dallas: Inspiring Teachers Publishing, Inc., 2000).

W.M. Fawcett-Hill, *Learning Thru Discussion*, (Beverly Hills: SAGE, 1986).

E. Jensen, *Teaching with the Brain in Mind*, (Washington D.C.: ASCD, 1988).

S. Kovalik, *Integrated Thematic Instruction: The Model (3rd Ed.)*, (Village of Oak Creek: Books for Educators, 1997).

K. Olsen, *Synergy*, (Village of Oak Creek: Books for Educators, 1998).

V. Troen and K. Boles, *Who's Teaching Your Children?: Why the Teacher Crisis is Worse than You Think and What Can be Done about It*. (New Haven: Yale University Press, 2003)

Maps, Charts, Graphs, and Diagrams, (Teacher Created Materials, Inc., 1990).

Inspiring Teachers Quick Order Form

Fax orders: 972-495-2702. Send this form.

Telephone orders: Call 1-877-496-7633 toll free. Have your credit card ready.

Internet orders: http://www.inspiringteachers.com/catalog/index.html Have your credit card ready.

Postal orders: Inspiring Teachers, 2510 Meadowridge Dr., Garland, TX 75044, USA

Products Available - View our online catalog at http://www.inspiringteachers.com/catalog/index.html

BOOKS
Survival Kit for New Teachers - $36.95
Survival Kit for New Secondary Teachers - $29.95
ABC's of Effective Parent Communication - $17.95
Mr. Tim's Tips for New Teachers - $12.95

Classroom Materials/Gifts
Yacker Tracker Traffic Light - $39.95
TAG Attention Getter - $18.95
Teacher Therapy CD - $15.00
Teacher Therapy Tape - $10.00

Please send the following products:

Quantity	Item	Unit Cost	Total

Please send more FREE information on:

☐ Staff Development Workshops   ☐ National Association for Beginning Teachers

Name: _____

Address: _____

City: _____ State: _____ Zip: _____

Telephone: _____

email address: _____

Sales tax: Please add 8.25% for products shipped to Texas addresses.

Shipping
U.S.: 15% of the total order. Order 4 or more, 10% of total. Order 10 or more, 5% of total
International: Same as above plus $15.00 to cover International shipping charges.

Payment: ☐ Check   Credit Card: ☐ Visa   ☐ MC   ☐ Amex

Card Number: _____ Exp. Date: _____

Signature: _____ Billing Zip Code: _____

About the Authors

Emma McDonald and Dyan Hershman, experienced classroom teachers and educational consultants from Texas, are known for their unique teaching strategies and techniques that motivate both teachers and students. Going beyond theories, these educators provide proven practical strategies to help teachers improve student learning. McDonald and Hershman have worked with and educated both children and adults over the past fifteen years. Currently, both mentor new teachers and work as Consultants with the Teacher Certification & Preparation Program for the Region 10 Education Service Center. Their strategies have been featured in Instructor Magazine and have been widely used by both new and veteran teachers. McDonald and Hershman now share their "tools" for success with educators all across the United States. They are well-known for their motivational, positive, practical, and energetic presentation style which inspires and encourages both new and veteran teachers.

About the Publisher

We are an organization of veteran teachers dedicated to helping the beginning teacher be successful in the classroom from the very first day of school.

Our mission is to empower new teachers with effective teaching strategies through resources and support services.

We believe a well-prepared teacher is an effective teacher.

We believe that new teachers who are given the right resources and support will stay in the classroom and make education a life-long career. This is important for our schools, our students, and our communities.

OUR SERVICES AND RESOURCES:

We provide many different services and resources to help new teachers. Learn more about these resources on our website at **www.inspiringteachers.com** .

Books

- Survival Kit for New Teachers
- Survival Kit for New Secondary Teachers
- ABC's of Effective Parent Communication
- Mr. Tim's Tips for New Teachers

Website - Free Resources -   www.inspiringteachers.com

- Tips, Articles, Inspirations, Recommended books and websites - updated monthly
- Ask a Mentor
- Professional Development - Book Studies, Links to additional resources
- Classroom Resources - Links to books and websites that are content related
- Classroom ToolKit - Gradebook and communication tool for students and parents
- Classroom Websites - Create a classroom or teacher website
- Teacher Preparation - Resources and links for becoming a teacher and getting a job
- Community - Email discussion lists and message boards to network with others
- Idea Share - A place to share great lesson ideas
- Mentor and Administrator Resources - articles and tips for working with new teachers (in progress)
- Teacher Trainer Resources - articles and tips for teacher preparation (in progress)
- NABT - National Association for Beginning Teachers (partnership)

Staff Development

- New Teacher Preparation
- Tools for Classroom Success
- Reading & Writing Across the Curriculum
- Student Assessment: Strategies and Ideas that Go Beyond Testing

NOTES:

NOTES: